English History Made Brief, Irreverent and Pleasurable

ENGLISH HISTORY
made
BRIEF,
IRREVERENT
and
PLEASURABLE

Lacey Baldwin Smith

ACADEMY CHICAGO PUBLISHERS

Published by Academy Chicago Publishers
An imprint of Chicago Review Press, Incorporated
814 North Franklin Street
Chicago, Illinois 60610

ISBN 978-0-89733-547-8

Library of Congress Cataloging-in-Publication Data
Smith, Lacey Baldwin, 1922–
    English history made brief, irreverent, and pleasurable/ Lacey Baldwin Smith.
        pages cm
Includes bibliographical references and index.
ISBN-13: 978-0-89733-547-8 (trade paper)
1. Great Britain—History. I. Title.

        DA30.S658 2006
        942—dc22
                            2006034420

Cover design: Sarah Olson
Cover illustration: George Cruikshank

TO

The powers behind the shaky throne: as always my wife
Jean, and nowadays my three children, MacAllister,
Dennison and Katherine Chandler

CONTENTS

Chapter I

WORDS OF ENCOURAGEMENT
AND COMMISERATION

No people have engendered quite so much critical acclaim or earned such unrestrained and bitter censure as the British. The tight little island has been extolled as the Athens of modern times, the cradle of ideas and institutions that have shaped entire societies and encompassed the globe. Conversely the British, secure in their island isolation off the western shores of the European Continent, have driven Europe and indeed the rest of the world to fury by their insolent self-satisfaction and perfidious hypocrisy. For many, the words attributed to Duncan Spaeth still ring true—"I know why the sun never sets on the British Empire: God wouldn't trust an Englishman in the dark." How then is it possible to reduce such a masterpiece of contradictions into an ordered narrative, to comprehend the incomprehensible? The answer, of course, is that you can't, without calling upon the magic and conceit of storytellers who select and shape their material into whatever form their imaginations and personal biases dictate. And so a double warning is in order.

First, the Anglo-Saxon component of the British Isles is unabashedly given stage center over the Celtic fringe. Ireland, Scotland and Wales appear in this story only when they impinge on English history or when it is impossible to disentangle Anglo-Saxon from Celtic culture and history. After all, the English Royal House of Stuart was Scottish, the Tudors were Welsh, and the Duke of Wellington was Anglo-Irish. Second, the warts and follies of English history, though not forgotten, are neither exaggerated nor treasured. As a specimen of his species, the English lion, who actually started off as an Anglo-French leopard, may today be more than a little arthritic and a heraldic parody of his former magnificence, but in the past he was a splendidly ferocious beast. Over the years he has proved to be a surprisingly resilient creature, possessed of an unparalleled talent for dressing his aggressive instincts in the deceptive mantle of good intentions. As a consequence, true Anglophiles are always inclined to ignore his appetite for raw meat, forgive him his pride, dismiss his tendency to regard anyone born in the Celtic fringe as slightly fey and all visitors from the United States, Canada, Australia, New Zealand, India, Pakistan and Africa as ex-colonials, and concentrate on the magnificence of his royal performance.

When the author of this slim volume asked his friends, mostly at cocktail and dinner parties, to free-associate on the essence of Britishness, a few elderly types answered "Empire"; a younger generation spoke of warm beer, tea, umbrellas and the Royal Family; but the most common response of all was simply to say "history." Great Britain may no longer be a great world power, but Britannia still possesses a great history and, except for a short chapter on a few indispensable facts and figures about the tight little island, that is what this book seeks to recount: the English part of British history made brief, irreverent and pleasurable.

Britannia and the English lion are more than a little arthritic

Chapter II

MATTERS OF GEOGRAPHY, DEMOGRAPHY AND TERMINOLOGY

We invariably speak of the British Isles as two islands: England-Wales-Scotland and Ireland. Actually they are an "Atlantic archipelago" of 400 islands, of which 200 are inhabited. At one time the two major islands were attached—at their closest point only ten miles divide them—and scarcely 10,000 years ago the entire archipelago was connected, probably in a fairly marshy fashion, to the European continent.

The name Britain stems from Brythonic, one of the two dialects spoken by the Celtic peoples of the isles: Brythonic was the language of England and Wales, Goidelic the tongue of Scotland and Ireland. The Celtic peoples inhabited most of Western Europe, and though later generations of Britons might bitterly resent it, British Celts were closely tied to their continental brothers and sisters in culture and kinship, the Parisi of Yorkshire being related to those Celts in Gaul who gave their name to the river settlement that eventually grew into the capital of France.

In size, the two islands are only slightly larger than New England and New York combined. England is 50,000 square miles, which is 900 square miles larger than the State of New York; Wales is 8,016 square miles, or almost the size of Massachusetts; Scotland is 30,400 square miles, about equal to Connecticut, New Hampshire, Rhode Island and Vermont combined; and Ireland (the Republic of and Northern Ireland) is 32,000 square miles, or the area of Maine. As a consequence, the British have difficulty comprehending the size of the rest of the world. The story is told that back in the days of sea travel, an English family sent their daughter off to New York. Not wanting to have their only child land unescorted in such a dangerous city, they telegraphed a friend in California asking him to meet her. He wired back, "Meet her yourself, you're closer."

By New World standards the tight little islands may be small, but in population, they are extremely crowded. The overwhelming bulk of the population—46.2 million—live in England. That is as if you added to the State of New York, with 19 million inhabitants, the entire population of Texas and threw in Massachusetts for good measure. Nowhere in the world can one find so much variation packed into such a small space. The island boasts some 30,000 place names of which at least a third are unpronounceable and the rest delightfully inane, as Blubberhouses, Chew Magna, Great Snoring, Leighton Buzzard, Piddletrenthide, and Stiffkey (pronounced Stookey).

Travelers to Britain rarely realize how far north they are venturing. All of the British Isles, except the Channel Islands located deep in French territorial waters, lie north of the contiguous states of the USA. London is north of Newfoundland; Edinburgh is less than a degree south of Juno, Alaska; and the Shetland Islands, the furthest point north in Britain, are the same latitude as Julianehab, Greenland. What makes the climate bearable is the Gulf Stream, which is so essential to British existence that when in the nineteenth century a canal across the top of Florida was proposed, the British Government objected strenuously for fear it might deflect the Gulf Stream by a few crucial degrees. The idea was dropped. The mixture of warm Gulf Stream water that circulates both through the English Channel and north of Scotland and the arctic location of the archipelago produces some of the most capricious weather in the world. As a result British weather reports tend to read either "generally sunny with occasional showers" or "generally cloudy with occasional bright spots." The traveler is well advised to bring an umbrella and a summer-winter wardrobe.

The traveller is well advised to bring an umbrella

Anyone who corresponds with a British friend knows how confusing it can be to address the letter. Should it be sent to England, Britain, Great Britain, or the United Kingdom? England is geographically limited to the southern and eastern two-thirds of the island of Britain, and Britain describes the entire island, including Wales and Scotland. (So don't call a Scotsman or Welshman an Englishman, but you may call an Englishman a Brit or British.) Great Britain is the legal political entity that came into being when England and Scotland were formally united in 1707, and the UK was created in 1801, when Ireland was absorbed into an even greater Great Britain. This is still the official designation, even though southern Ireland became an independent country in 1922, leaving only the northern counties as part of the UK. You stand a good chance of a friend in London receiving your letter addressed to England or Britain or Great Britain. Although the UK is the name you look for in an atlas or any official gazetteer, if you opt for UK, your letter is more than likely to arrive in the Ukraine, or even Uganda.

Britain used to be the land of the yard, the pound, the mile and the imperial gallon (larger than anybody else's gallon), all sacred measurements embedded in history. Legend maintains that Henry I (1100–1135) decreed the yard to be the distance between the tip of his nose and the end of his thumb. (The legal length of the yard, foot and inch are engraved in stone in Trafalgar Square, London.) Originally, the pound contained only twelve ounces, until Edward III (1327–77) rather arbitrarily decided it weighed sixteen ounces. The mile was first brought to Britain by the Romans and set at 1000 military double-steps, but was later redefined by Elizabethan statute to be exactly 5,280 feet. Local usage, and the nature of the liquid being bottled, determined the quantity of the gallon. But during the 1970s, British history and culture sustained an overwhelming defeat. The Kingdom was officially decimalized, leaving the United States to carry the historic torch almost alone. The rational, but alas "foreign," metric system, which had been part of the French baggage that followed in the wake of the Napoleonic conquest of Europe, finally triumphed, despite Waterloo and St. Helena. The meter, liter, and gram replaced the yard, gallon and ounce. As for pound sterling, that chaotic but endearing monetary system whereby there were 12 pence to the shilling and 20 shillings to the pound, vanished, when on February 14, 1971, the Queen's subjects were informed that there were now 100 pence to the pound and that the shilling was a victim of modernization. Only one archaic measure survives: the stone. True Britons still weigh themselves not in kilograms but in stones (14 pounds to the stone).

In one other area, however, the British have clung to their insular past: they still drive on the wrong, as opposed to the right, side of the road. For a time it looked as if in joining the European Union, the Kingdom would have to switch sides—the Swedes did—but now that the Japanese control the world's automobile market and themselves drive on the wrong side, the rest of us will have to worry about following suit.

English is still the official language of the Kingdom, but you may doubt it if you travel the London underground because London is the most cosmopolitan city in the world. Nevertheless, English-speaking tourists can generally make themselves understood, if only because English (much to the outrage of the French) has become the lingua franca of the world, which means everybody can understand us, but we don't have to understand them. It is important to remember, however, that the British don't speak American. Winston Churchill, George Bernard Shaw and Oscar Wilde have all been credited with the bon mot "England and America are two countries separated by a common language." How true this is quickly becomes apparent when Americans ask for gasoline, a drugstore, the toilet, a truck, a napkin or a diaper. They are answered by, "Oh, you mean petrol, chemist, loo, lorry, serviette, and nappy." Be particularly careful if your landlady asks you if you take "tarts"; she is not running a brothel but offering you a jam or meat pie! Don't be upset if a Britisher offers to "knock you up"; he is only offering to wake you up in the morning, presumably for tea; but watch out if someone suggests a "quick shag." On the other hand, stopping at a "layby" is usually quite safe. Finally, do not ask for English muffins; no one has ever heard of them.

One final point about the British: they are extremely touchy about Europe and are far from united about joining the European Union. David Frost and Anthony Jay, good Brits both, once said the British define hell as a world "where the Germans are the police, the Swedish are the comedians, the Italians are the defense force, . . . the Greeks run the government, and the common language is Dutch." As for the French and the Channel tunnel, "those whom God hath seen fit to cast asunder, let no man join together." So be careful when you refer to the UK as part of Europe. Brits get exceedingly irritated if you refer to them as Europeans.

Chapter III

HISTORY WORTH REMEMBERING
(TO 1485)

On the basis of research in innumerable pubs, at sporting events and at social functions, W.C. Sellar and R. J. Yeatman, the authors of *1066 and All That* (1930)—the happiest short history of England ever written—maintain that there are only two memorable dates in English history: Julius Caesar's invasion of the island in 55 BC and William the Conqueror's victory at Hastings in 1066. It speaks wonders for the British temperament that it can exercise such economy of memory and that it should prefer to memorialize only the two greatest defeats the peoples of Britain have ever sustained. Very likely the authors, could they have carried on their research into more current times, would have found favor for a third memorable date: Britain's disastrous defeat at Dunkirk in June of 1940 which, through an extraordinary concatenation of priorities, has been transformed into the island's finest hour. Although this narrative of British history cannot claim such stringency of means, it does seek to maintain the same principle of memorability: history is not what happened in the past, but what today is worth remembering about the past.

In the Beginning

Although the dedicated Anglophile might prefer to have history commence with the coming of the Angles and the Saxons and their coinage of the name Angleland—later corrupted into England—the Romans got there first and invented the term "Britain." Credit for starting British history goes to Julius Caesar, because the Celtic population, who had arrived after 1000 BC to replace or intermingle with the original Bronze Age Beaker Folk and Urnfield People, had no written language and never recorded what they called their island home. However, Caesar's role in the Roman conquest was largely restricted to spreading the word that the island was ripe for the picking. He crossed the Channel from Gaul in 55 BC and again the following year, but was far too busy crossing his own Rubicon and limiting the number of would-be emperors to one—himself—to worry about Celtic barbarians living a thousand miles from Rome and the center of politics and classical culture. Then, eleven years later on the Ides of March, he also was eliminated. As a consequence the serious conquest of the island did not begin until 43 AD when, eventually, a Romanizing force of 60,000 administrators and soldiers transformed some four to six million Celts into proper Roman citizens for the next 300 years. This was a "civilizing" feat matched only by the British themselves a millennium and a half later, when 160,000 Brits succeeded in anglicizing the 300 million inhabitants of the Indian subcontinent and making them proper subjects of the British Imperial Crown.

A Roman lecturing the ancient Britons on the advantages of Roman civilization

The Celtic peoples and their predecessors in Britain had been in evidence since 3000 BC, give or take a few centuries. What the Celts lacked in ability to express themselves in writing, they made up in stone. All over the British Isles are granite, sandstone and volcanic outcroppings arranged as burial sites and magic circles. The most famous and mysterious of these is Stonehenge.

Stonehenge

Stonehenge (Wiltshire) is possibly the most visited collection of rocks in the world. Placed in a series of concentric circles, they weigh up to 50 tons apiece, the smaller blue stones weighing in at four tons and quarried 135 miles away in Wales, the 50 tonners being mined locally and dragged a mere 24 miles. The original design goes back to the third millenium BC and was improved upon for the next thousand years. The picture of Druid priests making human sacrifices by moonlight is doubtless silly, but Stonehenge and the many other henge structures throughout Britain had something to do with burial rites, seasonal fertility ceremonies and possibly the worship of the sun and the figuring of astronomical calculations to predict solar and lunar eclipses. Alas, there are today so many tourists that visitors are no longer allowed within the magic circle, and are thus deprived of the right to add to British history by carving their names and sentiments in neolithic stone as countless generations have done. Close by, however, the traveler can visit Avebury Circle, the largest megalithic circle in Europe—over 11,000 feet in diameter—and Silbury Hill, the largest artificial mound in Western Europe: its 125-foot summit is large enough to hold all the stones of the two inner circles of Stonehenge. All these neolithic remains stand as enduring evidence of a people with few technological means "impelled by an overmastering impulse" to express themselves as best they could.

The Celtic spirit, if you know where to look for it, still pervades the land, locked away in the origins of town and river names. Avon means "river" in Celtic, and the Thames is Celtic for "dark one," while the River Dee, beside which the Roman walled city of Chester stands, is Celtic for "goddess or holy one." Devon was the territory of the Dumnonii, a Celtic tribe, and Dover gets its name from the local stream, the Dour, originally the Celtic word Dubran, meaning water.

The Comings and Goings of the Romans
(33 BC to 410 AD)

The Celts are remembered by Stonehenge, the Romans by more practical remains. They left 5000 miles of absolutely straight military roads, (good for marching but not for commercial use, because the grades were too steep for ox-drawn carts); the excellent bathing facilities at Bath; a few bits and pieces of exquisite floor mosaics that turn up in unlikely places (for example Winchcombe); and, most spectacular of all, Hadrian's Wall, a 15-foot-high, 10-foot-wide, 73-mile-long barricade designed to deprive envious Picts of the comforts of Roman life south of what is today the Scottish-English border. Rome also left behind the legend of Britain's first proper heroine and female patriot named Queen Boadicea who led a particularly bloody but futile Celtic attack in 60 AD against Roman rule. Appropriately, her statue adorns the parliamentary side of Westminster Bridge in London. The one thing the Romans did not leave behind was Christianity, which was replaced, except in Cornwall and Wales, by an assortment of Anglo-Saxon gods.

The Anglo-Saxons and Ethnic Cleansing
(410 to 1066)

During the decades following 410 AD, the year the Roman legions were called back to the Continent to help rival generals decide who would be the next emperor, the Germanic tribes along the North Sea—the Jutes, Angles and Saxons among them—decided to set sail or oar for Britain. For the next two centuries, Anglo-Saxon warriors "hated by man and God" systematically turned the island into a kind of 5th–6th-century Bosnia, ethnically cleansing the land of its Celtic people or intermarrying with them or both—killing the menfolk and raping the women. In time, their scorched earth policy licked "the western ocean with its fiery red tongue" and the Anglo-Saxons forged a Germanic majority in the more fertile south and east, but left a Celtic fringe in the inaccessible terrains of Scotland, Wales, Devon and Cornwall. Although the Celts and the Anglo-Saxons have learned to tolerate, not exterminate, one another (the exception being Northern Ireland today), they are not sure they constitute a single nation and still like to insult each other as the following definition attests: "The Irishman: he fights for a cause but does not know what he is fighting for; the Welshman: he prays on Sunday and on his neighbors the rest of the week; the Scotsman: he won't wear rubber heels on his shoes because they give a little; the Englishman: he is a self-made man who worships his own creator."

"No, Madam, a passport is not necessary for Scotland."

The Celtic population resisted the Anglo-Saxon invaders, and Arthur, an even more legendary and shadowy figure than Boadicea, looms as the second great Celtic hero, the warrior (not a king) who, at least during his lifetime, stemmed the onslaught of Anglo-Saxon conquests. Guinevere, the Knights of the Round Table and the evil Mordred never existed, but the Celts, with their Roman traditions and partially Christianized faith, may have been marginally more civil than the invaders whom the Romans thought stank because they groomed their hair with rancid butter. "Happy the nose that cannot smell a barbarian." Contemporaries describe these Anglo-Saxons as so "desperate and crass" and so ferocious that their "names [were] not to be spoken." There are those who like to believe that Arthur erected his Camelot at South Cadbury, situated on high grounds with a magnificent view of the Somerset downs and eighteen acres of military archaeological remains, and tradition insists that he was buried in the nearby monastery at Glastonbury.

The invaders proceeded over the years to divide Britain among themselves. The Saxons in the area of London broke up into the east, south and west Saxons—Essex, Sussex, and Wessex. The urge to box the compass generated the splendid, but alas apocryphal, story of a north Saxon kingdom called Nosex which naturally died out very rapidly, but doubtless inspired one of Britain's longest performing plays: *No Sex Please, We're British*. The Angles with their two subdivisions—the north and south folk (Norfolk and Suffolk)—settled in East Anglia. Given the magnificent wealth of one king of East Anglia, whose eighty-foot burial ship was found at Sutton Hoo in 1939, it is not surprising that the kingdom eventually gave its name, Angleland, to the entire island south of Hadrian's Wall. To the north emerged the kingdoms of Mercia (today the Midlands) and Northumbria (Yorkshire, Northumberland, and the Lake Country) while in the far south, the Jutes carved out what eventually became the county of Kent, in Celtic "the land of the armies."

With so many kingdoms, England was overrun by a pride of sovereigns with such unlikely names as Cenwulf and Ceolwulf, Aethelbald and Wiglaf, Bealdred and Ludeca, all of whose life expectancy was not great since they regularly fettered, blinded, imprisoned and mutilated one another. One Anglo-Saxon king, however, stands out, not so much because his name, Alfred King of Wessex (871–899), is more pronounceable than the others and he reigned for 28 years, as because he burnt some cakes (which all true Anglophiles know about) and in doing so was able to do something about the Vikings.

The life expectancy of Anglo-Saxon kings was not great

The Vikings and King Alfred

THE VIKINGS OR NORSEMEN WERE on the move everywhere, raiding, plundering, conquering and in Scotland, England, Ireland, Normandy and Russia, settling down and propagating. They arrived in England in the 780s determined to do to the Anglo-Saxons what the Anglo-Saxons had done to the Roman-Celts and, except for Alfred, they might have succeeded because they destroyed all of the kingdoms of England except Wessex.

Legend has it that in 878, at the low point in his efforts to save his kingdom from destruction by the pagan Vikings, Alfred was forced into hiding and wandered with a small band of men "through the woods and fen fastnesses" of Somerset. Separated from his soldiers, he stumbled upon a swineherd's hut where in Christian charity he was given food and shelter for several days by a husband and wife who had no notion who he was. One day while Alfred sat in front of the fire, the wife began to bake bread, expecting him to keep an eye on the loaves. Deeply depressed and endeavoring to console and encourage himself by meditating upon the patience of Job in the face of divine affliction, and praying to St. Neot to intercede with God to save his kingdom from the pagans, the King forgot his culinary duties, failed to turn the loaves, and let them burn. The wife was justifiably outraged and scolded her careless guest: "You fail to turn the loaves which you see to be burning, yet you're quite happy to eat them when they come warm from the oven!" Duly chastised for his negligence, Alfred humbly directed his attention to the unkingly task of watching the bread. The story is not only a delightful homily on humility and self-control—Christian kings were not expected to go around fettering, blinding or mutilating each other or their subjects—but also raises the question of how St. Neot got into the story, since Roman Christianity was meant to have been destroyed by the Anglo-Saxons and Heaven replaced by Valhalla.

Christianity

Christianity disappeared in Anglo-Saxon England, but not in the inaccessible areas of the Celtic fringe, and during the first half of the 5th century it was still a proselytizing missionary faith. St. Patrick, probably a Welshman or a Cornishman, finding it easier to convert the Irish than

Once more, King Alfred tells his favorite story of the burnt cakes

the Anglo-Saxons, and obviously reluctant to share Heaven and eternal bliss with such a monstrous crew, turned his missionary zeal toward Ireland. He not only rid the island of its snakes (if there were any) but also set in motion one of the more bizarre hairstyle wars in history—the battle of the tonsures. The great religious issue of the 6th and 7th centuries was whether Anglo-Saxon England would succumb to Celtic monks trained in Irish Christianity who shaved the entire front half of their heads, or to continental monks versed in Roman Catholicism who shaved their hair only on the top. The two sides reached pagan England almost in the same year. The Irish missionary St. Columba established a monastery on the island of Iona in 563, just off the coast of western Scotland. His purpose was to convert the heathen Picts, but Celtic Christianity quickly moved south into the kingdom of Northumbria. The Roman or papal version of Christianity, as the story is told, originated when Pope Gregory ran across fair-haired, blue-eyed Anglo-Saxon children being sold on the Roman slave market. When he asked their race and was told they were Angles, he retorted, "Angels, not angles" and said, "They should become fellow heirs with the angels in heaven." This has all the earmarks of Anglo-Saxon conceit, but indisputably Gregory, in 597, the year of St. Columba's death, sent St. Augustine and forty monks into southern England to convert the heathen Angles into Christian angels.

Both Celtic monastery missionaries from Scotland and Roman monks from Kent were immensely successful, and the two approaches to Christianity—differences in church organization, haircuts and the date of Easter—soon met and clashed, especially in Northumbria. In the end, the continental version prevailed, and at the synod of Whitby (664) the Roman ceremony triumphed. King Oswy of Northumbria agreed with St. Wilfred of Ripon's stern warning that St. Columba could not possibly compete with St. Peter, and he reminded Oswy that the Pope was Peter's successor as head of the Church. As Oswy put it: if he failed to do as the Pope commanded, "When I come to the gates of heaven, he who holds the keys may not be willing to open them."

King Oswy agreeing with St. Wilfred to adopt Roman Catholicism

Irish-Celtic Christianity bowed to Rome, but the mixture of the two produced one of the richest eruptions of art, literature and scholarship in British history. The most memorable name to emerge from this intellectual explosion was that of Bede (673–735), always called the Venerable, presumably because he made it to age sixty-two. He wrote the *Ecclesiastical History of the English People* which became a best seller for the next thousand years and taught everyone to distinguish between the past and the present by putting the initials "BC" (before Christ) and "AD" (anno domini or "in the year of our Lord") after all dates. This made history a lot easier and tidier.

Law and Order

But to return to Alfred and his cakes: he was sufficiently successful against the Vikings to be able to keep them and their laws north and east of one of those devilishly straight Roman roads that ran from London to northern Wales, and to force them to live in towns ending in "by" (Norse for village) and "thorp" (Norse for hamlet), such as Markby, Little Grimsby, Selby, and Woodthorpe, all safely in Lincolnshire and Yorkshire. By the time his son Edward (899–924) and grandson Athelstan (924–939) had finished with their conquests, all of England was united under Wessex rule.

Alfred and his successors maintained law and order, Alfred showing the way, and doing what came naturally to kings, when he collected all the old laws of the Kingdom and ordered that many of them, "which our forefathers observed, should be written down [and enforced] namely those I like."

Alfred and his descendants did more than write down the law. They tried to apply the Biblical dictum "an eye for an eye, a tooth for a tooth," and to curtail the expansion and escalation of vendettas and gang wars. If a Saxon lost a tooth as a consequence of an enemy's action, he or his family could demand a tooth in revenge, but could not up the ante and put the enemy's eye out as well. As an added incentive to law and order, Anglo-Saxon kings worked out a system of financial compensations, arguing that extracting your enemy's eye or tooth in revenge didn't do anyone much good—eyes rotted pretty fast—but if you could have your revenge in cash, that was something that you could keep and use. So a system of wergilds or revenge moneys or injury rates was worked out. If another person deprived you of a tooth, he had to pay 6 shillings; a big toe was worth 10 shillings; an ear 12s. and an eye 50s.

Alfred collecting old laws and
deciding on those he liked

A life was far more costly, depending, of course, on your social worth. The family of a freeman or woman could demand 200s. from a murderer, but that of a nobleman could call for 1200s. Once the wergild had been paid and the injury or death duly compensated, the King would issue his mund or protection or peace, threatening to punish any member of either family who sought to escalate or continue the fight. This system, as we all know, was rediscovered by modern juries and insurance companies and vastly expanded, adding mental anguish to the list of injuries. As a result of these efforts by the kings of Wessex, England by 1066 was the richest and ripest plum for the picking in all of Christendom, a point very much on William the Conqueror's mind at the time.

Duke William and the Norman Conquest
(1066)

When Alfred forced the Vikings out of Wessex, he thought he was done with them, but his descendants were not. One Viking King, Canute (1016–1035) actually sat for a short time on the Wessex throne, but, more important for English history, another Norseman named Rollo settled down in Normandy (the land of the Norse) and in 911 became the first Duke of Normandy, and therefore the great- great-great grandfather of William the Conqueror, the bastard son of Robert the Devil by a pretty French girl named Arlette, a tanner's daughter. Please note that there is more than a modicum of plebeian blood in the present royal family, especially if you look carefully.

The Wessex dynasty ran out when Edward the Confessor died on January 5, 1066. He is memorable for having committed the one unforgivable sin which all kings are warned against—although married, he lived celibate. When criticized for preferring the confessional to his wife, he answered, "The kingdom of the English is of God; and He will provide a king for it according to His will." The English have always maintained this conceit, and by the 19th century were even maintaining that God was an Englishman. In this case, when the great and wise men of the kingdom gathered to select a new king, God provided that they should elect Edward's brother-in-law, Harold Godwin. Edward's cousin, William Duke of Normandy, who expected to inherit the throne, was more than a little put out at what he regarded as a totally illegal act, claiming that the wise men of the realm could select as king only a member of the

Wessex family. William argued that he was
Edward's first cousin-once-removed because
his aunt Emma had married Edward's father.
What he failed to mention was that he had
no more Wessex blood in his veins than
Harold Godwin.

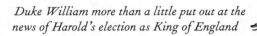

*Duke William more than a little put out at the
news of Harold's election as King of England*

William spread all sorts of nasty rumors about both Harold—he was
an oath breaker and brother killer—and about the Anglo-Saxons—
they sold "their female servants when pregnant by them either to public
prostitution or to foreign slavery"—and he persuaded the Pope to bless
his claim, thereby turning his invasion into a crusade of liberation.

The Duke gave teeth to his determination to become the rightful
King of England over the "usurper" Harold Godwin by landing a force
of over 10,000 men on the Sussex coast just west of the port of Hastings. As he waded ashore, he slipped and fell flat on his face—a terrible
omen—which a quick-witted observer transformed into a token of success by suggesting that the Duke had grasped England in his hands and
it now belonged to him and all his followers. On 14 October, 1066, in
the most momentous battle in Anglo-Saxon history, William met and
defeated an exhausted Saxon army. Only days before, King Harold had
vanquished yet another Viking invasion in the north of England led
by King Harold of Norway and Godwin's own brother, Tosti. Harold
had then marched his troops 250 miles in six days south to Hastings.
The battle lasted all day and could have gone either way until Harold
was killed, probably by an arrow in his eye. The Saxon militia broke
ranks and fled, but Harold's sworn companions guarded their king's
body until every one of them was slaughtered. "In the English ranks,"
wrote one Norman chronicler, "the only movement was the dropping
of the dead. . . . They were ever ready with their steel, those sons of the
old Saxon race, the most dauntless of men." (The actual location of the
battle was at Battle, six miles north of Hastings. There William founded

Battle Abbey with its high altar placed on the spot where Harold fell. If you like ruins and battlefields, the site is worth a visit.)

William the Conqueror grasping England in his hands

Harold died at Hastings, but his victory in the north assured that England would become Norman French, not Viking and Scandinavian. From 1066 on, the Anglo-Saxons fell to second-class status, and polite society began speaking nothing but French for the next 300 years. Lest her subjects forget the Norman Conquest, the Queen continues to this day to give her consent to acts of Parliament in French—"La reyne le veult" (the Queen wills it)—and when Parliament passes a money bill financing her government, she says, "La reyne remercie ses bons sujets, accepte leur benevolence et ainsi le veult." (The Queen thanks her good subjects, accepts their generosity and therefore wills it.)

Winning a Kingdom in a single battle, as is usually the case, proved easier than holding it. To control his new subjects, William, having dropped the name of Duke and Conqueror and settled for William I of England, did three very conquering things: he executed everyone who criticized him (this he called the King's Peace); he divided Saxon England up among his Norman barons (this is called feudalism by the historians); and he covered the land with a lot of castles to remind his new subjects who was in control.

William was a firm believer in law and order and issued a battery of statutes, one of the most memorable being his decision to divide jurisdiction over his subjects' bodies between himself and his barons and to make money doing it: "I forbid that anyone be killed or hung for any fault; but his eyes shall be torn out or his testicles cut off. And this command shall not be violated under penalty of a fine in full to me." This division of punishment—life and death reserved to the King, the bits and pieces to the barons—might strike modern readers as somewhat peculiar, and might well lead them to think the 11th-century Englishman was well advised to keep out of the hands of any authority, but this wasn't always easy, because Anglo-Saxon and early Norman law made no distinction between premeditated and accidental murder. Even if you invited a friend to dinner and on the way he fell off his horse and died of a broken neck, you were held responsible. You had committed murder because by your agency you had brought your friend "further from life" and "nearer to death." Under these circumstances there were not many dinner parties in 11th-century England.

Feudalism

In order to help his barons ensure that the English were at all times pious and obedient and that cutpurses and other kinds of hoods (Robin Hood is the most memorable) were properly cut up and/or executed, William and his henchmen built a vast array of massive and unromantic castles, the most historic being the Tower of London and Windsor Castle. English royal history is filled with instances where monarchs were thankful they had heavily fortified homes into which to retreat when either their barons or their subjects were thoroughly annoyed by their behavior. How carefully English kings guarded themselves can be seen in the ceremony of the Keys when the Tower of London is locked up each night. It is a fascinating ritual that has remained unchanged for 700 years and is open to the public if you write ahead for tickets.

William divided up not only his subjects' bodies but also their lands. Historians wax both eloquent and wrathful over whether William introduced, invented or discovered feudalism, but everyone is agreed that whatever he did, he made feudalism work better in England than did any other monarch in Europe. Feudalism is the most important single term for comprehending English medieval history, but as a system it is almost impossible to describe, some historians going so far as to question whether it actually existed at all. Possibly this is why students so often confuse it with the "futile system." Feudalism was both an attitude of mind and a political relationship supplying the human bonds that held medieval society together. In theory, it was a contractual but unwritten agreement between private individuals (the lord and his vassal) whereby the lord exchanged land for services, mostly military but sometimes legal and financial. Feudalism, although private, in the sense that the lord granted authority or dominium over land and the vassal in return took an oath of fealty to obey, was public in purpose. Its goal was to tie the political and military elite together into an organized and controllable unit that could be called upon to defend the Kingdom and enforce a minimum of law and order. It offered security in an era that was desperately short of ready money and had only land with which to pay for a professionally trained standing army.

Windsor Castle, the Norman way of reminding the English who was in control

As a private association between two contracting individuals aimed primarily at defense, feudalism tended to cultivate and extol two attributes: courage and loyalty. Although the vassal had important financial and judicial obligations to his overlord, the knight was above all a warrior. His reason for being was to fight, and therefore war was acclaimed to be a good and honorable enterprise and the proper stage upon which to display valor and loyalty. It is said that Duke William's troops as they rushed into battle against the Saxon army at Hastings sang "The Song of Roland," a singularly bloodthirsty tale of unyielding honor and bravery in which Roland and his tiny band of Christian heroes faced overwhelming odds against a Muslim horde. The vassal owed personal loyalty to his lord, and he tended to define himself in terms of the person to whom he had pledged his service and from whom he expected support. "Between lord and man there is only faith, and faith must be recognized and kept between them." This was the emotional cement that tied society together, and, as a result, any sense of obligation to a public authority, such as the state, was placed well below the private faith a man felt for his immediate overlord. The person and personality of the king were always far greater magnets for loyalty than was the crown he wore.

When William seized the Wessex throne, he strove to apply the organization of feudalism to his new domain and capitalize on its military and social values. During his reign, he kept about one-fourth of the island to maintain himself and his government. These are called the Crown lands or the private property of the monarch, and Elizabeth II still owns quite a few square miles of the Conqueror's conquest. (In all, the Crown owns today 250,000 acres.) William reserved another fourth of the land for the Church and then divided the remainder among 180 of his tenants-in-chief or top barons (ten received more than half the property) who in turn sub-infeudated their possessions among the lesser barons who owed them fealty and service. The "system" descended to the knight and his fief, the smallest jurisdictional unit large enough to support one armed knight and his retainers. In this way, William could, if necessary, raise a fighting force of approximately 5,000 knights to defend his kingdom and keep his English subjects peaceful and loyal.

Tidy and systematic in theory, feudalism in practice had two overwhelming drawbacks: 1) little or nothing was ever written down on paper—there were no lawyers available—which meant both sides could interpret the contract pretty much as they wanted; and 2) in a dispute,

real power tended to rest with the barons who had private armies at their disposal. Both these factors go a
long way in explaining the bloodiness and confusion of
most of English medieval history, because for the next
400 years the kings of England would do their best to
take advantage of the first weakness and minimize the
consequences of the second.

*A Norman baron insuring that the English
were at all times peaceful and loyal*

Medieval reality is hard for the 21st century to imagine, but visualize
a world without gunpowder that settles its international, social, economic
and private conflicts, not on the battlefield, but in the football stadium
where the winning team decides the dispute as it sees fit. Under these circumstances, the overriding concern of society would be how to induce
the players, once they are out of the stadium, to act in a civil manner. It
is difficult for us wimps to argue successfully with a professional athlete
weighing in at 250 pounds and encased in helmet, shoulder plates and padding. Even more serious—how does society control the owners of these
football teams whose players are defending us from foreign aggression?
Equate the owners with the great barons, and the players with the boiler-
plated knights clanking about the countryside doing pretty much as they
pleased, and you have a fairly realistic picture of feudal society. The central political issue of the day was how to get the vassals to live up to their
oaths of fealty and be honest, faithful and true to their overlords, and how
to get the top barons to wage war for the King and not against him.

Chivalry

Chivalry helped, but not much. Chivalry combined the macho warrior
code of courage, honor and loyalty—like Harold's companions giving
their lives to defend his corpse—with the religious code of piety, humility and duty to God. In breaking his feudal oath, the Christian knight had

God as well as his overlord to reckon with, and he risked his immortal soul. The theory then and now was that if you can't force a person to be good, you internalize the pressure and get him to enforce it himself. As every parent knows, there is nothing like a sense of guilt to discipline a child. The same held true for a knight. The English ideal was William Marshall, Earl of Pembroke, who served four kings faithfully and willingly, and when he died in 1219, Cardinal Langton said of him: "Behold, all that remains of the best knight who ever lived . . . . We have here a mirror, you and I. Let each man say his pater noster that God may . . . place him among His faithful vassals as he so well deserves." It was a great comfort to know that Heaven was the perfect feudal society where everybody lived by the rules.

Domesday Book
(1086)

Rules get broken, especially if they clash with the self-interest of armed men who possess power to make their own laws, and William tried to "improve" upon English feudalism—the barons might say he sought to take all the fun out of the system—by introducing a new set of regulations to force his vassals to be faithful and to tip the balance of political power in his favor. William asked each of the shires of the Kingdom to select a jury or committee of informed people to find out who owned what and how much in their county. He checked these findings against what his tenants-in-chief could tell him about how they had distributed the land he had given them. He then wrote everything down in a book. There was not "one yard of land, nor even—it is shame to tell—an ox, nor a cow, nor a swine was left that was not set down in his writ." The writer of this lament had cause to worry. Government by census-taking and fact-gathering was beginning, and Englishmen entitled William's work *Domesday Book* (1086) because it reminded them of the last judgment. But they were wrong; it turned out not to be the last but only the first of many judgments that governments would make about people's property.

Short-Circuiting the System

That same year (1086) William proceeded to play unfair and short-circuit the entire feudal system. At Salisbury, he gathered his top barons with all their vassals and sub-vassals together, and demanded from the entire gathering an oath of allegiance directly to him, the King. This meant that now vassals had a double loyalty, and henceforth when a great baron was fighting against his sovereign, it gave his vassals a good excuse for not fulfilling their duty to him; their first loyalty now rested with the King.

William was smarter, or possibly just plain luckier, than most feudal kings, because he was able to frustrate his barons by one final practice. In giving them land in return for service, he distributed their fiefs throughout the Kingdom instead of concentrating them in one locality. Thus a great English magnate might be as powerful as his baronial brother across the Channel—say a Duke of Burgundy or a Count of Flanders—in terms of the number of knights he could call to arms, but he could not capitalize on that military strength and carve out a sub-kingdom independent of the King. English barons had to watch their "P's" and "Q's," and in a conflict with the King the only way they could handle him was through collective action—barons of England unite, you have nothing to lose but your royal chains. This was a formula they would remember when, four generations later, they encountered King John, a thoroughly greedy king.

The Common Law and the Jury System

Because medieval kings were invariably both greedy and broke, they developed two ingenious ways of making or raising money. One was reasonably legal, the other demonstrably illegal. The legal method was to open up the King's justice to everyone for a price. This meant, of course, that justice was available only to those who could afford it. Henry I (1100–1135) started the process by making his justice mobile. Instead of requiring his subjects to come before him for justice, he sent his judges, called itinerant justices, out to them. This made the King's law common to the entire realm, thus creating the Common Law. It also enhanced the King's prestige, brought more business to the royal courts and increased his income. Although the top barons complained, the knights thought this an excellent extension of royal authority, because it safeguarded them against the local baronial bully, often their own overlords.

Henry II (1154–1189) went further. He invented the inquest jury to settle property disputes between his vassals. A plaintiff could now purchase a royal writ by which the King would order his sheriff to convene a jury to decide disputed inheritances and cases of illegal possession by an overlord. This was clearly a good thing, even if it gave rise to lawyers and litigation, because the traditional way of resolving such cases had been ordeal by combat in which presumably God granted victory to the person with the best legal claim. The Church thought it was asking too much of the Deity to decide legal cases, and supported the new system even though the process was considerably slower and more expensive.

Ordeal by combat

The inquest jury worked so well that Henry in 1166 decided to extend the procedure to criminal cases. Again, this was a vast improvement over the old system of accusation by whomever cried the loudest. Once the jury had determined that a crime had been committed and named the culprit, the defendant still had to prove his innocence or display his guilt by one of two kinds of ordeal. He might be required to hold a red-hot iron or put his hand in boiling water for a specified period of time. If after three days the hand had not healed, he was deemed guilty. (The hand by then was probably useless to him anyhow.) Or he would be chucked into a pool; the water was abjured to reject him if he were guilty and accept him if he were innocent. Therefore, if he floated he was guilty, if he drowned he was innocent (which by then was a mere technicality). This singularly unpredictable method of trial was not replaced by the trial jury for another hundred years, but inquest juries often refused to order the ordeal if they thought the accused was innocent, and the King could always banish a guilty defendant even if he had passed the ordeal.

Ordeal by boiling water

Upping the Fiscal Ante

These innovations were reasonably popular. What really irked everybody except the tax collectors, were the clearly illegal devices used by Henry II and especially his son John (1199–1216) to raise money. Every vassal owed his overlord three kinds of financial support. 1) If he could not fulfill his military obligations in person, he had to pay shield money or scutage with which the lord could finance a substitute. (Kings were delighted with scutage because they could use the cash to pay for a mercenary army instead of relying on uncontrollable feudal levies.) 2) He owed relief, a kind of estate tax, when he inherited a fief from his father. And 3) he owed aides whenever his overlord had really extraordinary expenses, as in time of war or when he needed extra cash for his daughter's dowry. Unfortunately, nothing was written down; and faced with ever-rising costs of government (as always), English kings upped the feudal financial ante, demanding more frequent aides and scutages and raising the cost of relief. John was the greediest of them all. His father, Henry II, had issued eight scutages in a reign of thirty-five years; John demanded eleven in eighteen years, several of which were for military campaigns he never fought. The barons thought this was grossly unfair.

Henry I's chief justiciar, Roger Bishop of Salisbury, is credited with designing the checkered tablecloth called the Exchequer on which English monarchs kept count of their feudal income coming in from aides, scutage and the like. In so doing, he invented something even more important: the bureaucratic mind that realized that the secret of power resides not so much in fighting men as in counting money and that money talks above all else. As another Exchequer official under Henry II put it, the power of kings "rises and falls as their portable wealth flows or ebbs. . . . Money is no less indispensable in peace than in war."

Magna Charter
(1215)

Under these circumstances, it is not surprising that the barons, who didn't understand counting money, were miffed at King John and said among other things, "Foul as it is, hell itself is defiled by the fouler presence of John." The trouble with John was not so much that he was a repellent human being—most early English kings come close to filling that description—as that he was a ruthless money raiser who failed to translate taxes into military victories. Instead, he lost most of his father's continental empire—about half of modern France—and earned the scornful baronial nickname of "soft sword." To make matters worse, he got himself excommunicated (this meant his vassals did not have to live up to their oaths of fealty); then he granted all of England to the Pope as a papal fief in order to win back His Holiness's favor; and, finally, he became the first wicked royal uncle in English history—he probably murdered his nephew, "little Arthur" (actually aged sixteen), who by right of inheritance should have been king.

The reason John got himself into trouble with the papacy goes back to the days of his father, who also had trouble with the Church and inadvertently created the most popular saint of the twelfth century—Thomas Becket, Archbishop of Canterbury. Church-state relations had always been troublesome, because God and Caesar were expected to divide body and soul between them, but no one could figure out where the one started and the other ended. Furthermore, bishops were not only spiritual figures responsible for the soul's welfare, but also feudal magnates owing military service to the King. (The archdiocese of Canterbury owed the King sixty knights.) Controversy erupted in 1150 when Henry

II appointed his Lord Chancellor, Thomas Becket, to be Archbishop of Canterbury. Thomas promptly announced he could not serve two masters at the same time, resigned the chancellorship and began propounding the most extreme arguments about the Church's independence from all state interference and its freedom from all secular and royal laws.

Two proud and willful men, one defending the honor of the Kingdom, the other the honor of God, fought to a standoff until Henry in a rash moment asked his barons, "Who will rid me of this low born priest?" Five of his vassals did exactly as he asked. They assassinated Becket as he was standing at the high altar of Canterbury Cathedral. The murder was an extremely impolitic action. Becket became a saint in record time (only St. Francis of Assisi made it faster); pilgrims flocked to his shrine in Canterbury (that is where Chaucer's pilgrims were headed); and for a short time the balance of church-state power dipped heavily against the state. Thus, when John quarreled with the Pope over who should be Archbishop of Canterbury, he was at a disadvantage and got the worst of it.

So John was a three-way loser. He lost to the papacy, he lost his inheritance in France, and he now lost out to the barons, who finally learned the importance of writing things down—"with a John you have to have paper." They insisted at sword point that he sign a document variously called Magna Carta or Charter (1215).

The barons learn the importance of writing things down

In this famous document, John promised to quit doing all those things that had outraged his barons, like raising rates, seizing property and forcing daughters and widows to marry whomever he decreed. He also pledged not to impose aides and scutages "except by the common council of our kingdom."

Promises are easy to make, but hard to enforce, and John was compelled to accept a committee of twenty-five barons to see to it that he keep his word and invite the whole community to "distress and injure us in every way they can," should he violate the Charter, which, of course, he did the moment he was out of swords' reach. He even got the Pope (now his friend since he had become a papal vassal) to absolve him of his oath, and he raised an army against the Magna Carta barons. The Pope's blessings, however, availed him little because the next year, not far from King's Lyn in Norfolk, he led his army across a small tidal inlet at low tide and in so doing marched his men into a stretch of quicksand. As a consequence, he lost his entire baggage and "everything in the world that he held most dear," including his crown. (Treasure hunters have been looking for it ever since.) Four days later, probably from getting so wet, he died of a combination of fever and, as every British school child knows, a surfeit of peaches and fresh cider. Little wonder no English king has ventured to take the name of John II.

Magna Carta resolved little, and the succession of a nine-year-old King did far more than a scrap of parchment to satisfy the barons and tip the political balance back in their favor.

But embedded in the Great Charter (four originals exist today; one each in Lincoln and Salisbury Cathedrals, and two in the British Museum in London) were the germs of two crucial ideas: 1) the historic customs and laws of the Kingdom stood higher than the King's will and, if he wanted to change those laws, the people (meaning at first the barons) had to be consulted—"without law a king is a tyrant"; and 2) if he violated the law, the people (again at first meaning the barons) had a right to chuck him out.

*The succession of a nine-year-old King did far
more than a scrap of parchment to satisfy the barons*

The Origin of Parliament

Henry III's reign (1216–72) is remembered because it was the third longest in English history (George III lasted 60 years, Victoria 64), and it is given credit for the birth of Parliament. How does one write about Parliament? The answer is very, very cautiously. It is indisputably memorable; everyone knows that England is the home of representative government, but historically it is almost unmanageable, because no one invented Parliament. It just happened. Parliament—which stems from the French verb parler, "to talk"—like Topsy, simply growed, because a lot of hard bargaining and talking were useful to both the barons and the King. Allegedly Winston Churchill, who should have known, stated the process in its most succinct and quotable form: "Jaw-jaw is better than war-war."

Like so many historical processes, the origin of Parliament is tied up with filthy lucre. The barons under John had insisted that he promise not to impose scutage and aids without convening his Great Council and discussing with it the need for taxation. (Not quite the same thing as asking permission, but close.) Later kings, especially Edward I, found that the easiest way of financially plucking the feudal turkey with the least amount of public squawking was to ask the people who had money—the barons and the knights of the shires. War made medieval sovereigns insolvent. When Edward I discovered that his military expenses over a period of four years had reached £730,000, while his yearly revenues were only £150,000, he found Parliament a useful, almost essential, way of preventing bankruptcy. Thus from the start, Parliament was both an organization to curtail royal power and an instrument to extend royal power, and it worked far better as a tool of the King than of the barons. A double paradox underlies the history and success of the institution. Only a strong king could make Parliament effective—initiate its statutes, enforce its laws and insist that it operate as a high court of justice—and only in England did Parliament survive because English 13th-century kings were so much more powerful than their cousins on the Continent.

Simon de Montfort in 1265 summoned the first Parliament, called the first because he invited for the first time not only the great barons and prelates of the Church but also two knights from every shire, and equally important, two burgesses from every chartered town, a sure sign that they were growing rich from trade and could be expected to contribute to the cost of the King's government. Over time these representatives of the Kingdom shuffled themselves into two groups—the House of Lords and the House of Commons, a unique arrangement, because elsewhere in Europe the clergy and the town folk sat separately from both the greater and lesser landowners.

Simon's purpose in calling this Parliament was to consolidate a baronial rebellion. He was a French baron and the brother-in-law of Henry III, and he led the protest and uprising against the King's scandal-ridden, extravagant and inefficient government. Baronial outrage reached the boiling point when Henry allowed the Pope to lead him down the garden path by offering the King's younger son the Crown of Sicily. Henry accepted the offer only to discover it had all sorts of strings attached such as: 1) Sicily already had an incumbent king, 2) the Pope expected the English to pay off his immense debts, and 3) His Holiness was quite prepared to excommunicate Henry if he didn't come up with the cash. It was a bad bargain, and precipitated a financial crisis in England that led to rebellion in 1264. Simon de Montfort's efforts to clean up the King's government did not last long; fifteen months later he was killed in battle by Henry's extremely competent elder son, the future Edward I, but the truth remains that England's first Parliament, as well as the word itself, came from France and was introduced by a Frenchman. Not something a real Anglo-Saxon cares to remember.

The Three Edwards
(1272–1377)

The English, Scots and Welsh remember Edward I (1272–1307) for very different reasons. English textbooks always refer to him as the model feudal king. But the English barons were not so sure; they were delighted by his military prowess, but deeply alarmed by his insistence that things needed to be written down in order to make them legal. Edward wanted to know by what warrant—Quo Warranto—his barons held their franchises (areas over which they had legal authority and could set up courts of law). The barons were outraged, and suspected the King was trying to encroach on their independence. One of them produced "an ancient and rusty sword and cried 'here my lords, here is my warrant! My ancestors came over with William the Bastard and conquered their lands by the sword and I will defend those same lands by the sword. . . .'" Edward wisely backed down, but his vassals were correct in sensing that the age of written documentation, lawyers and bureaucracy was fast approaching.

An outraged baron defending his title with his sword

The Scots gleefully recall Edward as "the hammer of the Scots" who missed the nail and hit his thumb. Edward tried for fifteen years to tame the Highland peoples and persuade them to recognize him as overlord of their bleak hills and misty dales, but he died before he could succeed. His sole triumph was the seizure in 1296 of the Stone of Scone on which Scottish kings had been crowned from time out of mind. (The Scots prefer to call it the Stone of Destiny, doubtless to differentiate it from a Celtic cake.) He carted the stone to Westminster Abbey, decided it was too uncomfortable to sit on, and built a splendid coronation chair around it for all future kings to be crowned on. Six hundred and fifty-four years later, on Christmas day 1950, the Scots managed to swipe the rock back, which was quite a feat since it weighs a tidy 458 pounds. They didn't return the stone, but made the English ridiculous by letting it be known where it was hidden in Scotland so that the English police could come and fetch it. Forty-six years later, the English were finally afflicted with a case of guilty conscience, and in 1996 formally returned the stone. In order to see it the tourist must now travel to Edinburgh. What future British kings will sit on when they are crowned remains to be seen.

Edward I carting off the Stone of Scone to Westminster Abbey

The Welsh have only to look out their windows at the sinister and not-in-the-least romantic castles (the most spectacular are Caenarvon, Conway and Harlech) that Edward built all over their country to remind themselves that it was Edward I who finally brought them to heel and made them part of England. By compensation, however, he promised them a Welsh-born future king. So he brought his pregnant wife to Caernarvon Castle and, when a son was born, he presented him as the "new Prince of Wales." Ever since, the King of England's eldest son has carried the title. Edward's gesture, however, did not soften Welsh hearts: in the 16th century they were still saying, "All these three live on blood—the flea, the mercenary and the Englishman."

Unfortunately for England and Wales, but not for Scotland, Edward's first born didn't survive, nor did his second or third, but his fourth son did. The second Edward (1307–27) is memorable for all the wrong reasons. He led an immense English army into Scotland to do what his father had failed to accomplish, and he got himself so badly defeated by a far smaller Scottish army at the Battle of Bannockburn (1314) that all English efforts to absorb Scotland ended for the next 400 years. Edward became so unpopular that eventually he was forced to abdicate as a consequence of yet another baronial uprising, led this time by his wife Isabella, her lover Roger Mortimer, and young Prince Edward, the King's fourteen-year-old son. Edward II did not long survive the palace revolution and was murdered, legend has it, in a most unpleasant way (see Royal Soap Opera, p. 202).

Edward II being murdered most unpleasantly

Edward III (1327–77) was a splendidly chivalric monarch who commenced his reign by executing his mother's paramour and incarcerating his mother in a comfortable prison for the rest of her life. Such unfilial behavior raises a heretofore unmentioned aspect of royal life—domestic friction. Family feuding was chronic throughout English royal history, because early modern governments combined family tensions and animosities with feudal and political conflicts. Public officials tended to be the King's private servants and/or personal cronies—as if the United States Secretary of State were also the President's valet, who played poker with him every Saturday night. Not only were the monarch's children his potential heirs, but they also helped him govern his Kingdom and often possessed incomes independent of the Crown—as if the President's sons were also the governors of New York and Texas. Consequently, family squabbles could and did erupt into feudal and political quarrels as when factions at court looked to the eldest son in expectation of his father's death or when a king presented feudal lands to his sons only to have them turn against him, both as vassals and offspring. This is what happened when Henry II divided up his various French possessions among his three elder sons. At the instigation of their mother, Eleanor of Aquitane, who was highly irritated that she had been evicted from the royal bed by Henry's mistress, the fair Rosamond Clifford, they rebelled against their father. To his dying day, he never resolved a civil war that was largely fueled by family hatred.

Edward III got along with his family far better than Henry II with his. He was devoted to his wife Philippe whom he had married at fifteen, and his six sons were surprisingly loyal, even after the chivalric romance of his early reign turned into the defeat and senility of his final years. Not only was Edward a good family man, but, more important, he was a good king as defined by the feudal standards of his age. He was macho, warlike and got along splendidly with his barons which was crucial to the success of any English king because, by the 14th century, the balance of political and financial power had dipped heavily in their favor, and a number of super barons were beginning to emerge.

As the ideal feudal knight, it behooved Edward to distract his barons with war in France, and consequently in 1338 he began a 115-year conflict which for no observable reason is always called the Hundred Years War, a conflict in which the cannon and longbow became more important than the armored and mounted knight.

The cannon becoming more important than the armored knight

The English won all the chivalric battles, but badly lost the unchivalrous war. The war was in effect a continuation of a conflict that started when the French baron and vassal of the King of France—Duke William of Normandy—became King of England in 1066. The aim of all future kings of England was to keep, or extend by battle or marriage, their French territories, and of all future kings of France to relieve their royal vassals of their French possessions. By 1338, England had lost everything except Gascony in southern France, and English-French relations had deteriorated to the point that the English were calling the French "frogs" (they ate slimy frog legs) and the French were countering with "God-damns" (the English used the expression so often). The English losing streak in France had gone on for so long that the French were convinced that England, as they said, had "the heart of a rabbit in the body of a lion" and was "the abode of popinjays."

Legend claims the fighting started anew when a highly dubious, free-wheeling French baron by the name of Count Robert of Artois presented Edward with a roasted heron (a symbol of cowardice), implying that the young King was afraid to claim and seize his rightful inheritance—the Crown of France. The direct male Capetian royal line had ended when Charles IV died childless. Edward III's mother was Charles's sister and he was therefore next in line, until the French suddenly remembered the Salic law—the French Crown could not pass through the female line—and the throne was given to Philip Valois, a good Frenchman and first cousin to the late Charles. With two powerful sovereigns, one sitting on the French throne, the other claiming it, and a war party egging the two sides on, war was predictable. By 1360, most of southern France and the Channel port of Calais were English and the flower of French armored cavalry had been dehorsed and deflowered by English longbows. Within two decades, however, these conquests melted away, and under Richard II, England would lose all its French possessions except Calais.

An English archer

Military victory on the Continent covered up the face of death on a terrifying level, because in 1348–49 the Black Death reached Britain, arriving first at Weymouth, today a delightful seaside town made famous by George III when doctors told him that sea-bathing would curb his growing madness. The plague was a virulent and mobile affliction transmitted by fleas to rats to man and spread pneumatically through direct contagion. It reduced the population by 40 percent—"We see death coming into our midst like black smoke, a plague which cuts off the young, and has no mercy for the fair of face." Worse, it was so fearsomely capricious that it could skip one village entirely, but wipe out another. The psychological impact of such a scourge, for which there was no explanation except the wrath of God, was devastating. England and the Continent slipped into two centuries of necrophilism, a fascination with death that was grounded on fear, not hope of resurrection, and the skeleton and cadaver replaced the recumbent figure of the pious Christian in Heaven as the favored tombstone effigy.

Piety and Progress

The arrival of war and disease on an unparalleled scale within a decade of each other is often said to have signaled the demise of medieval culture as a joyous and optimistic expression of man's faith in God and himself. During the 200 years before the Black Death and the Hundred Years War, Christians all over Europe had begun to open up their hearts and purses to help the Church in its struggle to transform 7th- and 8th-century Christianity from a ritualistic religion based on bartering with God—"if you give me victory in war or cure my cattle of hoof and mouth disease, I will worship you and not some pagan god"—into an internalized faith that viewed Christ's sacrifice on the cross and the suffering of the early Christian martyrs as the highest possible role models. True Christians were expected to ask not what God could do for them but what they could do for God. The monastery with its religious elite dedicated, at least in theory, to living out the Christian ideal of love, prayer and self-denial, and the cathedral which towered high above both royal palace and baronial castle, were the visual symbols of the new spiritual impulses of the era.

Medieval culture as a joyous and optimistic expression
of man's faith in God and himself

No visitor to England should miss the extraordinary magic of the ruins of Fountains Abbey hidden away in the rugged Yorkshire countryside or the magnificence of Lincoln, Salisbury and Wells Cathedrals with their lofty pointed arches and ribbed vaults designed to lead the eye upwards to God's grace, as it poured through a multitude of gorgeously colored stained-glass windows. Salisbury may well be the most graceful edifice in Britain, but it crawls with tourists who are forever being asked to contribute to its preservation fund. Lincoln, in contrast, is spiritually more pleasing, protected from hordes of gawking sightseers by its remoteness from London.

The cathedral was an expression of the renewed faith of the age, but it was equally evidence of its economic and social achievements. Before any monuments to God could be constructed or any monastery endowed, England (and all of Europe) had to move from a subsistence to a surplus economy which could support an expanding population and an increasingly complex civilization. Close to two million people had lived in England in 1066; by the year of the Black Death (1348) that number had certainly doubled, possibly tripled. Written records were more and more common; contracts and property rights were protected no longer by oral testimony or the sword, but now by written deeds and indentures; and society began to tax itself with greater and greater confidence that there was enough surplus money to pay for royal and clerical officials determined to remodel society in their own images. The growth of historical documentation is eloquent evidence of the extent of organizational and administrative change and the steady rationalization of society. By the 13th century, English kings were generating so much parchment work in the form of writs, warrants, summonses and royal edicts, that it became necessary to record how much wax the government was purchasing and using to seal royal documents. As one historian has noted, during the 46 years between "Henry III's coming of age and his death (1226–1272) the use of sealing wax increased ten fold." The managerial era had been born, if not yet come of age.

As reading and writing and rational thinking became essential to the proper functioning of society, the demand for education grew apace. Oxford University was fully established by 1163; Cambridge was founded two generations later by a band of disgruntled Oxford scholars; and by the 13th century, several hundred church and private schools had been established to teach the three R's. Even more remarkable, though government records continued to be written in Latin and French (the languages of the ruling elite), English was slowly reemerging as the dominant tongue. Anglo-Saxon English, incomprehensible to modern readers, had by the late 14th century developed into Chaucerian English, understandable with a little help, and it was in the English of Geoffrey Chaucer (the first writer to be buried in Westminster Abbey) that late medieval culture struggled with a world beset by death, heresy, economic stagnation, political turmoil, and social upheaval, for which neither church nor state seemed to have any answers

Sad Stories of the Death of Kings
(1377 to 1485)

Upon the death of Edward III in 1377, English history was afflicted with a drove of royal uncles and their quarrelsome offspring, and professional historians must share their account of what happened with the far more readable interpretation enshrined in the history plays of William Shakespeare. Richard II (1377–99) had a surfeit of uncles and a father who, known as the Black Prince because of the color of his armor, had died a year before Richard's succession to the throne.

Blackening up the Black Prince.
One of the most important and responsible duties at the court of Edward III

At age ten, the new King ruled a kingdom reeling from the cost of a losing war and a devastating death rate. Worse, he was confronted with over-mighty magnates—mostly, but not entirely, in the shape of his uncles and their ambitious children—who were bent on ruling in his name during his minority, dictating his policies when he came of age, and seizing his crown when he tried to resist. Shakespeare's *Richard II* concentrates only on the last baronial encroachment, when Richard sat upon the ground and told "sad stories of the death of kings," and omits the young monarch's earlier achievements, especially his part in the Peasants' Revolt.

The Peasants' Revolt invariably reminds historians that they have forgotten to mention the peasants—always embarrassing, since about 80 percent of the population fell into that category. The remaining 20 percent were mostly artisans and tradespeople and only one percent were what most historians write about—the ruling elite or some 4,000 people who left all the historical documents and made all the political noise. The exception is the year 1381 when suddenly the "great unwashed" made themselves heard. ("Unwashed" is an unfortunate misnomer since no one except an occasional monk or king went in

Potrait of an English peasant

for body washing—we know that King John was exceptionally clean; he took 23 baths at five pence a bath between 29 January 1209 and 26 May 1210.) For a month in late May and June, peasants and townspeople voiced their indignation in mayhem and murder. The Black Death had drastically reduced the number of farm laborers, which in turn forced up wages—good for the peasants but bad for the landowners. In reaction, the landed elite persuaded Parliament to enact a series of Statutes of Laborers (1351 and thereafter), freezing wages and prohibiting workers from leaving their manors in search of higher pay. Parliament then shifted the cost of the losing war with France onto the poor by introducing a one-shilling poll or head tax assessed equally on rich and poor.

The underprivileged sensed a deliberate conspiracy on the part of the well-to-do to use Parliament to their own profit and welfare. The result was the first and only kingdom-wide peasant-artisan uprising in English history. Monasteries were burned and manor houses looted. Mayhem took over the streets of London, where the crowds cut off 140 heads, mostly foreign merchants and lawyers, but also those of the Archbishop of Canterbury and Robert Hales, the King's treasurer.

Mayhem taking over the streets of London

At the height of the crisis, while the court cowered in the Tower of London, Richard, aged fourteen, went forth to negotiate with the rebels. Their leader, Wat Tyler, threatened the King with a dagger and was cut down for his bravado. The crowd, in shock and outrage, began to turn on the government negotiators, until Richard rode forward, offered himself as their new leader, and accepted many of their demands. He promised to abolish serfdom (a social system, already dying out, that bound peasants to the soil and obligated them to a fixed amount of labor owed to their masters) and to repeal the poll tax (which was clearly uncollectible). He also offered to discuss opening up what the rebels called "the great society" to the poor as well as the rich and powerful. The delighted crowd dispersed; and a vastly relieved Richard and his government returned to the Tower determined to undo all of the promises made in the King's name. As Richard himself said, "Villains you have been and are; in bondage you shall remain." Time and economic pressure proved the young King wrong, but not for another 500 years would the submerged 80 percent of the population be offered a place in "the great society." The poll tax, however, was never tried again until Prime Minister Margaret Thatcher in 1990 revived the idea, and though, unlike Robert Hales, she was allowed to keep her head, she was promptly thrown out of office.

Richard II was not the fumbling neurotic immortalized by the magic of Shakespeare's pen. The historic Richard fell victim to the basic constitutional riddle that had plagued the monarchy since the days of John and Magna Carta: a feudal king was both limited and unrestrained in his actions. The 13th-century version of the dilemma was voiced by Henry de Bracton—"the king himself ought not to be subject to any man but he ought to be subject to God and the law." Embedded in this formula was plenty of room for over-mighty magnates to interpret God and the law as they saw fit, and for sovereigns to insist that they had to be governors in their own realms. Richard sought, like all other successful feudal kings, to be master in his own house—but he overplayed his hand, claiming that "laws were in his own mouth" and that only he could make a law for his kingdom. And when he illegally sequestered the inheritance of his first cousin, Henry Bolingbroke Duke of Lancaster, the baronage of the realm rose in revolt. They sensed danger to all rights of property and inheritance. As Shakespeare's Duke of York warns Richard, when he ignored the right of Bolingbroke to inherit his father's estates, "landlord of England art thou now, not king."

Confronted by barons armed to the teeth, Richard was first forced to abdicate his throne and then was quietly murdered and replaced by an over-mighty subject, his cousin Henry Bolingbroke. As a consequence, the royal succession for the next 90 years was put up for auction while the descendants of Edward III's many sons made their bid for the Crown.

The new king, Henry IV (1399–1413), in his dying words, posed the question on everyone's mind: "Only God knows by what right I took the throne." The answer, of course, was by force of arms, and with Richard's abdication, English history falls apart, becoming increasingly violent, hopelessly confused and memorable only for those who can keep straight the names of the members of the royal family who drift in and out of Shakespeare's *Henry IV (Part I and II)* and *Henry VI*, in which the story gets so involved, it takes the Bard three parts to complete the tale. Kings get out of order, kingmakers come and go, people are forever changing their titles, the warring sides have to select different colored roses to tell themselves apart, and in the end a king is willing to exchange his kingdom for a horse. Not a pretty picture!

Not a pretty picture

One event, however, stands out as utterly memorable: the Battle of Agincourt (1415), where an array of heroes fought for "Harry, England and St. George." As England's "ideal king," Henry V (1413–1422) resolved his father's doubts about the legitimacy of the succession by reinstating the Hundred Years' War, distracting all his unruly barons by fighting in somebody else's land, and calling upon God to give England victory in the face of staggering odds—a French army of 50,000 against an English force of 8,000. The Deity was exceedingly obliging. When the battle was over, the French dead included three dukes, a grand constable, eight counts, 1500 knights and 4 to 5,000 men at arms; the English lost fewer than 300 men, one duke, one earl and seven knights. France lay prostrate, and Henry was able to dictate a peace settlement whereby he was named Regent of France, married Catherine Valois, the French King's daughter, and became heir to his Crown. Henry then expired at the ideal moment, leaving to his brothers the job of defending his nine-month-old son's dual title of King of England and France, a claim that English monarchs did not relinquish until the 18th century.

Henry VI's reign (1422–61, 1470–71) embodies a lesson: princes educated from birth to succeed their royal fathers generally do not do well when they reach the throne, but kings who mount their thrones as infants or children and are educated to be kings while they wear the crown do even worse. The most successful English monarchs have generally been younger sons or daughters, cousins, outright usurpers or some combination of the last two. This is a proposition that can be studied in Chapter VI—The Royal Soap Opera.

Given the fact that Henry VI was still in diapers (nappies), was descended from a French King who went insane, and endured fifteen years of minority government, it may not be surprising that he turned out to be a sovereign with absolutely no emotional or physical aptitude for being a 15th-century monarch. He lacked the "manliness to be a king." It is unfair to blame him for the loss of his French empire. England had neither the human and financial resources nor the political will to hold France—a Kingdom three times the population of England—once that country organized itself for reconquest. But from the moment Henry officially came of age in 1437, the Kingdom, as one contemporary confessed, "was out of all governance." Without the presence of a strong, charismatic sovereign who knew his own mind and commanded personal and military respect, royal government deteriorated into jobbery, corruption and bankruptcy, and the great magnates carved out semi-independent political-military organizations, called affinities, which transformed traditional feudal fealty and loyalty into a money-based patronage system often described as bastard feudalism.

Henry VI, aged nine months, receives his crown

Super barons, often Henry's cousins, built up private armies, used military force to distort the King's justice, intimidated judges and juries, and used their political clout at court and in the shires to settle old rivalries. Eventually, their competing affinities quit wrangling over who was going to control the King's government and began fighting over who would wear the crown. Two political dynasties clashed: the House of Lancaster (their roses were red) descended from John of Gaunt, Edward III's fourth son, and represented by the imbecilic Henry VI and his strong-minded wife, Margaret, who taught their young son "nothing else but cutting off heads or making war"; and the House of York (their roses were white) represented by Edward Duke of York who claimed descent from Edward III's third and fifth sons.

In the end York triumphed; Henry VI died mysteriously in the Tower of London; his son was killed on the battlefield, and Margaret packed off to France; but the dragonseed of Edward III's fecundity lived on in dozens of noblemen who could claim Plantagenet blood in their veins. The first Yorkist King, Edward IV (1461–1483) has been overshadowed in popular memory by his far more dramatized and notorious brother, Richard Duke of Gloucester, the infamous Richard Crookback and all-time wicked uncle. Whether Richard III was either hunchbacked or particularly wicked is extremely doubtful, but history can be devastatingly unfair, especially when written by one's enemies. In actuality, Richard was the product of a violent age when Shakespeare's proverb "uneasy lies the head that wears a crown" was a truism. When Edward IV unexpectedly died in 1483, he left behind five daughters, two sons—Edward V (April 9–July 6, 1483) aged twelve, and Richard aged ten—and his brother Richard, who became Lord Protector. From Protector to King was an easy jump, and on June 22nd he had young Edward and his brother declared bastards and two weeks later he mounted the throne as the rightful heir to his brother. Within the year, the two boys conveniently vanished. One hundred and ninety years later, the bones of two children were discovered in a chest buried under a staircase in the Tower of London, strongly suggesting murder most foul, and legend insists that Richard was the culprit. No matter who was responsible, the deaths of the two princes simply dramatized the inadequacies of a political system in which murder was the only way permanently to get rid of an ineffectual monarch, be he unstable Edward II, irresponsible Richard II, imbecilic Henry VI or child Edward V.

Richard III, the all-time wicked uncle

Even by 15th-century political standards, blatant usurpation of the Crown was unacceptable behavior, and there were plenty of Plantagenet heirs eager to put in their bid for the Crown, the strongest Lancastrian claimant being Henry Tudor Earl of Richmond. When it became clear that Richard had failed to establish a strong political base, Richmond decided to risk the throne of England and his life on the throw of the military dice. On August 22, 1485, at Bosworth Field, Yorkist luck ran out. Deserted by key magnates at the crucial moment, Richard III died defending his crown, which was picked up on the battlefield and placed on Henry Tudor's head. Bosworth Field did not augur well. England had endured eight monarchs in 86 years, and no one living in 1485 would have predicted that the dynastic wars between the Houses of York and Lancaster (the Wars of the Roses) were finally over, or that this newest usurper would die twenty-four years later, still King of England.

Chapter IV

MORE MEMORABLE HISTORY,
1485 TO 1964

◦◦

History used to be simpler, tidier, and far more optimistic than it is today. Nineteenth-century historians liked to credit Henry VII as the first of the so-called "New Monarchs." His triumph over Richard III at the Battle of Bosworth Field was heralded as a good thing, for it inaugurated modern times and the end of the Middle Ages, those dreary centuries which came between the glories of Greece and Rome and the even greater glories of the modern age of capitalism, constitutionalism, professionalism, democracy and technology. Today's historians dislike demarcating history in terms of battles and dynasties, or chopping up chronology into neat segments. They tend to see the first of the Tudors as just another medieval monarch, albeit a somewhat more efficient one, who profited from the memory of the civil wars of the roses and their political and human exhaustion, and they explain his success in reigning 24 years in terms of subterranean demographic, economic and social change which leave the reader depressed and confused.

Put in its simplest terms, somewhere around 1485, the English started to have more and better sex, and though there is no firm evidence that the poor became poorer, certainly the rich became richer. The population which had been reduced by a third, possibly even by a half, during the, second half of the 14th century, finally began to respond to the new economic impulses of the 1480s and '90s, and began an unprecedented rate of growth, rising from two to four million by 1600. Those fortunate enough to survive the bubonic plague were economically better off than ever before: more food and land to go around, fatter and healthier babies, and higher wages for all. Landowners confronted with a labor shortage turned from labor-intensive agriculture to sheep farming, where a single hired hand could watch over an entire flock. Sheep runs and a European-wide demand for English wool and broadcloth produced unprecedented prosperity—"I thank God and ever shall; it is the sheep has paid for all." Prosperity in turn began to undermine the old medieval regulation of trade and production that had sought to protect the consumer and establish, not a market or competitive price, but a just price for all. Finally, economic competition, inflation, and social mobility generated what society feared the most: change. New names, new blood, new methods were destroying the fabric of the medieval past. In the village of Apsley Guise, each peasant in 1275 had held equal holdings of 15 acres. By 1542, four lucky and hard-working families had increased their acreage to 60 acres or more; only three still possessed their original 15 acres; and all the rest had been forced to sell out, many of them migrating to London, the boom town of the Kingdom, where the population was quadrupling, rising from 50,000 in 1500 to 200,000 a century later.

Henry VII, The First of the Tudors (1485–1509)

The first of the Tudors may not have been a new monarch in the historical sense, but Henry VII was certainly the beneficiary of the new prosperity. It filled his royal coffers, and made him hard to unseat. Moreover, genealogically speaking, the seventh Henry contained a heavy dose of new and questionable blood (see the chart on p. 245). Like Henry IV and his heirs, he was descended from Edward III's fourth son, John of Gaunt, Duke of Lancaster, and in 1485 he was the only viable Lancastrian claimant to the throne. Unfortunately, his royal blood came from the wrong side of the blanket, his great grandmother having been Gaunt's mistress. Worse, their offspring, though legitimized, had been disbarred from the succession by act of Parliament. His paternal ancestry was equally questionable. His father was the product of the union of Catherine, the French widow of Henry V, and a lusty Welsh clerk of her wardrobe named Owen Tudor, but whether that son was born in or out of wedlock has never been established. Wisely, Henry claimed his throne primarily on the basis of God's will, as revealed in battle.

Presumably on the advice of his lawyers (a legal education was rapidly becoming essential to anyone who wished to rise in politics), Henry, the day after he won his Crown, declared that his reign had commenced on the day before the Battle of Bosworth Field, thereby turning Richard's supporters, who had loyally fought to save his throne, into traitors whose estates could be legally confiscated. Such dubious legal actions, plus his marriage to Edward IV's eldest daughter, and a final pitched battle two years later against the remnants of the Yorkist forces, secured Henry his throne and bestowed upon him the legitimacy his tainted blood had left in dispute, but they did not earn him widespread public support. His subjects applauded his success in making his government solvent, but they found it difficult to love a sovereign who paid such close and unkingly attention to details, both financial and legal, "that no one dared to get the better of him through deceit or guile." Henry's excessive reliance on lawyers ran counter to medieval and chivalric tastes, and the first thing his son did when he mounted the throne as Henry VIII was to execute two of his father's most efficient and unscrupulous lawyers, Empson and Dudley, anticipating by three generations Shakespeare's famous suggestion that "the first thing we do, let's kill all the lawyers." It was the most popular act of the new reign!

Henry VIII and the Reconstruction of England *(1509–1547)*

At his death in 1509, Henry VII left a Crown more secure and wealthier and a Kingdom more prosperous than either had been for over a hundred years. How personally responsible he was for these blessings is debatable but, since they happened during his reign, he gets the credit for them. He also left a son of magnificent physique and unimpeachable legitimacy (he united in his veins the blood of both York and Lancaster) whose sexual appetite, conjoined with great difficulty in siring a legitimate male heir, plunged the Kingdom into a political and religious crisis that transformed England forever (see the chart on p. 246).

Henry's tumultuous marital career and his unusual solution to his connubial problems—he divorced or executed four of his six wives— have excited the imagination for four and a half centuries. More important, his mixing of sex and politics when he determined to rid himself of his first wife, Catherine of Aragon, and marry Mistress Anne Boleyn, had dire and unexpected consequences. It swept away the ancient ecclesiastical structure with its head in Rome, opened up the Kingdom to Protestantism, and established the new nation state that demanded the undivided loyalty of all its citizens. On the surface, the problem in 1527 was simple. Henry at 36 was the father of a legitimate daughter, the Princess Mary, and an illegitimate son, Henry Fitzroy, Duke of Richmond; he was also husband to a Spanish wife five and half years his senior who could no longer bear him children. Equally important, he was in love with a vivacious young lady who refused to jump into his bed unless she became his queen. To do nothing not only deprived him of the pleasures Anne had to offer, but also left the Kingdom without a legitimate male heir and exposed the country to the dangers of civil war should Henry die, leaving the supporters of a legitimate daughter and a bastard son to fight over his Crown.

A Forgotten Deed of Valour: The King's remembrancer tactfully reminding Henry VIII that His Majesty has already been married five times

What Henry needed was an annulment, and he called upon his good friend the Pope to oblige him on the grounds that his marriage to Catherine was illegal from the start, since she had been previously wedded to his deceased brother. Not even, he said, a papal dispensation could allow such a union so clearly prohibited by the Bible. Henry expected little trouble. He was such a staunch supporter of Rome that only five years before, His Holiness had awarded him the title of Defender of the Faith, a pretension to which English monarchs have tenaciously clung to this day. Unfortunately, Henry did not reckon with his wife's family pride or the international balance of power. Catherine's nephew was the Emperor Charles V, the most powerful sovereign in Europe, and the man who controlled the fate of Italy and therefore the decisions of the papacy. Pope Clement VII weaseled and squirmed and offered to marry the Princess Mary to her half-brother or legitimize any children Henry might have by Anne, but he would not annul his marriage to Catherine.

Henry showed extraordinary patience: his courtship of Anne and his negotiations with the papacy had been limping along for five years. But in the fall of 1532, the timetable of events speeded up dramatically. Anne finally broke down and by December she was pregnant, and on January 25, she and the King were secretly married. If Henry wanted to avoid bigamy and legitimize his offspring, he had less than seven months to act. To achieve his purpose, he cajoled Parliament into passing legislation that decreed the archepiscopal court of Canterbury to be the highest ecclesiastical court of the land from which no appeal was possible. This prevented any possibility of Catherine appealing her case to Rome, and in May, Archbishop Thomas Cranmer pronounced his King's marriage to Catherine to be null and void. On the first of June, Anne was recognized as Queen, and on September seventh, much to the outrage of the father and the dismay of his astrologers, not to mention the glee of the Catholic world, the new heir turned out to be, not a son,

but Elizabeth Tudor. With ironic ineptitude, the Pope finally got around to excommunicating the father on the day the child was born.

Henry had risked his soul and defied most of Christendom for yet another worthless daughter to further complicate the succession.

Henry VIII inspecting the Princess Elizabeth, another worthless daughter

The King, however, once committed, refused to back down, and in March of 1534, an obliging Parliament passed the momentous Act of Succession which severed forever the medieval duality of State and Church, body and soul. For the first time, a purely secular institution sat in judgment of divine law, and by act of Parliament Catherine's marriage was "adjudged to be against the laws of Almighty God" and his marriage to his "most dear and entirely beloved Queen Anne" ordered to be "taken for undoubtful, true, sincere and perfect ever here-after." The logical conclusion to the destruction of the old Church came in November when the Act of Supremacy declared Henry to be the "Supreme Head of the Church of England."

A new polity was being shaped, in which diversity of mind or action was unthinkable, and the Act of Succession required all subjects to swear "without guile, fraud or other undue means" to "keep, maintain and defend this Act, and all the contents and effects thereof, and all other Acts . . . of this present Parliament." The loyalty oath had been born. For the first time in Western European history, a government was reaching down into the souls of its citizens and requiring a new kind of conformity to the will of society. Anne's marriage could no longer be accepted as fact. Now both approval of the wedding and the principles on which it rested were required: the break with Rome, the right of King and Parliament to speak for God, and Henry's authority as Supreme Head of the English Church.

At this point Sir Thomas More, Henry's ex-lord chancellor, author of *Utopia*, and England's most distinguished humanist, drew the line; he refused to take the oath. He said he did "nobody harm," thought "none harm," wished "everybody good," and "if this be not enough to keep a man alive, in good faith, I long not to live." A year later he got his wish. He was executed on Tower Hill. As he mounted the scaffold, he cracked the most famous sick joke in history: "I pray you, I pray you, Mr. Lieutenant, see me safe up, and for my coming down let me shift for myself." (Not far from his tomb in Chelsea Old Church on Cheyne Walk, there is a seated black-bronze statue of More with its hands, face, and medallion of office discordantly colored in gold.)

The man who directed Henry's political and religious revolution was, of course, not the King, who was far too busy doing what early modern monarchs did best, fighting (mostly in France and Scotland) and going on progresses to display their royal persons to their subjects, but Thomas Cromwell, a blacksmith's son who had led a feverish life soldiering in France, banking in Italy and practicing law in London before becoming Henry's Vicar General in 1535. It was Cromwell who oversaw the destruction of the monasteries and the confiscation of lands worth £2 million—the largest nationalization of property until the French and Russian revolutions—which made Henry the wealthiest sovereign per capita in Europe.

Henry VIII plundering the monasteries

Cromwell also introduced the age of statistics and census-taking. He ordered every parish priest to keep a register of births, baptisms, marriages and deaths. What had once been a spiritual obligation on the part of the clergy, now had become a secular order mandated by the State which was awaking to the realization that statistical knowledge was power, especially the power to tax and control.

The price Henry had to pay to legalize his marriage was to ally himself with the religious reformers who really did think the Pope was the whore of Babylon. And though the King never himself became a Protestant, when Anne miscarried her second child—thereby conclusively proving that she had failed to live up to her marriage vows to be "bonaire and buxom in bed and at board"—he had her executed on trumped-up charges of adultery, and married a lady-in-waiting of the reformed faith. Jane Seymour survived the birth of her baby by only a few days, but she did supply her husband with the son for whom he had risked so much, and he had the young prince Edward educated by humanist teachers with strong Protestant leanings. As a consequence, his new Church fell prey to the religious inclinations of his three heirs: devoutly Protestant Edward, equally devoutly Catholic Mary, and Elizabeth, who wavered somewhere between the two extremes.

The Pope as the whore of Babylon

The Little Tudors
(1547–1558)

Edward's and Mary's reigns are dreary evidence that good intentions are no guarantee of good results and as often as not end in disaster. At Henry's death in 1547, his son Edward was nine, and the government fell to his maternal uncle Edward Seymour, the Lord Protector. Seymour was a genial and politically naive nobleman, who innocently thought that reason and goodwill were in and by themselves sufficient to achieve success in government. Unfortunately, he presided over a government composed largely of unscrupulous land-hungry colleagues and militantly puritanical religious reformers. The results were blatant corruption, open disobedience, political infighting, and religious turmoil, as every tavern, alehouse, street corner, and pulpit became a forum to debate the true nature of the mass. Was it a miraculous reenactment of Christ's sacrifice on the cross in which the ceremonial bread and wine was literally transformed into the body and blood of the Savior as Catholics believed, or was it a commemorative service in which nothing changed except the hearts of the communicates as the Protestants maintained?

The Protector lasted only two years. In a palace coup engineered by John Dudley, Duke of Northumberland, he was arrested, deprived of office, and executed on fabricated charges of treason. Northumberland was closely allied with the Protestants (for political, not religious reasons since they advocated the sale of Church lands to the Duke and his cronies). And three years later, when it became apparent that Edward was fatally ill, Northumberland tried to save his political neck and prevent Catholic Mary following her brother on the throne, by arranging (with the dying Edward's fervent blessings) the succession of Lady Jane Gray, who was Henry VIII's grandniece, a devout Protestant and, best of all, the Duke's daughter-in-law. Her reign of only nine days was clear evidence that Protestantism, especially in the hands of politicians, had won over few hearts, and that the overwhelming majority of the Kingdom preferred to stick to the succession as Henry had willed it: Edward, then Mary, and finally Elizabeth.

Mary's reign was no more successful than her brother's. She sought to turn the clock back to the golden days when her mother was undisputed Queen and her father a dutiful and faithful son of Rome. She longed to return her errant land to the Catholic fold and to marry her Hapsburg cousin Philip, the future King of Spain and the son of her mother's stoutest champion, the Emperor Charles V (see the chart on p. 247). Mary achieved her ends, but they destroyed her reputation forever. Her marriage brought no heirs, only heartbreaks, and Philip at 28 is said to have remarked of his 38-year-old wife that "it would take God himself to drink of this cup." The marriage also involved the Kingdom in yet another war with France which Mary entered at the request of her husband, but which almost everybody in her government opposed. The war's only result was the military humiliation of England and the loss of its last continental foothold, the French port of Calais.

Philip learns of his wife's death

The unmaking of the religious revolution—the repeal of the Act of Supremacy, reunion with Rome, and the restitution of Catholic ceremonies—failed to achieve what Mary desired most, a Kingdom filled with loyal, loving subjects united by a common faith. She discovered that a policy of patience and understanding only encouraged obstinate heretics to greater acts of sacrilege, and confirmed her in the conviction that heresy and sedition were different sides of the same diabolical coin. In response, her government turned to fire—in the expectation that the sight of Protestant leaders, including Archbishop Cranmer, dying in agony at the stake would frighten the rank and file, dampen their zeal, and render them obedient. The policy backfired, creating martyrs who seemed to welcome the fire, not the desired spectacle of criminals receiving their painful but just deserts. Once lit, the flames proved difficult to extinguish, and, during the final years of the reign, some 288 heretics, mostly tradespeople, cloth workers and agricultural laborers, of whom 51 were women, were burned to death.

Mary's efforts to purge her realm with fire earned her the epithet of "Bloody," and when she died, all her dreams having turned into nightmares, her subjects rang church bells, lit bonfires, and rejoiced in the hope that the last of Henry VIII's children, the Princess Elizabeth, would do better than her siblings.

Elizabeth I, The "Unlooked-for Miracle" (1558–1603)

Elizabeth is a success story almost unparalleled in history, and it is made doubly extraordinary by the fact that at her succession on November 17, 1558 no one anticipated anything except disaster. Even her most loyal minister, Sir William Cecil, who served her for 40 years, predicted that the "end would be monstrous." An inexperienced Queen had inherited from her sister a bankrupt government and a losing war. The Kingdom was torn by religious dissention and was seen by many to be on the verge of civil war. Worse yet, Elizabeth was the wrong sex, and nothing could be expected of a lady who possessed most of the qualities attributed by 16th-century males to the female of the species: "light of credit, lusty of stomach, impatient, full of words, apt to lie, flatter and weep," and always desiring "rather to rule than be ruled."

So how did a bespangled woman of doubtful temper who suffered from almost pathological indecisiveness, threw slippers at her ministers, and possessed a vanity that would tolerate no rival in either dress or authority become a legend in her own time? Sir Francis Walsingham offered the only answer her contemporaries could conceive when explaining the success of that "weaker vessel," a mere woman. "God preserve her majesty long to reign over us by some unlooked-for miracle, for I cannot see by natural reason that her highness goeth about to provide for it." Elizabeth was indeed a supremely fortunate queen: lucky in religion, in diplomacy, in the felicitous timing of events, and most important of all, lucky in surviving for 45 years on the throne of a country that spawned some of the most remarkable minds of all times—Shakespeare, Spencer, Marlowe, Raleigh, Harvey, Bacon—and some of the most memorable events of the century—Drake's circumnavigation of the globe, the defeat of the Spanish Armada, and the first English effort to colonize North America.

Sir William Cecil predicting that the "end would be monstrous"

In religion, Catholics turned out to be better losers than Protestants. As Anne Boleyn's daughter, Elizabeth had little choice except to reinstate Protestantism and separate once again her Kingdom from Rome. Her religious settlement satisfied few and resolved little. It was an ambiguously phrased version of the Protestant formula under Edward VI and contained much of the outward trapping of Catholicism, but by the sheerest good fortune, it struck the magical balance between obscurity of doctrine and imprecise half measures designed to antagonize no one to the point of rebellion. Although every one of Mary's Catholic bishops resigned their sees, they did so without a fight, and of the 9000 parish priests, only 189 refused to go along with her settlement. Extreme Protestants, who would later be called religious purists or Puritans, also reluctantly accepted the settlement, in the expectation that once the succession crisis was over, their Queen would purge her Church of its papist corruptions. They miscalculated. Elizabeth liked her Church

exactly as she had shaped it, and the history of her reign became a prolonged struggle to muzzle a Puritan minority which began to question
the very foundations of her regal, and therefore divine, authority.

Elizabeth was the child of her age, and she accepted without question the divine nature of her kingly office, because in the 16th century
(as in previous centuries) all authority—the father over the family, the
sheriff over the county, the pastor over the flock, the sovereign over the
kingdom—ultimately stemmed from God. The Tudor State was far
more than a sterile collection of political institutions, social divisions,
and economic activities; it was conceived of as a living organism composed of obedient, loving and right-minded people who were, at least
in theory, expected to live in Christian harmony. The favorite political
metaphor of the age was the "body politic," in which the Prince func-
tioned as the head; the aristocracy the eyes and ears, and everyone else
the hands and feet. When the House of Commons stepped beyond its
proscribed bounds and tried to force the Queen to do the three things
she consistently refused to do—marry, name a successor, and reform
her Church more to the liking of the Puritans—she did not hesitate to
sternly inform its members that "it is monstrous that the feet should
direct the head" and "no king fit for his office will ever suffer such
absurdities." (The language of royalty even for Elizabeth remained
masculine.)

Elizabeth accepting without question the divine nature of her kingly office

Elizabeth, of course, did not rule alone. She governed directly through a personally selected privy council, a small administrative staff of less than 500, some 1750 appointed, unpaid and amateur justices of the peace, and indirectly through Parliament. The mystical union of King in Parliament was seen as the "highest and most absolute power of the realm" because "every Englishman [note, not Englishwoman] is intended to be there present . . . from the prince to the lowest person in England." This claim to masculine universality was more imaginary than real. Parliament represented the will of only the ruling elite, probably no more than five to ten thousand individuals in a kingdom of four million, but it did at times recognize the welfare of the feet of the body politic. A country devoid of an effective police force and standing army could not afford economic and social dislocation for fear it would lead to political rebellion. The Tudor State perceived that obedience and respect on the part of the underprivileged depended in large measure on full bellies, fat children and job security.

Elizabeth's government did its ineffectual best to implement a policy of benevolent paternalism. The Statute of Apprentices (1565) sought to regulate working conditions, setting wages and hours, and controlling labor relations between master and apprentices. The Poor Law (1601) was directed at the unemployed, allocating money for poor relief and instructing justices of the peace to control prices so that the victims of famine, economic dislocation, accident and old age would not starve. Both laws remained on the law books until the 19th century, when government rejected paternalism and state interference as being economically, socially and morally wrong.

More effective than parliamentary legislation in maintaining a harmonious Kingdom populated by obedient and loving subjects was mind control. The key to the well-ordered commonwealth was the family, because it was there that children learned the cardinal principles of the body politic—respect for and obedience to one's betters. The family unit on average contained only 4.75 individuals—husband, wife and two to three children—a statistic that has meaning only when one recognizes that a host of sociological factors kept the family small. A quarter of all married couples were childless; adult offspring and widowed parents rarely remained in the family nest; of the two to six children born to a typical family, 25 percent died before the age of ten; and the average marriage lasted only 17 to 20 years. Death—especially the wife in childbirth—did to the 16th-century family what divorce does today: one-fourth of those marrying had been married at least once before. Grim as these statistics are, relative to the rest of the world, Elizabethan England was a healthy country, and its life expectancy of 41.7 years was not exceeded until the early decades of the 19th century.

The family, over which the father was supreme, was seen as the Kingdom writ small. In learning obedience to and respect for their parents, Tudor children learned deference to authority on every level of society. Thus the inferior bowed to all forms of superiority, the freshman stepping aside for the senior, the bachelor of arts for the master of arts, the master of arts for the doctor of divinity or civil law, and all six for the professor, a way of life that high-ranking academics today regret has disappeared.

The Gentry

In this ordered and hierarchical world, the element that prospered the most and to whom the future belonged was not the great aristocrats who sat in the House of Lords, but the landed country gentlemen who monopolized the House of Commons and, as justices of the peace, controlled county government. This element, known in history as the gentry, contributed the most to the stability of Elizabeth's reign, was largely responsible for the political and religious explosion that occurred 38 years after her death, and was the principal beneficiary of the world that would emerge following the Restoration of the Stuart monarchy in 1660. The gentry increasingly set the social and cultural atmosphere of the Kingdom, and their confidence in the future, both in this world and the next, is splendidly displayed in the magnificent stone effigies with which they adorned their tombs and sought to emblazon their social and political status for all to remember and respect.

Membership in the gentry was variously defined by blood, birth, family lineage, personal reputation, and most particularly by the ownership of sufficient land to permit a clean-fingered life style. Included in their ranks were Crown officials, physicians, lawyers, and, begrudgingly, academics and clergymen. The commercial and urban elite might qualify if they had the money to mimic gentility, were married to landed families or held high municipal office. The gentry were a growing segment of society and by 1700 represented about two percent of the population. In the mid-15th century, they possessed possibly 25 percent of all arable land; by the end of the 17th century that percentage had doubled, the Crown and Church being the primary losers.

A gentleman's life style was not cheap. His estates had to sustain what was described as the four "causalities" of gentility: the burdens of lawsuits to protect his property in a highly litigious age; the cost of acquiring government office (he had to entertain and bribe the right people); the expense of arranging socially acceptable marriages for his children, and, the greatest expenditure of all, the construction of a country mansion that would display his social worth, an enterprise that could financially destroy a gentleman "without the help of any enemy."

Of all his expenses, a gentleman's home meant the most to him, because his ideal, which only the richest could attain, was to "set his house aloft on the hill, to be seen afar," and to display the magnificence of his residence throughout the land.

A sixteenth-century gentleman displaying his new country house

Compared to the Continent, Tudor and Stuart England had few public mansions, but what it lacked in public parade it made up in private ostentation. Architecturally, the age admired size, symmetry, novelty, and above all else, windows. The gentry built their homes as if they were lanterns, glittering with candlelight from within and sunlight from without. Here was the visual proof of their security and status in an ordered society: they no longer needed high walls and narrow windows to protect them. Outwardly, a gentleman's home gave proof to his wealth and social position; inwardly, it reflected a fundamental change in domestic organization. In the medieval past, the master and his family had mingled with their guests and servants. In the more structured and hierarchical world of the 16th century, servants were assigned to "below stairs," guests were given their own rooms in a separate wing, and the master and his family possessed their own space appropriate to their gentle status. Labor was cheap and plentiful, and a gentleman might maintain a staff of 50 to run his household and estate, while a great magnate might jog along with three times that number. Servants were almost always male, and not until the late 17th century did their numbers decline and their domestic duties be taken over by women. Only male servants wore livery—maids' uniforms were a Victorian invention. Maids wore their mistress's castoff clothing, which led to frequent and embarrassing confusion between the two, a favorite theme of 18th-century drama. The stately home was a way of life that lasted well into the 20th century and can be viewed today in all its nostalgic splendor, but with few of its warts and flaws, in the television series *Upstairs, Downstairs*. The visitor to Britain is well advised to purchase *Hudson's Historic Houses & Gardens, Castles and Heritage Sites*, and visit such stately piles as Longleat in Wiltshire, or the even more spectacular Hardwick Hall in Derbyshire (built by the Countess of Shrewsbury, the richest woman in England next to the Queen) to name only two out of the hundreds that are open to the public.

Hot and Cold War
(1567–1603)

If Elizabeth was lucky that her religious settlement, much to everyone's surprise, endured somewhat shopworn to the present day, and the existing cosmic and social systems supported her kingly authority, she was even more fortunate in the diplomatic gyrations of the century. In 1559, just when it looked as if Catholic France and Spain might team up to exterminate Protestant heresy wherever they found it, an unlooked-for miracle took place: two French kings died within 20 months of each other—one from a sliver of wood from a broken jousting spear which entered his eye, the other from an abscessed ear—and the country was plunged into two generations of civil and religious war. Almost overnight France fell from being the primary Kingdom of Europe and England's greatest threat, into a diplomatic and military cipher. Suddenly Philip of Spain emerged by default as the burdened colossus of Europe, immensely powerful but distracted and perplexed by the obligations of world supremacy. Although the riches of the Indies poured into his coffers and Spanish troops were regarded as the best on the Continent, Philip's domains were scattered far and wide among Italy, the Iberian Peninsula, the Netherlands, and the New World. More serious, Spain, with a population half that of France but twice that of England, was a divided and economically backward land, and the King's geopolitical responsibilities were overwhelming.

Fortunately for Elizabeth, Philip's most pressing problem was the Turkish menace in the Mediterranean, and not until the Spanish naval victory at Lepanto in 1571, did he have the time or resources to think about his one time sister-in-law, the Queen of England, who was becoming an increasingly irritating thorn in his side. It was bad enough that English pirates (Elizabeth called them heroes and privateers) were poaching in Spanish New World waters and plundering his treasure ships. What upset the King the most was England's strategic position athwart his sea lanes between Spain and the Netherlands, and Elizabethan's blatant violation of international law in first sending money and volunteers and then troops to help his rebellious Protestant subjects in their attempt to break from Spanish and Catholic rule. Philip, however, was a prudent and patient man, preferring intrigue and caution to open war. He sensed that the moment that fatally irresistible lady, Mary of Scotland, forsook her chilly lochs and rebellious subjects and arrived in England, Elizabeth's Kingdom would boil over with schemes to unseat its heretical sovereign.

Mary Stuart had been educated French and Catholic, and as the grandniece of Henry VIII she regarded herself as the legitimate heir to the English throne, and Elizabeth as a Protestant usurper. Unfortunately, when her husband, Francis II of France, died and she was bundled back to Scotland in 1561, she discovered that her Kingdom was rapidly forsaking its Catholicism and traditional French orientation, and turning to Presbyterian Protestantism under the belligerent and Calvinistic leadership of John Knox. As Queen, Mary Stuart mixed sex and homicide in fatal proportions, conniving at the death of her second husband, Lord Darnley, and eloping (some claim she was kidnapped) with his murderer, the Protestant Earl of Bothwell. Scottish public opinion, both Protestant and Catholic, was outraged; the streets of Edinburgh rang with the cry "Burn the whore"; and in 1567, Mary had no choice but to abdicate in favor of her infant son, James VI, and flee for her life. The moment she crossed the border as England's unwanted and dangerous guest, she became the darling of Catholic Europe and the focus of endless plots to dispatch her cousin Elizabeth.

That Bess of England survived a plethora of schemes to assassinate her by a variety of unlikely means, including deadly perfumes, poisoned gloves, balls of fatal incense, and silver bullets allegedly blessed by the Pope, was one of those unlooked-for miracles which her ministers had in fact come to expect. The source of this treason they knew to be that "daughter of sedition," Catholic Mary, and they urged their Queen to "cut off her head and make no more ado about her," but it was not until February of 1587 that Elizabeth reluctantly signed the warrant of execution. Philip by that time had come to the realization that he could not reconquer his Dutch provinces without first disciplining Elizabeth, and he determined that if she could not be removed by the assassin's blade, then Spanish ships and troops would have to do the job.

The Armada sailed for England in July of 1588. The Spanish fleet, at least on paper, was impressive: 130 vessels, collectively weighing 58,000 tons, carrying 32,000 soldiers and sailors, and mounting 2,431 cannons. The fighting core of the Armada, however, was limited to 21 battle galleons and four giant galleasses propelled by sail and oar. These were more than matched by 18 of the Queen's galleons which were technologically and tactically superior to anything the Spanish possessed. Tactics and technology won the day, because Philip's great ships were built in the medieval and Mediterranean style—high in the bow and stern, to give musketeers an elevated platform from which to fire when grappling and boarding the enemy. They were slow, clumsy, and designed for fighting a land war at sea. Even the fleet's commanding officer, the Duke of Medina Sidonia, was a general who had never before been to sea. In contrast, English galleons were designed to sink, not board, the enemy. They were small, relatively streamlined, and maneuverable, possessing more firepower than the Spanish because they carried no boarding troops.

Medina Sidonia managed to get his vessels through the English Channel to Calais where he hoped to meet up with Spanish ground forces and combine them with the 25,000 troops on board the Armada, but on the night of August 7th, English fireboats dislodged his ships from their safe haven. The Spanish set to sea in confusion, and next morning encountered the full English fleet, with disastrous results. Five of Philip's great galleons were sunk or driven ashore, and only a sudden shift in the wind saved the Armada from being driven on to the shoals along the Dutch coast, and allowed it to escape into the gray waters of the North Atlantic. But there, as Medina Sidonia turned his squadrons north in an effort to round the tip of Scotland and return to Spain, his fleet was destroyed by wind and waves and the rocky coasts of Scotland and Ireland.

The defeat of the Armada was the apex of Elizabeth's reign. Thereafter the long recessional began. Philip learned to construct better galleons and protect his treasure ships. War in Ireland strained the Queen's finances to the limit, and she had to sell a fourth of her father's patrimony to stay solvent; even so, she left her successor, James Stuart of Scotland, £422,000 in debt. Her court became ridden with factions and infighting, and Elizabeth began to lose her magic. Her young favorite, the Earl of Essex, in a rage at his difficult sovereign, dared to pose the one query that no subject was even allowed to think: "What, cannot Princes err? Cannot subjects receive wrong? Is an earthly power or authority infinite?" The Earl was executed in 1601 after an abortive rebellion to prove his words, but the epitaph of the divine right monarchy had been voiced, and two generations later a sizable portion of Stuart society would answer his first two questions with a resounding "yes" and his last with an adamant "no."

James I and VI or Mary Stuart's Revenge
(1603–1625)

James Stuart, who spelled his family name of Stewart in the French style because his mother, Mary Queen of Scots, had been educated in France, regarded his inheritance as "the promised land," a country with revenues six times that of Scotland, which he had every intention of spending as lavishly as he could. James was the most successful of his ill-starred Stuart line. His great grandfather, James IV, had been killed in battle fighting the English; his grandfather was said to have died of shame after being defeated by the English; and his mother had been executed by order of her English cousin. James VI survived a plethora of plots to murder or kidnap him (he came to his throne at 13 months), and he lived to rule over the English for 22 years as James I of England. The news of Elizabeth's death in March of 1603 and his succession to her throne "sounded so sweetly" to his ears that he "could alter no note in so agreeable an harmony." The note that sounded sweetest was the chance to redress history and give his mother equal billing with Elizabeth in Westminster Abbey. At a cost that would have horrified Gloriana, he constructed a sepulchre for Mary of Scotland that prominently displayed the fleurs de lis of France and placed it beside the gilded bronze effigies of Henry VII and his wife, Elizabeth of York. There lies the first of the Tudors flanked by his grand and great granddaughters, a century of drama frozen in stone.

When James mounted the throne, he was immediately confronted with a constitutional dilemma. He did not possess an income sufficient to support himself in the style which he felt became a King of England, but Parliament refused to accept responsibility for the solvency of his government. James was expected to live on the historic revenues of the Crown and call upon Parliament only in time of gravest emergency. Elizabeth had resolved the problem by tact, frugality and the ability to clothe her demands in the magic of majesty. James was neither frugal nor majestic. He was hopelessly extravagant, knew nothing about cajoling money out of Parliament, had the instincts of a cranky pedagogue, and was about as charismatic as a potato boiled with prunes, which along with tea were the new delicacies of the age. If James could not control his urge to lavish vast sums on his Scottish cronies and court favorites, Parliament could not refrain from nagging or developing the exasperating habit of attaching all sorts of conditions to its financial support in order to force the King to reform his government and adopt policies to its liking. The result was a stalemate. James, on the basis of his prerogative powers, turned to unpopular means of raising money, and Parliament refused to vote taxes until he quit doing so. To make matters even more explosive, the House of Commons began to assert a new and alarming notion: "The voice of the people, in the things of their knowledge, is said to be the voice of God." Hesitantly, often awkwardly, Parliament, since it claimed to speak for the people, was propounding a rival claim to the Divine Right of Kings. King and Parliament could not both speak for the Deity.

Puritans welcomed the new King with paeans of praise. He was Scottish, had been educated in the Presbyterian faith, and therefore could be expected to strip the Church of England of all its papal trappings. James possessed an irritating talent for going to the root of a problem—not for nothing was he called the "wisest fool in Christendom." He worried: if Puritans really believed that each individual covenanted directly with God and was responsible for his own salvation, what would happen to the serried ranks of authority and hierarchy ranging from the father to the King and culminating in the Deity? The answer was that all intermediary authorities between man and God would be short-circuited. If you questioned the authority of bishops to interpret the Bible, the next step would be to call into question the Divine Right of Kings: "no bishops, no king." James found the episcopal organization of the Church of England peculiarly suited to a monarchy, and when the Puritans suggested the need for a Presbyterian organization in England, he bluntly told them that Presbyterianism "agreeth as well with a monarchy as God with a devil." He knew the truth whereof he spoke, for he had endured the lecturing of the Scottish Presbyterian Church for 36 years. Actually, James was far more tolerant of Puritans than Elizabeth had been, and the 35 Puritans who accompanied the other 66 passengers on board the *Mayflower* came from Holland, where they had fled to escape edicts laid down by the old Queen, not the new Stuart sovereign.

The Planting of Colonies

In the 16th century, English eyes for the first time turned from the Continent to the New World. Imaginations were no longer held captive by the memory of Agincourt and the conquest of France. Now they were enthralled by the legend of a direct sea passage over the top of the globe to China and the Orient; by stories of fabled civilizations where kitchen utensils were made of gold, and by Sir Walter Raleigh's dream of planting an "English nation" beyond the seas.

The treasured American picture of God-fearing pilgrims, dressed "in black plug hats," founding with grim determination a Puritan paradise in the wilderness, is not strictly true. God's people were clothed in the height of Stuart fashion and came to the New World seeking the profit of their purses as well as the welfare of their souls. Colonial settlements were expensive, requiring long-term capital investments. The

Jamestown expedition of 1607 spent £100,000 in the first 15 years of its existence and went bankrupt. Not until the Virginia settlers sent home the dried tobacco leaves smoked by the Indians, and the English acquired the habit, did the colony become profitable.

"Then, if the people got to like it, you could always put a tax on it."

The planting of nations "where none before hath stood" would never have been possible had not the urge to colonize coincided with an era of commercial and industrial expansion that generated the venture capital necessary for financing the pioneering spirit. Between 1540 and 1640, the capitalist and the entrepreneur prospered mightily. Iron production multiplied fivefold and coal sevenfold. "Correct your map," it was said, "Newcastle is Peru," meaning that the black gold buried in England's back yard was far more precious than all the riches plundered by Spain in South and Central America. The coal mines of Yorkshire kept London hearth fires burning, converted ore into iron, cane into sugar, ocean water into salt, and made fortunes for the mine owners. On the high seas English shipping doubled, and the East India Company, originally founded to cash in on the East Indies spice trade, but forced by the Dutch to settle for the subcontinent of India, was by 1607 earning profits of 500 percent in a single year.

Money propelled the exodus. The English were on the move to the granite outcroppings of New England, the fisheries of Newfoundland, the red earth of Virginia, and the West Indies, rich in sugar to sweeten their craving for tea. By the end of the century 250,000 English men and women lived along the North American coast from Maine to the Carolinas.

In this migration, the first two Stuart monarchs took little interest, with one exception—Ireland—where James I is remembered to this day as the originator of the decision to populate the province of Ulster with Scottish-English immigrants. The conquest of the Emerald Isle, that graveyard of English military reputations, had commenced under Henry II. Elizabeth had fought a bitter and costly war to subdue the Irish clans, but James selected nearly a hundred Scottish and English "undertakers" and granted each between one and three thousand acres on condition that they populate their estates with godly Protestant immigrants. In the end, more English and Scots left for Ireland in the 17th century than for any other place in the world, and James's policy of enforced colonization was carried on with a vengeance under the Cromwellian Protectorate during the 1650s. Thousands of Cromwellian soldiers and English immigrants settled in the wake of his military victories, expelling the Irish peasants and forcing them to resettle in the wilds of western Ireland. The Irish still speak of Oliver Cromwell as being where he can light his pipe with his finger.

Charles I—A Better Martyr than Monarch
(1625–1649)

If the ship of state was leaky and ill handled by James I, his son Charles, with considerable help from Parliament, ran it straight upon the rocks of civil war. The gale that in the end destroyed both King and Parliament had less to do with constitutional principles than with psychology. Fundamental disagreements over where the taxing power lay—did it reside only with Parliament or could the King legally raise forced loans and extra-parliamentary taxes—and over the independence of the executive from interference by the legislature in matters of foreign and domestic policy, seriously crippled the ship of state, but distrust and suspicion, heightened by religious hysteria, created the emotional climate that led to mutiny and revolution.

James had believed in enjoying what God had bestowed upon him and was content to leave his inheritance more or less as he had found it. Charles in 1625 felt obliged to improve upon it, taking seriously his responsibilities as the divine and paternalistic sovereign of an organic society in which the King knew best and was always right. He resented any questioning of his prerogative powers or having to justify his policies to the House of Commons before it would grant him money. He and his chief minister, the Duke of Buckingham, a particularly rapacious specimen left over from his father's reign, had embroiled the country in two short but hopelessly bungled wars with France and Spain, and nothing irritated Parliament more than paying for losing wars. By 1629, King and Parliament were at such loggerheads that the House of Commons tried to pass a resolution branding anyone who paid custom duties or enforced loans as betrayers of "the liberties of England." When in response Charles ordered Parliament to be dissolved, Commons forcibly kept the Speaker of the House in his seat, informing him that "you shall sit till we please to rise." The words were tantamount to mutiny, for the Speaker was a royal official, and in preventing him from rising, Parliament was claiming the right to prorogue and dissolve itself, historically a right that belonged only to the King.

Charles's solution to the constitutional crisis was to rule for the next 11 years without Parliament. The historic habits of obeying the King and paying taxes were still ingrained social instincts, but if the King were to fulfill his duties as the head and heart of the body politic and keep the confidence of the country, he needed a consistent and rational policy, money to finance it, and efficient and honest officials to administer it. Money was found through "fiscal feudalism," the rummaging through long-forgotten medieval charters and feudal obligations with an eye to monetary gain. The most notorious and rewarding was the extension of the historic obligation on the part of certain Channel ports to pay ship money for naval defense, during times of great national crisis, to inland towns whenever the King demanded, irrespective of military need.

The King's policy was high on idealism, but abysmally low on application. The trouble was twofold: among the King's ministers, only Archbishop William Laud and Thomas Wentworth, Earl of Strafford approached anything resembling efficiency and honesty, and the policy itself was so corruptly applied that it destroyed all government credibility. The two ancient prerogative courts of Star Chamber and High

Commission were used to enforce the Elizabethan concept of a balanced and paternalistic commonwealth. But without a paid and trained civil service, the King's Book of Orders instructing justices of the peace to offer relief to the deserving poor, freeze prices in time of famine, and prevent landlords from evicting their peasants in the name of more efficient farming methods, fell on the uninterested ears of men who had nothing to gain from such orders, and who had sat in a Parliament that had been dissolved against its will by the King. Equally serious, the Crown indulged in financial practices that would have landed the leaders of any other organization in jail. High-minded economic and social regulations were used, not to keep the body politic healthy, but to raise money by fining violators (rather like speeding tickets today).

Charles I indulging in financial practices that
would have landed any other leader in jail

The King's ramshackle rule might have staggered on indefinitely had it not been for religion. In a way, royal policy generated the seeds of its own destruction, because it was predicated upon a principle dear to

Charles's heart—uniformity of faith. The King and Archbishop Laud began to impose upon England and Scotland a High Church form of Protestantism which smattered, especially in the eyes of Puritans, of Catholicism. In England, Puritans fled to the New World, but in Scotland Presbyterians threw chairs at the Dean of Edinburgh Cathedral, defied the King, and worsted him in battle.

*Charles I's Scottish subjects throwing chairs at the
Dean of Edinburgh Cathedral*

War revealed the rot that was eating away at Charles's government, and forced him to call Parliament. With a Scottish army on English soil, and unable to raise money to defend his Kingdom, Charles had no choice, and in November of 1640 the Long Parliament was convened. It lasted in one form or another for 23 years, first sweeping away the King's prerogative powers, then claiming sovereignty for itself, and finally executing the King in the name of law. After eleven years of inept and unpopular royal rule, during which the King's credibility in the eyes of the governing elite had sunk to the vanishing point, Lords and Commons were united in their determination to fundamentally change the relationship between Crown and Parliament. In 1641, Charles bowed to the inevitable. He sanctioned the dismantlement of his prerogative courts; he permitted his servants, Laud and Strafford, to be condemned to death by act of Parliament; he signed legislation guaranteeing that Parliament would be called every three years and could not be prorogued or dissolved without its consent; and he gave up all forms of non-parliamentary sources of income except from his Crown lands.

Parliament achieved a shattering victory without firing a shot. Yet within the year war would break out. Why? The answer has to do with religion, bad timing, fear, and the internal dynamism that governs the life cycle of any revolution and places it in the hands of its most extreme elements.

By the time Charles's eleven-year effort to rule without Parliament collapsed, the King was seen, not just by Puritans but by Protestants generally, as being soft on religion, even being a crypto-Catholic. His wife, Henrietta of France, was a Catholic and was allowed to hear mass at court; he promoted Catholics to high office; he had tried to destroy Scottish Presbyterianism; and his Archbishop Laud seemed to be in league with Rome. The Pope was the Antichrist, and that had been proved 26 years before, when on November 5th, 1605, Guy Fawkes, along with a band of Catholic cohorts, had attempted to exterminate King, Lords and Commons in a single spectacular explosion, which is reenacted every year by British schoolchildren, determined to blow themselves up with modern fireworks. No more than 1.5 percent of the kingdom was actually Catholic, but in the eyes of most Protestants, numbers did not count when dealing with the Catholic menace, especially if the King himself was supping with the devil.

Suddenly in October, 1641, latent religious hysteria merged with a fresh constitutional crisis. Reports arrived from Ireland of a bloody uprising of Catholic peasants against their English and Scottish Protestant landlords. Thirty thousand men, women and children were said to have been horribly murdered and unspeakable atrocities committed. The figures were hopelessly exaggerated, but the rebellion confronted Parliament with an emotionally charged dilemma. Irish Catholic rebels had to be punished, but historically responsibility for military action belonged to the King and parliamentary leaders did not trust Charles. They feared lest he turn an army designed to discipline papists in Ireland against God-fearing Protestants in England.

Controversy over who controlled the military went to the root of the constitutional struggle, forced moderates to take sides, and stampeded Parliament into directly attacking the King's sovereignty. In February of 1642, it passed the Militia Act by 23 votes, stripping Charles of his ancient and historic right to command in time of war and placing all naval and military appointments under parliamentary control. Charles's sentiments were dead on the mark. If, he said, he lost the power to appoint his own officials, "we may be waited on bare-headed, we may have our hand kissed . . . and please ourselves with the sign of a crown and sceptre . . . but as to true and real power, we shall remain but on the outside, but the picture, but the sign of a King."

Political and religious moderates, interested in limited but constitutional monarchy, were shocked by the Militia Act's attack on the King's historic sovereignty. They were also deeply disturbed by parliamentary threats to impeach the Queen, abolish episcopacy and introduce Presbyterianism into the Church of England. A King's party began to emerge, and when Charles raised his standard at Nottingham on August 22, 1642, in defense of the Tudor-Stuart monarchy—exactly 157 years after Henry Tudor's victory at Bosworth Field—239 out of the 507 MPs and most of the House of Lords walked out of Parliament either to join their King in the defense of the ancient constitution and the Church of England, or to remain as neutral as possible.

Parliament eventually won the war, but in doing so it created the instrument of its own destruction—Oliver Cromwell's New Model Army. It helped that Parliament controlled the wealthiest parts of the country, the city of London and the navy, and that it had the money to pay a Scottish army to do much of the fighting. But not until Cromwell forged a military force filled with troopers who actually believed that the King was the devil's disciple, did the tide of battle turn. At the battle of Naseby in 1643, Charles's cavaliers (named after the brutal Spanish cavaliero) were resoundingly defeated by Cromwell's roundheads (named after the short cropped hair of London apprentices). A year later, reminding them that he had been born in Scotland, Charles surrendered to the Scots, who promptly and ungratefully sold him for £400,000 to the parliamentary forces.

A cavalier ("wrong but romantic") and a roundhead ("right but repulsive")

Victory came with a price: the victors—Parliament, the Scots and the New Model Army—began to quarrel among themselves. Conservatives in Commons and Lords, who favored constitutional monarchy and Presbyterianism in the Church, fell out with their more radical colleagues who advocated absolute parliamentary supremacy, republicanism and congregationalism in religion. Worse, the parliamentary conservatives earned the undying hatred of the army by trying to dismiss, without pay, the very organization that had won the war for them. Not a dissenting voice was to be heard in the military ranks to the charge that Charles's years of mismanagement were "as a molehill to a mountain in comparison of this everlasting Parliament."

In the midst of this bickering, Charles played the dishonest broker, making promises he had no intention of honoring and arranging a three-way alliance in 1648 between himself, the Scots and the Presbyterians in Parliament against the army and religious and political radicals. For a second time Charles was defeated, but with a difference. At the end of the first civil war he was still accepted as King, albeit a misguided one. At the conclusion of this second civil war, he was viewed by Cromwell and the military as a "man of blood" who had to "account for the blood he had shed, and mischief" he had done to God's cause and "the good people of England." In the eyes of the military, the conservatives in Parliament were just as evil as the King and had to be purged. On December 6th, Colonel Thomas Pride arrested 47 members of the House of Commons and barred the doors to 96 others. Many more, appalled by the Colonel's actions, refused their seats, leaving only a "Rump" (scarcely a quorum) of 56 godly and right-minded men who would harken to the Word of God and the will of the army. A month later, and urged on by Oliver Cromwell and the other grandees of the military, the "Rump" launched a revolution that dismantled the ancient constitution of King in Parliament. It decreed itself to "have the supreme power in the nation"; tried and convicted Charles of war crimes and of being a "traitor to the people of England"; executed him on January 30, 1649; and almost as an afterthought, in February legislated the House of Lords out of existence.

Nothing was left of the historic constitution except a "Rump" controlled by the military, and the next ten years is the history of the army's footless efforts to devise some form of constitutional structure that would act as a respectable fig leaf to naked force. For all his multiple sins, Charles had been quite right when he said, first at his trial and again at his execution, that if his rights as King were violated and his life forfeited, he "did not know what subject . . . can be sure of his life or anything that he calls his own," and that therefore he died "the martyr of his people."

Cutting off the King's head did not end the bloodshed, and the body politic gave a final convulsive spasm. In September of 1649, Catholic Ireland brought upon itself the vengeance of God's self-ordained elect when Cromwell's troops stormed the Irish stronghold of Drogheda and slaughtered its garrison. Two years later, Scotland rose to defend its new sovereign, Charles II, only to be defeated and garrisoned by New Model Army soldiers, its 19-year-old King fleeing, dressed first as a woodsman, then as a household servant. (The sapling, presumably from the famous royal oak tree in which he hid from heavily armed Roundheads, still stands at Boscobel House, near the cathedral city of Worcester.) The destruction of the Stuart monarchy was costly beyond imagination. Of the King's three kingdoms, England lost 3.7 percent of its population, Scotland 6 percent and Ireland 41 percent where 616,000 people perished; and the financial price was, according to one authority, "not exceeded until the world wars of the twentieth century."

The Interregnum and the Search for Legality
(1649–1660)

With all the army's enemies chastised and obedient, the military declared itself to be not "a mercenary army" but a body that had taken up arms "in judgment and in conscience." According to its conscience, it judged the parliamentary "Rump" to have done nothing "for the public good," and Cromwell vowed "to be done with it." Thus, on April 20, 1653, he cleared the house of its members, and next day posted a sign on the door reading, "This house for Lett now Unfurnished."

Oliver Cromwell dissolving the Long Parliament

The last vestige of the old constitution was gone, but nothing the military could devise to replace it seemed to work. Lord General of the Army Cromwell, even when he changed his title to Lord Protector, discovered that he had even more trouble raising money than Charles, and that saints and Puritans disliked paying taxes as much as sinners and royalists. Like the dead King, he too was forced to go it alone, but while royal Charles's so-called "tyranny" had endured for eleven years, Protector Cromwell's rule of the major generals survived only two. With the habit of obedience gone, it soon became apparent that military dictatorship, no matter how godly, was no substitute for historic legality even when exercised by an inept monarch. Slowly the same men who had destroyed King, Lords and Commons began to inch their way back to a historic monarchy in all but name. They constructed a lower house based on the ancient electoral franchise, a house of peers filled with the grandees of the army and Cromwell's friends, and a Lord Protector who declined the title of King but settled for "His Highness" with most of the regalia of royal office. The new structure, however, still lacked legitimacy, and when the Lord Protector, "a puzzled atlas" who had labored devoutly, but fruitlessly, in the Lord's vineyard to persuade an errant nation to do the right as he saw it, died in September, 1658 the protectorate died with him.

In an atmosphere of near-anarchy in which men of property, both royalists and republicans, came face to face with the "giddy, hot-headed, bloody multitude," the "better part" of society came to the conclusion that the only way to keep the "more part" in proper obedience to "degree, priority and place," was to reinstate the historic monarchy. And so in the spring of 1660, General George Monck marched his troops into London and restored an elderly and disgruntled "Rump." He instructed it to open its doors to the members evicted 12 years before, stood by while the partially resurrected Long Parliament established the machinery to invite Charles II to remount his throne, and finally ordered it to quietly dissolve itself.

To this day the eleven years following the execution of Charles are regarded as an aberration, an Interregnum between periods of legality during which no new laws had validity. The British learned their lesson: the dangers of tampering with the historic constitution and the even greater danger of a standing army, and ever since they have done their best to avoid both. But the drama of the King's death and the destruction of the monarchy have proved to possess such an enduring fascination that not until the second half of the 20th century have the ghosts of the two main protagonists been fully laid to rest. The anniversary of Charles's death as a day of "fasting and humility" was celebrated by the Church of England until 1858, and services for the dead sovereign were not deleted from the Book of Common Prayer until 1928. In a more corporeal vein, the coffin of Charles was opened in 1813 by Sir Henry Halford, the royal surgeon. He could not resist liberating the King's fourth vertebra, and he turned it into a macabre salt shaker to entertain his guests at dinner. When Queen Victoria, who was partial to the Stuarts, heard of this desecration, she was not amused and forced him to make her ancestor whole again. (One wonders whether she would have done the same for the eighth

Henry.) Cromwell's head had similar peregrinations. After the restoration of the monarchy, the Lord Protector was executed post mortem
for regicide and his skull impaled over the entrance to Westminster
Hall (the building in which Charles had been tried and condemned
to death). Twenty-four years later, it fell off in a windstorm. It bat-
ted about for decades, was purchased for £230 by a consortium that
hoped to make money displaying it, and finally fell into the hands of
the Wilkinson family, who kept the skull for years in an oak box lined
with red silk and in 1960 turned it over to Sydney Sussex College,
Cambridge (appropriately Cromwell's own alma mater) where it was
discreetly buried. The spirits of Charles and the Lord Protector may
have finally been laid to rest, but by one of those strange twists of
chance, the visitor can view the King forever confronting his nemesis.
In a niche above the east door of St. Margaret's Church in London, a
bronze bust of the monarch, serene but fastidiously obstinate, looks
directly across Parliament Street at the stern-faced statue of Oliver
Cromwell. He stands with a sword in one hand and the Bible in the
other, appropriately placed with his back to the Houses of Parliament,
a statue erected by private, not public, money.

Charles II and the Restored Monarchy
(1660–1685)

Never before in history has there been such a concerted effort to turn
back time and pretend that two decades of treason had never existed.
Symbolically, Charles I's bronze equestrian statue (the handsomest in
London) that had been completed just as the civil war broke out and
buried in order to prevent it from being melted down by the King's enemies, was disinterred and placed in the center of Whitehall leading directly to the banqueting hall where the King had been executed. Appropriately, it was located on the spot where his regicides in their turn had
died as enemies of the monarchy and historic constitution. Charles II's
restoration was unconditional, except for his royal pledge that he would
disband the army, offer "liberty to tender consciences," and leave retri-
bution to Parliament. Otherwise, the Stuart monarchy was resurrected
intact as Charles's father and the Lords and Commons of the Long Parliament had settled it in 1641: 1) a King who still possessed all his divinely and historically ordained prerogative powers, but who had given

up much of his ability to enforce those powers when he had graciously signed the Habeas Corpus Act protecting his subjects from arbitrary arrest and had permitted the abolition of his courts of Star Chamber and High Commission, and 2) a Parliament that monopolized the right to tax, had taken upon itself the responsibility to fund the government, and was guaranteed to meet at least every three years.

Although the constitution looked much the same and the mystical union of King in Parliament had in theory been restored, the spirit of that union had been profoundly altered. No one could deny that a revolution had taken place in which a King had been executed by his own Parliament. The monarchy had been restored not by divine interference but by the will of Parliament, and that body had not forgotten the words of one of its more revolutionary members, John Pym, when he declared "a Parliament is to the commonwealth which the soul is to the body." The Tudor body politic might still exist, but the King was no longer its spiritual leader. At most he was only its administrative head.

The Kingdom was fortunate in its new King, who was determined never to go on his travels again, understood that he had to operate within a highly unstable constitutional system in which a multitude of issues between King and Parliament remained unresolved, and who possessed the charm, tact and cynicism to survive 25 years of politicking that sometimes bordered on rebellion. Three ongoing problems destabilized the reign. The most immediate was that Parliament had granted Charles a £1.2 million annual income from excise taxes and custom duties, but the economy failed to actually generate that amount. As a consequence, the King was desperately short of cash and remedied the situation by becoming the pensioner of his cousin, the King of France. Louis XIV's money came with a price tag. Charles was expected to promote a pro-French foreign policy that placed him at odds with his Parliament, which was deeply suspicious of French military and religious intentions. Louis was busily doing away with the legal safeguards that protected French Protestants (Huguenots) at home, and Parliament feared that he had plans to re-Catholicize England as well.

More serious in the long run for both Charles and Parliament, was the failure of the Restoration to resolve the thorny question of the relation of the taxing power (possessed by Parliament) to the policy-making power (belonging to the Crown). Parliament could raise money, but not appropriate it for specific policies; the King could spend money as he saw fit, but not raise it. Only slowly did Charles give up his right to dispense money as he liked; only slowly did Parliament develop the machinery to enforce its financial will and require a public accounting from the Crown.

Finally, Charles very nearly went on his travels again over a mixture of religion and his inability to sire a legitimate heir to the throne. (He had no trouble with illegitimate heirs.) Since the Crown and religion were inseparable, any restoration of the ancient constitution required the reestablishment of the old Church, and Charles's new "Cavalier" Parliament was determined to enforce conformity to the official Anglican creed despite Charles's promise of liberty for tender consciences. The monarch was once again named Defender of the Faith and Head of the Church of England. Catholics and Puritans who dissented from the new Act of Uniformity were severely penalized, if not openly persecuted, Puritanism finding in defeat its grandest voice in the poetry of the blind John Milton. *Paradise Lost* is the cry of disheartened Puritanism; *Paradise Regained* is the renewed hope of spiritual, not political, victory, and the regaining of Heaven.

Religion and religious hysteria remained almost as pervasive and intense as in the past, and during the last decade of the reign, fear of Catholicism, largely fostered by Anthony Cooper, Earl of Shaftesbury, united with bitter political debate over the succession, to create yet another constitutional crisis. The nub of the issue was that Charles's legal heir was his brother James, and James was a Catholic convert. Shaftesbury and his political organization known as the Green Ribbon Club (which later evolved into the Whig Party) sought, by whipping up anti-Catholic hysteria and distributing vast quantities of free beer, to elect a Parliament that would pass an exclusion bill barring James from the succession. Charles staked his political reputation and his Crown to save his brother's inheritance, and only the King's close call with death in 1679, and the realization that, should he die, civil war between his illegitimate, but Protestant, son, the Duke of Monmouth, and Catholic James would ensue, shocked the Kingdom into recalling the dangers of tampering with legality and legitimacy. The King recovered; the exclusion crisis simmered down; and Charles finished his reign, heavily financed by France, in peace and security. Even so, the most popular of the Stuart monarchs gloomily predicted that his brother would be lucky to last four years on the throne. He was short of the mark by only 45 days.

The Glorious Revolution
(1688–1691)

If there was ever a monarch designed by an ill-natured Deity to lose his Crown, it was James II. He was stodgy, stubborn and stupid; even his brother thought that James's mistresses were so ugly and stultifying that they must have been assigned "by his priest for penance." But his throne in 1685 was as stable as it had been when in 1603 the first James crossed the border to enjoy his inheritance. The second James, however, achieved the near impossible. Within 36 months, he had so antagonized everybody who counted that Parliament invited a foreigner, a Dutchman, to replace him and engineered what history calls the Glorious Revolution.

If there was ever a monarch designed by an ill-natured
Deity to lose his Crown it was James II

When James succeeded to the Crown, his Catholicism was carefully forgotten, because his heirs were his two Protestant daughters, Mary and Anne, by his first marriage. What could not be forgotten or forgiven was the viciousness with which he suppressed his Protestant nephew's (the Duke of Monmouth) ill-starred effort to unseat him; his

failure to disband the army raised to crush that rebellion; his appoint-
ment of Catholics to high military and public office in direct violation of
statutory law; his use of the Crown's suspending powers to set aside the
law of the land; his tampering with the electoral process so as to pack
the House of Commons and undermine the control of men of wealth
and respectability; and most important of all, the unexpected appearance of a Catholic son and heir to the throne. This last, the birth of
the Warming-Pan Baby (Whigs and Protestants always questioned
whether James's second wife, Mary of Modena, ever actually gave birth
to a son and insisted that she had had a baby smuggled into her birth-
ing chamber in a warming pan), and James's unbelievable flouting of
Protestant sentiments by making the Pope the child's godfather, galva-
nized both Whigs and Tories into common action. Whigs (a derogatory
name referring to Scottish horse thieves and rebels) regarded the King
merely as the administrative head of state, real power resting with Parliament; Tories (an equally insulting label referring to Catholic bandits
in Ireland) continued to adhere to the Divinity of Kings; but together
they controlled Parliament, and both parties represented men of property and the traditional leaders of society. In their eyes, James's actions
were clear proof that he was hell-bent on reestablishing absolutism and
Catholicism, and was deliberately undermining their historic right to
rule. He had to go. The problem was how to rid the Kingdom of a legal
King without breaking the law or inviting civil war.

The solution owes much to good luck and James Stuart's panicky dis-
inclination to stay and fight for his Crown. The trick was to find a legitimate replacement, and on June 30, 1688, six Whig and Tory peers and
an Anglican bishop wrote William of Orange, Stadholder of Holland (he
had already indicated he would be happy to receive such a letter), asking
him to rescue their country from a King who avowed that Elizabeth I
had been as much a usurper as Oliver Cromwell, and who seemed to be
"guided solely by the Virgin Mary." William was Charles I's grandson,
and, equally important, was married to Mary Stuart, James II's Protestant
daughter. Together they embodied the essence of legitimacy.

William landed in England in November with a disciplined force of
15,000 soldiers, replete with a mold to mint coins prominently displaying his hooked nose in profile, and a portable press to flood the country
with the news that he had come to protect "the Protestant Religion and
the Liberties of England." James's support melted away, and when his

younger daughter Anne and John Churchill, his best general, declared for William, he fled the realm, taking with him his wife and son. As he left for France and the protection of his first cousin, Louis XIV, he dropped the Great Seal of England into the Thames River. It was a symbolic act allowing Parliament to announce that James had abdicated his Crown, the only debate left being the terms under which a new claimant (or claimants) would ascend the throne.

A three-way tug-of-war ensued. Whigs wanted the throne declared vacant, Mary elected Queen, and William designated simply her Prince Consort; Tories desired William only as regent ruling in James's stead, thereby preserving the principle of absolute legitimacy; and the Stadholder declared that he would not hold "anything by [his wife's] apron strings" or act as regent, and told both Whig and Tory that if he could not rule in his own right, he would go home and "meddle no more in their affairs." William won, (or almost won) and he and his wife Mary were declared joint monarchs. Since Mary was an obedient spouse and, according to one contemporary, had a mind "as sluggish as an inland river," William had the throne pretty much to himself. He preferred to claim that he ruled by right of conquest and legitimacy, but it was difficult to dismiss the words of "Honest Tom" Wharton, a shrewd Whig election monger and politician, who bluntly told him "we [Parliament] have made you king," and he accepted in 1689, none too graciously, a "Revolutionary Settlement" dictated by Lords and Commons. A Bill of Rights curtailed, but did not abolish, his prerogative powers and right to suspend law. He signed legislation making it impossible to maintain a standing army for more than a year without parliamentary consent. He accepted an unrestricted yearly income of £600,000 (half that of Charles II's), and acknowledged that all the rest had to be appropriated on an annual basis for specific purposes. And he signed a Toleration Act, now an absolute necessity since William was a Calvinist and his wife an Anglican, lifting most, but not all, of the penal legislation directed at religious dissenters (but not Catholics or Jews).

Dutch William had little liking for his English subjects, and they responded in kind. Nevertheless, the bestowing of joint sovereignty on a married couple was an immensely successful piece of political legerdemain. England was allowed to enjoy constitutional monarchy while maintaining the comforting myth that the two Protestant grandchildren of Charles I were superior in divinity and legitimacy to his Catholic son. And William was permitted to fulfill his hidden agenda: defend his precious Holland from French aggression, and bring England into the Continental orbit to rectify the balance of power upset by Louis XIV's ambitions to extend France to its "natural" borders—the Pyrenees to the south, the Alps to the east and the Rhine River to the north, which entailed gobbling up bits of the Holy Roman Empire, all of the Spanish Netherlands (today Belgium) and a large hunk of the Dutch Republic.

The "modification" of the succession may have been glorious, but it was certainly not bloodless. The Lowland Scots accepted William with no great enthusiasm after extracting from him legal recognition of their Presbyterian Church, but the Highland clans clung tenaciously to the original Stuart line, exhibiting their loyalty in a series of bloody but footless rebellions in 1689, 1715 and a final convulsion in 1745–46 when the power of the clans was destroyed once and for all at Colloden by a vastly superior English army led by William, Duke of Cumberland. Thousands upon thousands of Highlanders died, and the fatal mystique of the Stuart line was smashed forever. The clans were cruelly deprived of their bagpipes and kilts, but since the kilt was an English invention scarcely a generation old in 1745, and the bagpipes were originally an English instrument of musical torture, their outlawing was not as inhuman as later legend likes to maintain. Nevertheless, when the English proudly named a flower for Cumberland calling it Sweet William, the Scots countered by naming a weed Stinky Billy in memory of the Duke's savagery at Colloden.

A fierce Scottish Highlander making the most of his bagpipes and kilt

Ireland was even bloodier. William III could not afford to have the island used as a staging ground either for a French invasion of England or the reconquest of the throne by James. In 1691, for the third time in a century, Protestant English troops crushed Catholic nationalist rebellion, and for the next 230 years the island became tantamount to a English colony to be garrisoned and exploited, only one-seventh of the land being left in Irish Catholic hands.

Sir Isaac Newton and the "Happy Childhood of Science"

Despite his ill-tempered and introverted ways, William III was one of England's most successful warrior kings, and he would have been more than a little surprised to be told that 300 years in the future *Time* magazine, in its analysis of the second millennium and listing of the wheelers and dealers who shaped it, would name, not him or the Sun King of France, but Sir Isaac Newton the man of the 17th century. (Two other figures in English history earned this distinction: William the Conqueror for the 11th and Elizabeth I for the 16th century.)

Sir Isaac Newton (in a frivolous mood).
"My good woman, I never buy apples—they come to me."

Newton (1642–1727) and his famous, if somewhat apocryphal, apple proving the theory of gravity, along with his scientific colleagues in the Royal Society (founded 1660), are the giants upon whose shoulders modern science stands, because they introduced a revolution in human thought, transforming the Deity from a spiritual cartographer into a Divine Mechanic whose clockwork universe operated on predictable, discoverable and universal laws of nature, and was subject to human understanding and control. They set the intellectual standards for the 18th-century Enlightenment when sages and scientists throughout Europe confidently proclaimed: "From music to morals, from the scholastic disputes of theologians to matters of trade . . . everything has been discussed and analyzed, or at least mentioned."

As Alexander Pope quipped, "Nature and Nature's laws lay hid in night: God said 'Let Newton be!' and all was light." No wonder Albert Einstein spoke of "Fortunate Newton, happy childhood of science!" God and man, revelation and reason were in perfect accord, and philosophers, bishops and kings all optimistically chanted with Pope: "And, spite of pride, in erring reasons spite, Whatever is, is right." The only trouble was that 17th- and 18th-century monarchs spent far more time and energy making war than questing after "universal good," but, of course, they were happily ignorant of *Time*'s 21st-century priorities or that the 20th century would belong to a mild German theoretical physicist who complicated the cosmos beyond comprehension but clung, like Newton, tenaciously to the faith that "God does not play dice with the universe." (Newton's statue is part of the decorations of the City of London School opposite Blackfriar Bridge. Close by stand John Milton and John Stuart Mill.)

War with France, The First Phase
(1689–1713)

War was the major preoccupation of 18th-century states. England between 1689 and 1815 would be at war for 63 years, largely in an effort to contain France both on the Continent and throughout the world. Since Agincourt and the conquests of Henry V, England had sunk to the level of a second-rate player in the European game of power politics. Even the reign of Elizabeth I was no exception, her successes being more the result of French dynastic collapse and religious wars than English geopolitical strength, and in the 17th century the island returned to its peripheral status. But after 1690, all this changed with startling international and domestic consequences. England, the new player on the block, emerged as the paymaster of the grand alliance against France, and its most powerful member.

Out of the long duel with France, the so-called Second Hundred Years War, a description just as imprecise as the first, grew the cardinal principles on which English foreign policy would rest until well into the 20th century. 1) The Lowlands (Holland and the Spanish Netherlands) must not be allowed to fall into the hands of an unfriendly power (until the 20th century this meant France). 2) Naval command of the sea; this included not simply preventing invasion from the Continent and protecting England's vital sea lanes, but also guaranteeing the flow of arms and supplies to her continental allies. And 3) England would use her insular position and control of world commerce to bankroll her friends in Europe, and—depending on who happened to be her ally—would fight, as the witticism goes, to the last Austrian, Prussian, Russian or Dutchman to keep France, or any other power, from dominating Europe.

There is a very ancient truism: war takes three things—money, more money and still more money. William's government found the answer to feeding the beasts of war, especially rebuilding the navy and hiring foreign mercenary troops, by taxing the propertied classes on an unprecedented scale and by creating the consolidated national debt, a system of deficit financing whereby the money supply never ran dry because the debt never had to be paid off. Financially speaking, England in the 18th century was the world's first modern state. The traditional way to borrow money was through short-term loans for specific purposes. During the 1690s and thereafter, the English Crown began to offer for sale interest-bearing securities guaranteed by the stability and solvency of the government. This was possible for the first time, because Parliament after the Glorious Revolution held a firm rein on the national purse strings and could dictate royal policy. Consequently, the financial and commercial interests, heavily represented in Parliament, were willing to invest in government securities. Everybody benefited. The moneyed classes received handsome incomes from high-yield stock; the Crown could use the money at any time, for any purpose; and best of all, the government was never called upon to pay out hard cash—if a stockholder wanted his money back, he simply sold his stock to another investor.

Having devised the national debt, the Crown needed an organization to administer it, and when a pride of London financiers offered to lend

the Crown £1.2 million at a rate of interest lower than that paid by government securities, a deal was struck. They received a charter granting
their bank the sole right to administer the national debt and giving it the
right to issue bank notes or paper money guaranteed in pounds sterling
by the government. Thus was created the Bank of England, the Old
Lady of Threadneedle Street, a private institution, but at the same time
an arm of the state. By 1760, 60,000 security holders were investing in
the future of the Kingdom, and the wedding of the state and the moneyed classes had been accomplished: yet another sign of modernity.

Stock holders thronging the Bank of England

Borrowing paid for part of the cost of war; taxation—property and
excise taxes and custom duties—carried the lion's share of the burden.
The English Crown was unequalled in Europe in financing its military,
foreign and naval policies, because the executive and the legislature were
in accord with one another for the first time in a hundred years. There
was, however, a price. The property tax fell heaviest on landowners (especially the gentry), not merchants, and 18th-century English politics
constituted a prolonged struggle to control foreign policy. The Tories,
who felt that their landed constituents were being unduly taxed to pay for
war, preached peace, and the Whigs, who represented financial, commercial and imperial interests, favored a more militant approach. Those who
could not abide either party were left in political darkness to complain

with the Earl of Dorset "the long and the short of the story [was that] the fools might be Whigs [but] none but knaves should be Tories."

War not only costs money, it also requires domestic solidarity, and war explains the timing of the Act of Union which joined England and Scotland. Despite a hundred years of Siamese-twins existence, joined together only by a common sovereign, the two parts of the island seemed in 1700 to be falling apart, and faced the choice of union or full separation. The two kingdoms reluctantly gave up a thousand years of mutual distaste and in 1707 chose partial union for two reasons: 1) England could not risk the possibility that when Queen Anne, the last of the Protestant Stuart monarchs, died, Scotland would declare for James Stuart, the son of the exiled James II, and become once again a French dagger pointed at the English back. And 2) Scottish merchants desperately wanted access to English and colonial markets. By the terms of unification, Scotland retained its legal system, local government, State Presbyterian Church, and the right to issue its own paper money (which to this day looks different from the English pound), but gave up its Parliament in return for 45 seats in an enlarged Westminster House of Commons of 554 members and 16 new peers in the House of Lords, selected from the Scottish peerage.

For a Kingdom that covered one-third of the island and contained one-sixth of its population, the terms of union seemed particularly galling. But Scotland possessed only a tiny fraction of the new union's wealth, and Scottish commercial interests were granted a heaven-sent chance to take over Britain and its emerging empire, which they promptly did. The new political entity known as Great Britain constituted the largest free-trade bloc in Europe and received a new flag: a merging of the crosses of St. George and St. Andrew. (Today's Union Jack is the result of the union in 1801 with Ireland when the cross of St. Patrick was added to the design.) Not everyone greeted the union of the two flags with praise: Jonathan Swift called the new commonwealth "a vessel with a double keel" and predicted "tossing faction will o'erwhelm one crazy double-bottom'd realm." (He may yet be proved right—see pp. 184–85.)

The Treaty of Utrecht brought the war with France to a reluctant and temporary end in 1713, eleven years after the death of William III and only a year before his sister-in-law and successor died. By then England had become a major Atlantic and Mediterranean power, acquiring Gibraltar and Minorca and large tracts of New World territory in Newfoundland and Nova Scotia. She extracted from Spain partial commercial penetration of its South American possessions, and rapidly became the dominant slave carrier for the New World. Ships left the port of Liverpool for the west coast of Africa loaded with firearms, textiles and manufactured trinkets to be exchanged for slaves; this human freight was transported to the West Indies and the mainland and sold for rum, molasses and sugar; then back home with a cargo worth a fortune in Britain. The triangular journey was immensely profitable (one slave could produce nearly a ton of sugar in his lifetime) since it entailed little capital, and the Caribbean sugar plantations were so unhealthy that slave owners had to constantly replenish their labor supply.

Britain also emerged with the largest navy in the world, which everybody admitted was responsible for her new military position in Europe and throughout the globe, but no one wanted to pay for, especially in peacetime. One-half of the money that funded the Bank of England had gone to building this war machine of 300 vessels and 50,000 sailors, and its maintenance was the single largest industry in the land. Significantly, however, the most enduring monument to Britain's new power status was not a public navy but a private home, Blenheim Palace, the residence of John Churchill, Duke of Marlborough, the Kingdom's greatest general and the man who almost single handedly kept the grand alliance against France alive and brought Louis XIV to his knees. A grateful Queen Anne presented her handsome soldier with the titles and moneys to build what may be the largest and most spectacular private pile on earth. When the Duke died in 1721, Jonathan Swift, who detested the man, crowed:

> *Come hither, all ye empty things,*
> *Ye bubbles rais'd by breath of Kings;*
> *Who float upon the tide of state,*
> *Come hither, and behold your fate.*
> *Let pride be taught by this rebuke,*
> *How very mean a thing's a Duke;*
> *From all his ill-got honours flung,*
> *Turn'd to that dirt from whence he sprung.*

But Blenheim (situated on the 16,000-acre royal manor of Woodstock, eight miles outside Oxford) is more than a gaudy five-acre Palladian panache to Marlborough's fleeting military triumphs, that every tourist must see in order to believe; it is also a celebration of the robust egotism and extravagance of Britain's Augustan Age driven by the wealth of commerce and Empire.

Blenheim Palace—It must be seen to be believed

London, "The Emporium of the World"

London, as the visitor sees it today, rose like the phoenix from the great fire of 1666 which destroyed two-thirds of the metropolis. It was rebuilt, not of thatch and wood but of brick and stone, and financed by the immense commercial wealth that the city generated. Reconstruction and growth were the work of aristocrats, developers and merchants; no royal or central planning directed the reincarnation. London became unique in Europe because it was the governmental center of the Kingdom, the heart of the world's largest Empire, and the hub of global commerce. No other city could compare in size, wealth, prestige or importance. Historically, its only rival might have been classical Rome or Constantinople (today's Istanbul) at the height of the Byzantine Empire. And no subject better conveys the mercantile grandeur that Great Britain attained in the 18th century. By 1700, London rivaled Paris as the largest metropolis in Europe; 50 years later it far exceeded it, with a population of 675,000. The city dominated its Kingdom as no other capital did. It housed one-tenth of the population and was larger than the 60 largest provincial towns added together. As London spread beyond its medieval walls, it became the first metropolis to segregate rich from poor, residential from commercial and industrial, and build quality suburbs—today's West End.

The great fire destroyed four-fifths of the old city, not stopping until it had burned westward beyond the medieval walls as far as Fetter Lane, just east of the Royal Courts of Justice and Lincoln's Inn. Gone were 87 parish churches, 44 guildhalls, the Royal Exchange, 13,200 houses, and the old cathedral of St. Paul's, magnificent to look at from a distance but falling apart within. It all happened in three days; "the saddest sight of desolation that I ever saw," wrote Samuel Pepys in his diary. Thanks to Christopher Wren and his magnificent new St. Paul's, finished in 1710 and dedicated to a new understanding of God and man embodied in the Enlightenment, the old city was given fresh life and attractiveness, but the heart of the metropolis had moved from its medieval center to the West End, where "the houses are mostly new and elegant, the squares are superb, the streets straight and open," the throughways paved and lighted with oil lamps, and the atmosphere fit for men and women of quality. Gone were the stink, squalor, smoke and slums of the old city and its industrial East End.

The West End grew out of the great aristocratic estates that clustered around the King's palace and Westminster Abbey. The Earl of Southampton developed Bloomsbury and the areas now containing the British Museum (originally Southampton's town residence) and the University of London. The Earl of St. Albans created St. James Square; the Earl of Bedford, Covent Garden; and the Earl of Leicester, Soho (a hunting call) and Leicester Square. Sir Thomas Bond gave his name to Bond Street; Lord Gerrard developed Gerrard Street, and Richard Grosvenor, the heir to a hundred acres in Mayfair, laid out Grosvenor Square, the largest in London and site of the jarringly inappropriate American Embassy.

Land in the West End became so valuable that the Georgian narrow, but deep, four-story town house evolved—basement for the kitchen and servants' hall; first and second floors reserved for reception rooms; third floor for the family living quarters; the attic for a nursery and servants' bedrooms; and a muse or alley in back with a stable for the horses, carriage and grooms (now, of course, valuable garage apartments). Since not even the well-to-do could afford extensive private gardens, the communal square became standard, and though it is not quite true that the visitor can walk from one end of London to the other without leaving green turf, the city with its parks and multitude of squares is one of the most open metropolises in the world. By the late 19th century, the elegant homes overlooking Bedford, Berkeley, Hanover and Grosvenor Squares and throughout Mayfair, had been broken up into flats or maisonettes, but even today the vibrancy of Georgian West End life is still very much present as one reads small plaques noting that Clive of India died at No. 45 Berkeley Square (allegedly of an overdose of opium but, more probably of cutting his throat—he was 49), and the poet John Dryden resided at No. 44 Gerrard Street, or discovers that Dr. Samuel Johnson's residence still stands on Gough Square just off Fleet Street. There, in the eloquence of Georgian London, the new commercial wealth of the century indulged in an unsurpassed extravaganza of spectacular clothing and coiffeuring. For a brief moment even the ladies took second place to the men of high fashion—the Macaronis, who appeared in the 1770s, their only permanent mark in history being their presence in the satirical rhyme about "Yankee Doodle Dandy who put a feather in his cap and called it macaroni."

A macaroni in 1773

The West End, that bastion of gentility, lived off the real muscle of the metropolis located in the old city, the docks along the Thames, and the grimy industrial East End. The port of London monopolized 80 percent of the nation's import and 86 percent of its re-export trade, and daily some 1400 ships tried to find space in a harbor designed for 500 vessels. By 1750, London was burning annually 650,000 tons of coal to fuel its distilleries (Booth's and Gordon's gin), sugar refineries, and breweries which regularly produced seven million barrels of various kinds of beer and ale. Mr. Thomas Chippendale employed 400 apprentices in his furniture factory, and 5,000 craftsmen manufactured 120,000 watches, a number that represented half the world's yearly production. (The Swiss did not take over until the 19th century.) The East End produced soap, glue, paint and dyes, all "odious stinking businesses." During the 1760s, William Fortnum, once a footman to Queen Anne, set up a grocery store with his good friend Hugh Mason, and 240 years later it is still the city's most elegant food store. In the same decade, William Hamley established his toy shop, "Noah's Ark," in High Holborn before a branch store was set up on Regent Street where it is still located, and James Christie, an ex-naval person, opened his rooms in Pall Mall to compete with Samuel Baker, the founder of Sotheby's, and sixty other auction houses. The tea, coffee and chocolate merchant R. Twinings established his office on the Strand in 1706; today his company is the oldest continuous real estate taxpayer in the West End. And in 1757, James Lock, a hatter's apprentice, married his boss's daughter and gave his name to a hattery already 81 years old, which in 1805 manufactured a cocked hat for Nelson with a special "eye-shade" to conceal the Admiral's blind eye. Lock's store is still located at No. 6 James Street.

As the center of world finance, London swarmed with agents, brokers, discounters, remitters, ticket-mongers and stockjobbers. Nicholas Barbon founded the first fire insurance office in the 1680s, charging a yearly rate of 2.5 percent on brick and 5 percent on wooden homes, and Edward Lloyd established his maritime insurance company, and ten years later began printing London's oldest continuously published newspaper, *Lloyd's List and Shipping Gazette*. How Mr. Lloyd's insurance business has grown, prospered and modernized itself over the centuries can be sensed by a glance at the new (1986) Lloyd office building, a science-fiction structure looking more like a shotgun wedding between an oil refinery and an intergalactic rocket than the home of the world's oldest insurance company.

London of the 18th century was dangerous, disorderly and drunken. Thames river pirates annually plundered East India Company ships and warehouses of £250,000 worth of goods; the city boasted 8,659 brandy shops and 5,875 pubs; and mob violence was a way of life. The age has been described as one of aristocracy tempered by rioting, and most of that rioting took place in London, partly because the city was the seat of Parliament, but more because sheer numbers gave force to the will of King Mob.

There were riots in support of John Wilkes and his efforts to reform Parliament and allow the publication of its proceedings; riots against giving citizenship to Jews; and riots over the calendar. (The mob wanted back its lost eleven days when England finally went on the Gregorian calendar, changing September 3, 1752 into September 14 and altering the first of the year from March 25 to January 1.) Rotten apples were hurled at George III, peers had their carriages overturned, and the Houses of Parliament were blockaded. During the famous Gordon riot of 1780 in response to legislation granting partial religious freedom to Catholics, Lord Mansfield's wig was torn off, the Archbishop of York's gown ripped apart, and the Duke of Northumberland's watch and purse stolen as the three men tried to enter the House of Lords. When the mob started burning the homes of prominent Catholics, Justice Hyde tried to stop them only to have his own house burned to the ground in retaliation. Newgate jail was assaulted, its prisoners released, and the building burned; even the residences of the Lord Chancellor and Prime Minister were attacked. The week-long riot came to a crescendo when a Catholic distillery was burned, its flaming barrels of gin rolled about the streets, and everyone, as the saying goes, got drunk as lords. Only when the mob finally attacked the Bank of England, did the government bring the orgy to an end by ordering the troops to fire on the rioters. Oligarchy floated uneasily on a sea of discontent which, fortunately for people of property and London's West End, was moved far more by the instinct to vandalize than by any desire for constructive reform.

"That will be five years—with ten days added because of the change-over to the Gregorian calendar."

Two Out of Four Georges
(1714–1760)

Any reform of the government was almost unthinkable, because people of gentility had, in their estimation, achieved the perfect equilibrium between King, Parliament and the legal rights of Englishmen, a balance painstakingly recorded and enshrined in the American Constitution as the separation of powers among the executive, legislature and judiciary. The British 18th-century system was the result of time, accident and personality. As a consequence, it was constantly in flux, but by mid-century, the result was very much to the liking of property owners and the denizens of the West End. Central to the proper functioning of government was the presence of a sovereign who spoke almost no English, and was uninterested in and ignorant of all domestic and foreign policies except when they touched upon his sole concern, the Electorate of Hanover.

George I, Elector of Hanover, came to the British throne at the mature age of 54 because he was James I's great grandson and a Protestant, the only remaining Stuart who was. The Act of Settlement passed in 1701, the year the last of Queen Anne's six live-born children died, dictated that the King could not be Catholic (should some future sovereign either convert or marry a Catholic, it would take an act of Parliament to legalize it), and settled the succession on the Hanoverian-Stuart line. In mounting the throne in 1714, George inadvertently resolved a constitutional issue left unsettled by both the Restoration and the Glorious Revolution: how to manage a marriage of convenience between a King who devised his own policies and a Parliament that controlled the purse strings that made those policies possible. The resolution derived from the personalities—or more accurately the deficiencies—of the first two Georges.

George I trying on the crown of England

The modern office of Prime Minister evolved because the King's chief adviser took over the responsibility for creating royal policy and generating support for it in Parliament. Such a person had to possess three qualities: 1) He had to be personally agreeable to the monarch who selected his own advisers, and have access to his private chambers because the King still ruled in name and, more important, controlled royal patronage, consisting of annuities, honors, pensions, sinecures, government offices, and contracts for the army and navy; 2) He had to be able to manufacture a working majority in Parliament to finance his policies, and this was done in part through his popularity in Parliament, and in part through his manipulation of royal patronage which he used to influence (read "buy") the necessary votes in Lords and Commons; and 3) he had to possess the executive ability to preside over a cabinet of the King's officials and turn it into an effective executive organ to administer his policies. Originally, no office of Prime Minister existed; he was simply the King's chief adviser, usually the Lord Treasurer, later the Chancellor of the Exchequer. He presided over a cabinet of the monarch's most important officers who were responsible solely to the sovereign. Not until the early 20th century was the position of Prime Minister recognized as a separate office with ceremonial precedence after the Archbishop of York, and only slowly did the cabinet acquire corporate identity and collective responsibility for its decisions.

The Prime Minister was more than a policy maker; he was a politician whose success depended on a mind-boggling electoral system that was marvelously chaotic and bore absolutely no relationship to the massive demographic changes of the century. Medieval towns (called boroughs), which over the centuries had become tiny villages, had the same representation in the House of Commons as new and fast-growing industrial cities, some of which had no representation at all. In a few extreme cases, boroughs had actually disappeared but still had the right to send representatives to Parliament, the towns having moved or fallen into the ocean and elections being held in a tent pitched on an empty meadow or in a boat floating over the original site. A few towns had universal male suffrage, but most limited the electorate to less than 500, and in many, only the mayor and town officials could vote. The result was an electoral system where the electorate could be easily bribed and manipulated, and as a consequence half the seats in Commons were "pockets boroughs" controlled by 154 individuals.

Chaotic as the system appears to modern minds, to the 18th century it made perfect sense. John Locke, the philosophical godfather of the age, wrote that the purpose of all government was to protect "life, liberty and estate." (The "pursuit of happiness" was a later, American, adaptation of Locke's famous formula.) "Estate" included all kinds of property—land, money, birth, social status and office—and those with the greatest "estate" in society, it was argued, should have the greatest voice in government, because the purpose of government was to protect their estates. The monarch, as the possessor of the weightiest title in the realm and as still the largest single landowner, deserved a heavy say in how the government was run. So did the great peers whose voice was guaranteed in the House of Lords. Lesser landowners and commercial interests were heard in Commons, but it did not seem odd that 307 of those seats should be controlled by 154 men, mostly peers, who possessed vast wealth and estate. Moreover, it seemed eminently sensible in 1716 to extend the duration of Parliament from three to seven years (today it is five), thereby making it easier and cheaper, since elections were expensive, for both the King's chief minister and the borough masters to control the lower house. The 18th century would have dismissed as nonsensical the notion that representation should be equal and uniform or that mere citizenship should give either the right to vote or a voice in government equal to everyone else.

As an additional safeguard that government should be of, by, and for men of estate and gentility, both the military and the Church were successfully harnessed to property and money. Determined that the army should never again turn on its creator as it had done after the Civil War, the ruling elite, as soon as Charles II was secure on his throne, introduced the purchase system, making high military ranks marketable, thereby guaranteeing that officers would always be gentlemen with a proper financial stake in society. The navy was exempt: promotion was based largely on merit, and the navy's performance was noticeably more successful throughout the century than the army's. Even so, it is well to remember that Britain's greatest generals—including the Dukes of Wellington and Marlborough—bought their way into the military. The Church was equally tamed. The Church of England became the bastion of gentility, a form of outdoor relief for the younger sons of the landed aristocracy, preaching obedience to one's betters and offering God's blessings to that all-important social distinction: if you "walked across an estate, you were trespassing, but if you rode across the same property on horseback, you were gentry."

The man who mastered the political system, in many ways embodied it, in that he successfully shaped royal policy under the first two Georges, looked after his political friends in Parliament, and rewarded himself in a grand fashion, was Sir Robert Walpole. For a generation (1721–1742), the nation was governed by a hard-drinking, womanizing political boss, almost in the American style, who boasted that he was "no savant, no saint, no reformer," and who conducted both domestic and foreign policy on his famous motto—"Let sleeping dogs lie." (Jonathan Swift put it rather differently: "Oppressing true merit, exalting the base, and selling his country to purchase his peace.") Walpole's legacy is enshrined in two buildings: No. 10 Downing Street (named after its developer, Sir George Downing, a graduate of Harvard), given him by George II as the residence of the first Lord of the Treasury, and his Norfolk home—Houghton Hall—a splendid, but rather stark Palladian structure. The hall housed a magnificent display of nouveau riche artistic ostentation and a collection of paintings which, alas, was sold by his grandson to the Empress of Russia and now is one of the treasures of the Hermitage museum in Saint Petersburg.

Walpole's Policy

Walpole's peacefully sleeping dogs were rudely awakened in 1739 by yet another round of international wars: conflicts which, except for a few intervals of fitful resting, would continue until 1815. The military sparring partners had a hard time deciding on their opponents, but by 1756 the warring teams had been fairly well fixed: England and Prussia against France and Austria, who received occasional help from Russia and Spain. The bones they fought over were three-fold: the presence in central Europe of a highly aggressive Prussia, which, in the apt words of Napoleon, had been "hatched from a cannonball"; the dynastic accident of the Electorate of Hanover, so dear to the first two Georges, which made Britain vulnerable in Europe; and the commercial and colonial rivalry between England and France in India and the New World. The Seven Years War broke out in Europe in 1756, but had already started in America two years earlier when Lieutenant Colonel George Washington of the Virginia militia led a small company of men to establish a military outpost on the Ohio river, now the site of Pittsburgh, only to be captured by the French who were already there. A year later Great Britain's effort to avenge Washington's defeat and capture resulted in an even greater debacle, when General Edward Braddock's expedition to seize the French position ended in his ambush and death.

Undeclared war erupted into declared conflict when French troops overran Hanover in the expectation that the Electorate could be used to blackmail Britain into returning any French colonial losses throughout the world at the war's end. The French badly miscalculated. As a consequence of her naval and financial power, plus the victories of Robert Clive in India (his bronze statue stands in King Charles Street overlooking St. James's Park) and General Wolfe in Canada, and the wartime leadership of William Pitt, Great Britain emerged from the conflict in 1763 the world's first superpower. By the treaty of Paris, France had to cede Canada, Cape Breton and all her claims to the lands between the Allegheny Mountains and the Mississippi River. She also gave over to Spain New Orleans and the vast Louisiana territory west of the Mississippi. In return, Spain ceded Florida to Britain. In India the war was equally disastrous for France, leaving Britain the dominant European power and paving the way for the eventual Imperial takeover of the entire subcontinent. As one American citizen of the new Empire proudly proclaimed, Britain had "attained to a degree of wealth, power, and eminence, which half a century ago the most sanguine of her patriots would hardly have made the object of their warmest wishes."

Britain Cut Down to Size: The American Revolution
(1776–1781)

Victory, however, was short-lived. Within a generation, Britain lost her most important colonial possession—her American shore-line colonies—and the most valuable portion of the territories extracted from France because 1) she never learned how to manage her immense and varied Empire; 2) no one likes a top-dog, and the European family of nations was waiting to cut the new superpower down to size; and 3) as Edmund Burke told the House of Commons, "a great empire and little minds go ill together."

Imperial defeat had its roots in domestic turmoil when the high-minded, over-educated, 22-year-old grandson of George II succeeded his grandfather to the throne in 1760. The third George upset a 40-year tradition established by Walpole and Pitt that the King ruled through his chief minister, who determined national policy. As the first fully English George, who dismissed Hanover as "that horrid electorate" and gloried "in the name of Britain," George III was determined to be his own chief executive, save his Kingdom from moral corruption, and restore it "to virtue, freedom and glory." The result was a generation of feeble cabinets, inconsistent policies, and endless political bickering. Worse, George's efforts to exert his constitutional right to rule his Kingdom through a party of the King's friends in Parliament and a cabinet picked for its loyalty to the monarch personally (not for its political or administrative competence) meant that the monarch was no longer protected by his chief minister from political mudslinging. The cry went up that George aimed at restoring royal tyranny and subverting the liberties won at the Restoration and the Glorious Revolution. Pressure both within and without Parliament mounted to limit the monarch's authority, especially his power over royal patronage, and to reform a corrupt electoral system that allowed the King to maintain so many of his friends in Parliament. Into this political quagmire the colonial issue was introduced, with lethal consequences.

After the peace treaty of 1763, Great Britain realized that she possessed an Empire that had tripled in size but had no Imperial policy to go with it. Not only had the Empire grown in area, but it had also increased in wealth, population and importance to the domestic prosperity of the mother country. In 1700, 250,000 Brits, or one out of every 17 of the King's subjects, lived overseas in the American mainland colonies. Three generations later, that population had swollen to 1.7 million, or one in every four, and their economic value as a market for British goods and a source of supplies for raw materials had risen from £532,000 to £2.8 million annually. In terms of Imperial (but not European) trade, this represented about one-fourth of the Kingdom's imports and exports, slightly more than India, but less than the West Indies, and equal to Ireland. With so much at stake, it was clearly time to reconsider the relationship of the various parts of the empire to the whole. Unfortunately, that policy was befuddled, bemused and bedeviled. As Adam Smith, the father of modern economic theory, said, it "looked ever for the present gain; it overlooked colonial aspirations and needs; it took too much for granted."

Indeed, Britain took too much for granted. Seven years of war had left her victorious but exhausted, staggering from taxation and a debt of £133 million. George III's budget-minded cabinet bleakly noted that during this life-and-death struggle, the American colonies, which had benefited so much from the elimination of the French (and Indian) menace by British triumphs in Canada, had contributed almost nothing to victory. For every penny paid in taxes by the colonists, taxpayers in Britain had divvied up 50; the colonies had grown rich and independent under the protection of the British navy; and, worse, they had defiantly gone on trading illegally with the enemy's sugar islands in the Caribbean. Surely the least they could do now was to pay a fair share of the cost of defending and administering the Empire, the only question being how to pluck the colonial goose with the least amount of provincial squawking.

After a number of abortive but irritating attempts, the British government settled on a stamp tax on newspapers and legal documents and a reduced, but enforced, import charge on sugar from the Caribbean, in order to raise £145,000 or one-third of the cost of defending the Empire in America. On paper these taxes made perfect sense: moneys spent on the navy would stop smuggling, thereby guaranteeing revenues from the sugar import tax, and only the wealthy, who could best afford it, would be affected by the new Stamp Act which fell on Brits as well as colonists. The result, however, was catastrophic. With smuggling stopped, taxation in effect rose 200 percent. Worse, the most vocal elements of colonial society—lawyers, publishers and merchants—were the hardest hit. The ensuing hue and cry of indignation was deafening: "If taxes are laid upon us in any shape without ever having a legal representation . . . are we not reduced from the character of free subjects to the miserable state of tributary slaves?" In the face of a colonial boycott of British goods, and growing criticism in Parliament where the colonial cry of "no taxation without representation" meshed with opposition to George's so-called tyrannical domestic policies, the government backed down. By 1770, the stamp tax on the colonists and all import duties (except a small levy on tea, symbolizing that Parliament still had the right to tax the colonies) were repealed.

As in most conflicts, misunderstanding on both sides stood at the core of the controversy. The British government was woefully ignorant about the American colonies. Mr. James Otis of Boston complained that Imperial administrators did not even know whether Jamaica "lay in the Mediterranean, the Baltic, or in the moon." During the Seven Years War the British had become convinced that the American colonies were so chauvinistically independent and self-centered that they were incapable of "the concept of self-sacrifice, of service to the common cause." "Fire and water," it was said, "are not more heterogeneous than the different colonies of North America," and many Brits predicted that "there would soon be a civil war from one end of the continent to the other." Worse, both the King and his cabinet were scornful of Benjamin Franklin's warning that obedience depended far less upon "forts, citadels, garrisons or armies" than on affection. The colonists, he said, "were led by a thread." On their side, the colonists vastly overestimated their importance as a market for English goods. Their definition of a federated Empire in which George III presided over politically equal and separate units held together solely by economic self interest and loyalty to a common Crown, was totally at odds with the British reality of a single Imperial Parliament situated in Westminster.

For the next three years, the mounting tension between the mother country and its colonial offspring simmered, until Britain made yet another "enlightened" attempt to gently pluck the colonial goose. The East India Company was in financial difficulties, and the government offered it the chance to sell its tea directly in American ports without going through middlemen in London. Everyone was expected to benefit: the company would acquire a handsome profit, the colonists cheaper tea, and the government a modest revenue. Unfortunately, the colonies, as one historian expressed it, were "wary of Greeks bearing gifts." Even at a reduced price, the tea still carried a tax imposed by Parliament, and equally serious, it undercut tea previously purchased by such patriotic American merchants as Mr. John Hancock of Boston, who were now substantially out of pocket. As every red-blooded American knows, the result was the dumping of 342 chests of East Indian tea into Boston harbor.

Lord North administering a strong dose
of tea to the reluctant colonies

The Boston Tea Party of December 1773 was not simply an act of vandalism; it was a profoundly symbolic gesture, for East India ships had also been turned away in Charleston, New York and Philadelphia, and far more tea was burned throughout the colonies than dropped into Boston harbor. Tea, by 1773, had become the national drink for rich and poor, and the parliamentary tax that added to its price touched everybody. As a consequence, the boycott of tea became the clarion call for unity, and the Massachusetts Colony went on record, stating that tea was "the baneful vehicle of a corrupt and venial [British] administration [sent] for the purpose of introducing despotism and slavery into this once happy country, and that every individual in this province ought totally to disuse the same." The colonists had finally found their service to a common cause, a cause which explains why Americans to this day prefer coffee to tea.

For their part, George III and his government were outraged; even the opposition in Parliament was shocked. Not only had the authority of the King in his Imperial Parliament been flouted, but private property had now been vandalized, and everyone knew that the primary purpose of government was to protect property. Almost without a dissenting vote, Parliament ordered the closing of the port of Boston to all shipping and revoked the Massachusetts charter. To enforce these actions, troops were recalled from the Ohio valley; the administration and policing of that area was turned over to the provincial government of Quebec; and Generals Johnny Burgoyne, Henry Clinton and William Howe, a triumvirate of such unbelievable incompetents that defeat in war was almost guaranteed, were sent to reinforce British soldiers in Boston. Colonial opinion exploded: Boston was being tyrannically punished for standing up for colonial rights, and Britain was deliberately thwarting colonial manifest destiny to expand into the Ohio Valley and westward to the Mississippi, by turning over control of the area to Quebec.

George III and his chief minister Frederick, Lord North, 2nd Earl of Guilford (of whom Dr. Samuel Johnson acidly remarked, "He would not say that what he did was always wrong but it was always done at the wrong time"), were not responsible for the initial skirmishes at Lexington and Concord or Britain's Pyrrhic encounter with colonial troops at Bunker Hill in June of 1775, let alone the Declaration of Independence the following year.

*"I may not be able to hit anything—but this is ONE shot
that's going to make a lot of noise."*

The British government was 3000 miles away and the victims of their underlings' local panic and incompetence. But the way they conducted the war, the constitutional crisis they were generating at home, and everyone's misunderstanding of the nature and seriousness of the conflict— "The native American is an effeminate thing, very unfit and very impatient of war"—inevitably led to defeat. The British could not make up their minds whether they wanted to force or negotiate the colonies back into the Empire, or how to go about doing either. Of one thing, however, they were certain: they wanted to achieve their purpose as cheaply as possible. Both the war and Lord North's government were increasingly unpopular, partly because war disrupted trade, partly because large sections of the country agreed with the colonists, and partly because opposition factions in Parliament regarded the war as being the King's war. As a consequence, British war policy was a monument to the maxim, "too little and too late." The navy was allowed to flounder in a conflict that demanded the sea lanes be kept open; generals never had enough supplies or men; strategies were never synchronized; chains of command were not enforced; and a civil war within the Empire was allowed to turn into a world war when all the maritime powers—France, Spain and Holland—joined in to revenge themselves on "perfidious Albion."

A badly conceived and worse-conducted civil war came to an ignoble end at Yorktown on 19 October, 1781, when General Cornwallis (who later went on to become Governor General of India) allowed himself to be blockaded by George Washington by land and a French fleet by sea. As he surrendered, the British band appropriately played "The World Turned Upside Down": the superpower had been ignominiously humiliated. Although no one realized it at the time, the world had not simply been turned upside down, it had also been changed forever. Had Britain won and the thirteen colonies remained in the Empire, European, even world history, would have been unimaginably different.

Two years later, on January 20, 1783, Britain made formal peace with all the combatants in typical 18th-century compromise fashion. She could not disguise the extent of her defeat—the loss of her American seaboard colonies—but she had the satisfaction of preventing her archenemy France from regaining territory on the North American continent by ceding all lands east of the Mississippi to her one-time colonies and returning Florida to Spain. Britain, moreover, remained the economic giant of the globe; her trade with her lost colonies doubled during the 15 years following 1783 (plus she no longer had to pay to defend or administer them); and what she lost in the New World, she compensated for in the world down under by Captain James Cook's discovery in 1768-71 of Australia and New Zealand. It speaks wonders for the mixed-up nature of the war as well as the tolerance of the British that they have been willing to live with a statue of George Washington, prominently located in front of the National Gallery just off Trafalgar Square.

Four Revolutions:
Industrial, Agricultural, Demographic, and Spiritual

Great Britain lost the American Revolutionary War (the British still call it the War for Independence), but she was the spectacular winner in another revolution. She was the first country on earth to experience the Industrial Revolution, and she reaped the rewards and consequences of being first. Extraordinary industrial growth gave her victory in the final duel with Napoleonic France and established the foundations for the Pax Britannica throughout the 19th century. But, being first, Britain also went into the revolution blind, and the price in terms of human suffering was shockingly high.

The Industrial Revolution, in its starkest definition, is the use of the coal-fired steam engine in conjunction with heavy iron machinery and a regimented labor force fettered to the time clock and factory whistle, to vastly increase human productivity. The interaction between steam and iron revolutionized production and the society it served, changing an agricultural labor force into an urban proletariat, generating unimaginable wealth, and turning tiny villages into huge industrial cities. Depending on your point of view, the industrial behemoth created either a marvel of economic and social engineering and human ingenuity, or "the curse of Midas" and "the moral atmosphere of the slave trade."

Parallel with, but not directly caused by industrial change, were three other revolutions: the agricultural, demographic and religious. The first, with loud laments from idealists and farm workers (but not farm owners), did away with the old medieval communal method of farming, privatized the land, collected isolated fields into more efficient blocks, and introduced scientific breeding and farming techniques which increased agricultural production by 50 percent. The second, closely connected to the increased food supply, resulted in an unprecedented human explosion. The population rose from 7.7 to 10.5 million during the last 50 years of the 18th century and then proceeded to double during the next half century. The third revolution was a religious revival that transformed the spiritual landscape, brought hell-fire religion into the new industrial slums, and in the next century became the spiritual underpinnings for Victorian morality in the home, in the factory and in politics. The Anglican Church, reestablished as the state religion of England in 1660, had allied itself intellectually, socially and biologically with gentility and aristocracy. It preached obedience to and respect for one's betters; supplied the second and third sons of the well-to-do with cushy clerical livings; and favored sermons which were either so dull or so erudite that no one listened to them. Going to church was a social habit, not a spiritual experience. Starting with John Wesley's conversion in 1738 to high-intensity religion which spoke to the soul, not the mind, and offered salvation equally to rich and poor, the religious atmosphere began to change. Rejected by his own church—"It is monstrous," complained an outraged duchess, "to be told that you have a heart as sinful as the common wretches that crawl the earth"—Wesley founded his own: Methodism, which offered hymn singing and born-again Christianity to the ever-growing industrial population of the new factory towns. So emotionally satisfying was the movement, that the egalitarian ideals of the French Revolution found little support among Britain's industrial masses.

Statistics cannot hope to conjure up the emotional impact of these revolutions, but they can convey a sense of their magnitude. During the final decades of the century, commercial and industrial productivity rose 160 percent and foreign trade tripled. Cotton consumption soared exponentially: £8 million in 1770, £37 in 1795 and £250 by 1830 when half a million workers made their living in the cotton mills. The number of blast furnaces experienced the same kind of growth, rising from 20 in the mid-18th century to 372 by 1830, and by that year Britain was producing three-fourths of all the coal mined in Europe. The factory system became so productive that it was estimated that 750 unskilled operators in a single cotton mill could manufacture what 200,000 skilled cottage workers had accomplished in the past, and that a lace-making machine supervised by two laborers could produce as much as 10,000 hand weavers. By 1850, Britain commanded 25 percent of the entire world's trade, sending textiles and clocks, cutlery and china, steam engines and firearms to the four corners of the earth. Mr. Josiah Wedgwood was not alone when he prayed that "the winds and seas" would waft his fine china cups and plates "to their destined Markets" and rejoiced how rapidly their use had "spread almost over the whole globe and how universally" they were liked.

Within two generations the Kingdom became a nation of urban dwellers. By 1800, 27 percent of the population, in contrast to France's 11 percent, lived in towns, and by 1850, half the country had flocked into such new industrial cities as Manchester, the home of the cotton industry, in search of higher wages. Manchester in 1757 was a bustling town of 17,000; by 1800 it had swollen six-fold, and fifty years later reached over 300,000. London experienced the same explosion. By the turn of the century its population was just short of a million; 50 years later 11 percent of the nation, or 2.4 million people, lived in the capital city. Urbanization, especially in the new industrial cities, came at a terrible price: no sewers, drains, streetlights or parks. Houses were jerry-built, constructed back-to-back with no ventilation, often following ditches to reduce the cost of digging cellars, "not for storing wares but for dwellings for human beings." From such squalor the mill owner, banker and lawyer fled, abandoning, as one observer noted, the city to "publicans, mendicants, thieves and prostitutes, merely taking precaution to leave behind him a police force." Nevertheless, from such filthy sewers poured pure gold. (There are dozens of railroad and industrial museums in Britain, but Ironbridge in Shropshire has the best outdoor exhibition and is the location of the world's first cast-iron bridge: 1779.)

For better or for worse, Great Britain was transformed and learned to worship the new juggernaut. Swept away was the old organic, paternalistic, hierarchical and family-oriented society with its roots going back to Tudor times and beyond. The Kingdom was projected into the fluid, atomized, fiercely competitive and mass world of the 19th century, where the individual sought to survive, either by joining highly class-conscious labor unions and mass political parties powerful enough to influence public policy, or by taking advantage of the economic freedom that favored self-help, hard work, calculated ruthlessness and good luck.

For better or worse, Great Britain was transformed and learned
to worship the new industrial juggernaut

Revolution French Style

While Britain was struggling with its own social upheavals, another
revolution was taking place across the Channel in France. There the
Kingdom was being transformed first into a Republic and then into an
Empire by those three intoxicating, if ruthless, sisters: Liberty, Equality, and Fraternity. The mere fact that political revolution came with a
French label was sufficient to discourage reform in Britain, and when
French ideals led to a reign of political terror, the guillotining of a King,
and the heralding of a variety of deism which smattered of atheism, all
British reform was muzzled. War between the two countries in 1793
turned any mention of the rights of man into seditious talk, and for the
next generation Brits harkened to "A Word to the Wise" which warned
in dreadful paronomastic doggerel:

> *Ye Britons, be wise, as you're brave and humane*
> *You then will be happy without any Paine.**
> *We know of no despots, we've nothing to fear*
> *For this new-fangled nonsense will never do here.*

*Tom Paine, author of the *Rights of Man*.

In 1793, the British had to prepare themselves for a new kind of war—a conflict that sought to capture the mind as well as the body of Europe—but, true to form, they did so both slowly and ineptly. Like the other kingdoms of Europe, Britain took an eternity to awaken to the realization that the French Revolution had disastrously upset the international balance of power—vastly enhancing French capacity to wage battle—and had changed both the nature and goal of war. Eighteenth-century wars had been fought with highly trained, semi-mercenary troops, drawn from the least productive elements of society (the aristocracy, the unemployed, and criminal elements) for highly limited goals—readjusting borders, reassigning colonies, and preserving the status quo.

With the French Revolution, all this changed: the nation in arms was born. The levee en masse introduced the modern drafted army in which every citizen was a soldier and every soldier a citizen. Patriotism could now be substituted for draconian discipline because, as one historian put it, "the French state was transformed from a public utility into a goddess," for whom her worshippers gladly sacrificed their lives. War approached totality, involving all segments of society: "Young men will go forth to battle; married men will forge weapons; women will make tents . . . and serve in hospitals; and [most important of all] old men will . . . arouse the courage of the soldiers, while preaching the unity of the Republic and hatred against kings." The goal of war was no longer to win a few battles and maintain the existing order of things. It was now to destroy the enemy totally and reshape its society, to attack not simply Britain's armies but also "her manners, her customs, her literature, and her constitution." Before Britain and her allies—the Dutch Republic, Austria, Prussia, Spain and on occasion Russia—woke to the full magnitude of the French menace, French ideas and armies, either in the name of the new Republic or of Napoleon's Empire, had inundated Western Europe.

Still More War With France
(1793–1815)

That Great Britain finally won the ordeal that lasted 22 years (with a brief respite in 1802–03) had less to do with British heroism in battle than with three other prosaic but more dependable factors: 1) a navy of 400 vessels and 129,000 seamen that blockaded and strangled France;

2) financial resources that made it possible for her allies to regroup and raise new armies every time Napoleon defeated them in battle; and 3) industrial and commercial might that made her manufactured goods and re-export trade indispensable to Europe. Napoleon's only recourse was a new kind of economic warfare—close the entire Continent to British exports. He asked Europe to give up sugar, coffee, tea, chocolate, all shipped in British vessels, not to mention the industrial marvels streaming out of English factories, for the dubious benefits of liberty, equality and fraternity as interpreted and enforced by French bureaucrats and soldiers. Obviously, time was on the side of the tight little island so perversely immune from French conquest. (Napoleon planned but could not construct a tunnel under the English Channel to get at his enemy.) Costly as the war was (excise taxes quadrupled, the land tax doubled, a graduated tax on all incomes over £60 was introduced, the debt soared from £247 to £861 million, and bad harvests, inflation and economic dislocation brought hundreds of thousands to the edge of starvation), in 1815 Great Britain triumphed.

In the midst of a struggle of such magnitude, Britain may be forgiven for scarcely noticing that it had inadvertently embroiled itself in a war with its one-time colonies. The issue was the right to search U.S. ships for contraband (goods being shipped from French colonies) and for English seamen who had deserted and been hired by American ship owners. (Such was Britain's desperate need for sailors to man her swollen navy.) Even though the *USS Constitution* worsted the British frigate *Guerrière* (a French warship captured by the British), and British troops attacked Washington, burning the White House and inspiring "The Star-Spangled Banner," one of the world's most unsingable anthems (the music was written by an Englishman), the so-called War of 1812 made so little impression on British history that it is said that when a 20th-century Brit was reminded that his country had burned Washington, he replied: "Really? I know, of course, that we burned Joan of Arc but George Washington?!"

Far more memorable for British history than the attack on the American capital was the creation of the United Kingdom in 1801 when, as with Scotland in 1707, the French menace led to the incorporation of Ireland into a greater Great Britain. The man who initiated union with Ireland was William Pitt, the austere, hard-working second son of Britain's leader during the Seven Years War. Pitt the younger, who had been the King's chief minister ever since the debacle of the American Revolution and Lord North's resignation in 1783, was an inveterate administrative reformer. He reformed the Kingdom's finances just in time for Britain to become once again the paymaster of Europe in the long duel with revolutionary France, and in India he curbed corruption and established the foundations of the British Raj: an appointed Governor General, a small band of administrators, and a large, well-trained, British-officered native (Sepoy) army.

In Ireland, Pitt was confronted with a series of French efforts to break through the British blockade and land troops on the Emerald Isle in order to give teeth to endemic Irish rebellion. His solution was to propose the political union of the two islands and full Catholic emancipation, permitting Catholics to sit in the Westminster Parliament. He got political union—100 Irish members were added to the House of Commons and 28 peers, elected for life, and four bishops to the House of Lords—but he failed to achieve religious emancipation, largely because George III regarded the Catholic vote to be a violation of his coronation oath to defend the Church of England. The right to send Catholic representatives to Parliament had to wait another 28 years, thereby ending any chance of Catholic Ireland ever giving up its sense of identity and willingly merging itself into a United Kingdom.

Final Triumph and Peace Settlement
(1815)

Napoleon's imperial dream of a world where English was never spoken, French was the top language, and Parisian mean time replaced Greenwich zero meridian, collapsed after the Emperor's ill-starred 1812 invasion of Russia. In 1814 Paris was occupied, and the tubby little Corsican corporal was bundled off to Elba, only to return the following year for a final spectacular go at making France top nation once again. The attempt was thwarted at Waterloo (June, 18, 1815) when the Duke of Wellington—who had to order his officers not to go into battle with their umbrellas, described his troops as "composed of the scum of the earth," and rather mysteriously claimed he won the battle on the playing fields of Eton—thrashed (with considerable help from a German army under General Blucher) the French for the last time. The Emperor was shipped off to St. Helena in the South Atlantic, a tiny island where nobody ever went except occasionally to make astronomical observations or to revitalize on the long trip to India.

The war left Great Britain (now the United Kingdom) the undisputed commercial and industrial giant of the world, but one almost pathologically wedded to 18th-century values. During the war she had seized the Dutch, French, Portuguese and Spanish colonial empires, and now used the offer of their return to insist on the three old-fashioned principles which underlay the Vienna peace settlement: legitimacy, compensation and the balance of power. In the name of legitimacy, the Bourbon monarchy in the form of Louis XVIII was restored and France was returned to her pre-war boundaries instead of being carved up by its enemies. By way of compensation, the great powers—Austria, Prussia and Russia—dipped their sticky fingers into the European grab-bag of lesser states (today Germany, Italy and Poland) and pulled out rich plums. Finally, in order to insure a proper balance of power and thwart any future French aggression, Holland and Belgium were joined in a union that lasted only until 1831, and Sardinia was enlarged to include the Republic of Genoa, thereby becoming the nucleus around which a later unified Italy would take shape. In return, Britain graciously restored most of its colonial conquests (the American experience had taught her that colonies were not worth their administrative and military cost), keeping only those bits and pieces essential to her sea route to India, most notably the Cape of Good Hope. Though the settlement satisfied none of the major European powers except Britain, it managed to prevent another world war for the next hundred years.

The Aftermath of War
(1815–1832)

Napoleon Bonaparte was securely ensconced on his volcanic, 47-square-mile island, 1100 miles off the west coast of southern Africa, where he spent his last six years finally learning English. The British for the next generation spent their time reminding themselves of their military and diplomatic triumphs, displaying the trophies of war and constructing monuments to victory. An immense collection of Egyptian antiquities, including the famous Rossetta Stone, captured from the French, was placed in a new wing of the British Museum. A splendid equestrian portrait of the Duke of Wellington by Goya, along with a huge, larger-than-life, appropriately nude statue of Napoleon and a lavish dinner service made for the Emperor to commemorate his Egyptian campaign, were placed in No. 1 Piccadilly (Apsley House) which had been given the Iron Duke by a grateful nation. An entire square was constructed (1839–42) to celebrate Horatio Nelson's defeat of a combined French-Spanish fleet at Trafalgar, its central feature a 17 ½ foot statue of the Admiral atop a 167-foot-high column (a precarious perch for a sailor who was always sick at sea) surrounded by four bronze lions and more pigeons than any place on earth. The commander in chief of the army, not Wellington, but George III's insolvent son the Duke of York, got himself an equally fine column (located in Waterloo Place just off Pall Mall) with his portly figure at the top. London wits said he was placed at the top of a 112-foot-high pedestal to prevent his creditors from reaching him. Rather belatedly (1878), Cleopatra's Needle (the twin of the 3500-year-old obelisk in New York's Central Park) arrived in London and was placed on the Victoria Embankment beside the Thames. It was the gift of the Egyptian government to celebrate Nelson's victory over the French at the Battle of the Nile.

Napoleon on the island of St. Helena with nothing to do except learn English

Just to prove that British taste in monuments was not limited to macho erections in the sky, first George IV and then Victoria turned to commemorative arches to remind the Kingdom of its past glories. Marble Arch (1825) was originally designed by John Nash to embellish George's newly renovated residence—Buckingham Palace. Unfortunately, Nash got his measurements wrong and the arch was not wide enough for state processions to pass through and had to be carted off to Tyburn, once the location of the city gallows, but today the north entrance to Hyde Park. At the opposite end of the park is yet another victory monument, Constitution Arch (1846), which once acted as a massive plinth for the mounted figure of Wellington. Alas, he was dethroned in 1912 and replaced with a more generic representation of Victory. The Duke had to make do with a new location across the street from his home at Apsley House and another equestrian representation in front of the Bank of England.

No matter how many monuments to Victory the British raised, the Kingdom discovered that peace and victory were singularly bitter pills, and learned the truth of the warning voiced by Edmund Burke, the father of modern conservative political thought: "A state without the means of some change is without the means of its own conservation." Fettered by a government that viewed any suggestion of social or political reform as tantamount to revolution in the French style, Britain was ill-prepared to handle not only a host of post-war economic problems—falling prices, declining trade, unemployment, bad harvests, sky-rocketing cost of poor relief, and mobs surrounding Parliament shouting "No starvation! No landlords!"—but far more serious, the human and political consequences of industrial change. Society was in an ugly mood. Violence erupted in Manchester in 1819 when mounted militiamen, brandishing their swords, rode into a crowd of 60,000 men, women and children bearing banners calling for "liberty or death." The charge left eleven dead and 400 wounded. At one extreme, old-fashioned cottage workers, especially weavers, bitterly resented the advent of the machine and factory age, which left them either destitute or degraded, and they turned to violence. At the other extreme, factory owners, many of whom had started life as my lord's stable boy but now could buy up my lord, house, park and stable, wanted their new industrial wealth, not the historic ownership of land, to count in politics and the control of national policy.

Disturbing ideas were in the air. Such thinkers as Adam Smith, Jeremy Bentham, David Ricardo and Thomas Malthus spawned a new and revolutionary mentality that preached free trade and the iron laws of supply and demand, advocated the economic and moral benefits of liberating the individual from all historic and governmental restraints, and believed that "the nation is only the aggregate of individual conditions, and civilization itself is but a question of personal improvement"—a far cry from the 16th-century body politic and paternalistic state. And finally, bloody mindedness, that pugnacious hallmark of Britain class-consciousness, was emerging, whereby aristocrats, industrialists and factory workers delighted in despising and disparaging one another and cared only for their own well-being.

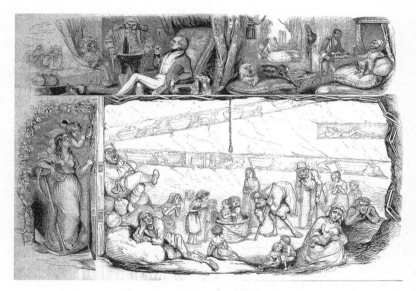

The two extremes of English society

The Flood Gates Are Opened
(1832)

Although willing in the name of humanitarian and religious indignation to make certain social concessions—Catholic emancipation, the depoliticizing of royal patronage, and the abolition of slavery throughout the Empire with, of course, due respect for property, to the tune of £20 million (more than the nation's annual military budget) to compensate slave owners—the government stubbornly held out against any political change. Only in 1832 did the old guard capitulate in the face of social revolution. Gripped by the hysterical fear that if the House of Commons were not reformed, "the nobility and principal gentry and everyone who possessed anything" would be "guillotined without remorse," and goaded by the threat that enough new peers would be created to force reform legislation through the House of Lords, Commons under the Whig leadership of the second Earl Grey (he lent his name to an aromatic tea) reluctantly passed (by a single vote) the great Reform Bill of 1832. One hundred and forty-one borough seats were abolished and redistributed to reflect the demographic and industrial changes of the past century. Equally important, the electoral process for all boroughs was standardized, all house owners and anyone paying £10 in rent receiving the vote. In the counties, the franchise, historically limited to those who owned land worth 40 shillings in income, was extended to include well-to-do tenant farmers. Separate legislation for Scotland was even more dramatic, raising the voting population from 4,000 to 64,000.

The old guard gives way before social and industrial change

On paper the great Reform Bill seemed impressive, yet never was a political revolution achieved with such economy of means or with fewer immediate results. The upper middle class was given the ballot, raising the English electorate from one in ten to one in six, but the new voters persisted in sending their old aristocratic representatives back to Parliament. The House of Commons remained a highly exclusive gentleman's club for another generation (not until 1911 did its members receive a salary), and until 1874, the membership of every cabinet was heavily aristocratic. The great landowners may have lost some of their control over the nation's electoral machinery, but not until their immense wealth from land disappeared, did their political clout decline. During the 1870s, British agriculture was overwhelmed by a flood of cheap grain and meat from the United States, Canada and Argentina, and aristocratic incomes fell precipitously. Even so, in 1895 2,500 land owners possessed more than 3,000 acres apiece with annual incomes of at least £3,000; of this number 115 privileged souls, of whom 65 were peers of the realm, owned over 50,000 acres, while seven dukes, three marquises, three earls, one baron and one baronet jogged along with revenues of over £100,000. Clearly, up to 1914 and the First World War, "the name of a lord" was still great in Britain.

Anticlimactic as the Reform Bill was, a silent revolution had taken place, because the principles upon which the old political system rested had been violated. The doctrine of statistical uniformity was beginning to replace the sanctity of historic idiosyncrasy. Those with the greatest stake (or estate) in society no longer possessed the unquestioned right to govern. A quantitative, not qualitative, approach to politics was appearing. And most disruptive of all, a precedent had been set: the constitution could be changed. As one elderly commentator noted as she looked back at the event, "The flood gates were opened in 1832 and never since has the current stopped."

The Angry Path to Political Democracy
(1832–1913)

The current of political change became a torrent when, first in 1867, the electorate was doubled (1.3 to 2.4 million) by enfranchising urban workers, and then doubled again in 1884 when agricultural laborers received the vote. Universal suffrage, however, was not approached until 1918 when women over 30 received the ballot. Only in 1928 did the Kingdom accept the principle of one vote, one citizen, irrespective of age, sex, education or wealth; but it took a Labor Government in 1948 to finally finish off the last vestige of the old electoral system going back to James I: Oxford's and Cambridge's two seats in the House of Commons were abolished and with them the right of Oxbridge graduates to two votes in a general election.

Commons adapted to the democratic tide, but the House of Lords allowed the current of economic and social change to pass it by until the constitutional crisis of 1909–11, when it risked its very existence by vetoing what it regarded as the Liberal Government's socialistic budget. The Lords had changed in size and character after 1832. More and more peers of ancient lineage were investing in industry and their ranks were being swollen by an influx of factory owners, bankers, shippers and brewers in search of social respectability. The 630 members of the upper house had by 1909 not only become a bastion of the Conservative Party, but also such a blatant anachronism in an era of increasing democracy that W.S. Gilbert and Arthur Sullivan wrote an entire operetta satirizing blue blood. In *Iolanthe,* a pride of haughty lords sing with gusto that they are "paragons of legislation, pillars of the British nation," but wisely fly off to fairyland with their new fairy brides, fearful lest the peerage be thrown open to competitive examinations. In real life they were far less adept, blundering into a power struggle with a House of Commons controlled by the Liberals and were badly worsted.

A paragon of legislation and pillar of the British nation

The struggle came to a head when Commons passed Chancellor of the Exchequer Lloyd George's "People's Budget" to finance new battleships in the naval race with Germany and to fund national health and unemployment insurance and old age pensions. What hurt was the introduction of an income tax as the government's primary source of revenue; worse, the tax was graduated with a "super tax" imposed on the very rich; and worst of all, a 20 percent capital gains tax was levied on the sale of land. The budget struck at the hereditary aristocracy for whom Lloyd George had no respect, questioning their qualification for sitting in the upper house. They had, he said, no credentials. "They do not even need a medical certificate. They need not be sound either in body or in mind. They only require a certificate of birth, just to prove that they are the first of the litter. You would not choose a spaniel on those principles." In 1909, the Lords vetoed the budget by a vote of 350 to 75, thereby creating a constitutional crisis, because ever since 1676 it was understood that the upper house never interfered with a money bill.

Two general elections later, plus the threat of creating 400 new peers, the House of Lords caved in. During a heat wave when the temperature reached 100 degrees (the highest ever recorded in Britain), the upper house accepted not only the budget, but also the Parliamentary Act of 1911 that stripped the Lords of its veto powers. Henceforth, the will of Commons would be supreme. The power of the upper house was reduced to delaying a money bill for a month and other legislation for two years (later reduced to one). Parliament had in effect become a unicameral organization, reflecting, at least in theory, the voice of the people.

Conservatives vs. Liberals: Disraeli vs. Gladstone

The existence of a mass electorate expressing its will in an all-powerful House of Commons changed the way politics was conducted in Britain. Until 1832, Parliament had been filled with highly idiosyncratic members who called themselves Whigs and Tories and voted either their consciences or individual self-interest. Occasionally, during moments of crisis, they coalesced into something resembling political parties, but even in 1832 individuals did not hesitate to cross ideological lines. Whigs in both houses of Parliament, looking back to the Glorious Revolution, were willing to accept moderate political change, and tended to be sympathetic to the commercial and financial interests of the Kingdom as they had been during the 18th century. In the midst of their ranks were two other groups: the philosophical radicals (followers of Classical Liberalism, see pp. 133–36) and a cluster of Catholic Irish MPs under the leadership of Daniel O'Connell, who appeared after the Catholic Emancipation Act of 1829 allowed them to sit in Commons. The Radicals favored the secret ballot, the extension of the franchise, the disestablishment of Anglicanism as the State Church of England and Ireland, and the removal of governmental interference from the free operation of the so-called "natural laws" of economics. The Irish were allied to the Whigs because O'Connell thought them the most likely to grant Home Rule to Ireland. Out of this unlikely assortment of interests, William Ewart Gladstone's thunderous magnetism and righteous morality forged the Liberal Party during the 1850s and 60s.

The Tories were more homogeneous. They were the party that reflected the philosophy of Edmund Burke, having a deep respect for the sanctity of history and believing that government was "a partnership between those who are living, those who are dead, and those who are yet to be born." With the advent of mass democracy, and under the theatrical leadership of Benjamin Disraeli, they preached Britain's manifest and romantic destiny as the world's greatest Empire, took up the paternalistic cause of the common man, and changed their name from the Tory (with all its reactionary connotations) to the Conservative Party.

The two parties had to respond to and influence the will of the electorate, and both of them developed elaborate machinery to marshal the vote of their respective followers. As national elections depended more and more on party organization and funding, and less and less on the personal qualities of the man standing for election, parliamentary parties changed from loose collections of individuals into solid blocs held together by party loyalty and money. The whip who disciplined his colleagues and got out the parliamentary vote according to the party's wishes, and the leader who spoke for the party as a whole were all-powerful. At one time the Prime Minister had been the King's chief minister who could, in Disraeli's words, collect a majority "God knows how, voting God knows why." Now he was the leader of that party in Parliament which had mustered the most votes in a national election, and the Crown had no choice but to accept him as its chief minister.

The King's power to interfere in the political process had been declining ever since the disaster of the American Revolutionary War. The process was accelerated by George III's madness and the increasing difficulty the Crown's ministers had in creating a king's party in Commons as royal patronage was reformed and dried up. By 1829, the Duke of Wellington, as Prime Minister, was complaining that "no government can go on without some means of rewarding services. I have none." By Victoria's reign, a republic had come into being in the guise of a monarchy, and the Crown's authority had been limited to "the right to be consulted, the right to encourage and the right to warn," rights which the Queen, throughout her interminable reign (1837–1901), did not hesitate to exercise in such a meddlesome manner that it drove her long-suffering ministers to distraction.

While the disposition of the monarch declined as a primary political factor, the personality of the Prime Minister became a matter of ever increasing public interest, although never to the extent a U.S. president is subject to media scrutiny. During the decades between 1860 and 1880 two men, as different as the lion and the unicorn, pranced up and down the political arena. Benjamin Disraeli (1804–81) was born to a middle-class Jewish family of Italian extraction which had converted to Anglicanism. He tried and failed to make a success first at the law and then as a novelist before entering Parliament. He married a rich wife 12 years his senior, climbed to the top of what he described as "the greasy pole" of politics by a combination of wit, charm and talent, and, when asked where he stood politically, truthfully answered "on my head."

To Victoria he was "full of poetry, romance and chivalry," winning her heart through egregious flattery which he confessed he laid "on with a trowel." Never content except when in the limelight, he dressed like a dandy in "green velvet trousers, a canary coloured waistcoat, shoes with silver buckles, lace at his wrists, and his hair in ringlets," a most unusual looking Conservative Prime Minister. He vastly preferred glamorous foreign to dreary domestic policy, and thoroughly disliked Mr. Gladstone, saying by way of explaining the difference between a misfortune and a calamity, that "if Gladstone fell into the Thames that would be a misfortune; and if anybody pulled him out, that would be a calamity."

Benjamin Disraeli achieving his ambition of becoming Prime Minister

William Gladstone (1809–98), in contrast, was the deeply religious son of a wealthy Liverpool merchant, who almost went into the ministry but instead won a seat in Parliament at the age of 22. He felt most at home as Chancellor of the Exchequer, being the only man who could wax eloquent over the budget while addressing the House of Commons. He took up a variety of causes, ranging from reforming prostitutes to Home Rule for Ireland, with the zeal of a religious crusader, and he possessed a rigid Calvinistic work ethic, regularly putting in a 15-hour day and chopping wood in his spare time. As Prime Minister, instead of flattering the Queen, he lectured her as if, she complained, she were "a public meeting." Even his humor was heavy-handed: he once apologized to Victoria for being late, by joking that he possessed three hands, his right and left hands and a "little behindhand." Known as the Grand Old Man ("God's Only Mistake" to his enemies) he was, much to the Queen's discomfort, Prime Minister three times to Disraeli's two. (The rivalry between the Prime Ministers has passed into bronze. Gladstone warrants two bronze statues, one 16 feet in height, placed on a 38-foot pedestal, but neither is near the heart of government or Empire—Aldwych in the Strand and Bow Churchyard in the old city. Disraeli's single monument, displaying his peer's robes and Order of the Garter, is across from the Houses of Parliament and surrounded by four other Prime Ministers, including Churchill and Palmerston.)

Unlike his rival, Gladstone went on and on, until in 1894 he came close to destroying the Liberal Party he had almost single-handedly created 30 years before, over Irish Home Rule. Ninety-four Liberal MPs broke ranks and voted against Irish Home Rule, first establishing their own party—the Liberal Unionists—then joining the Conservatives. At stake was more than Irish independence; a revolution was transforming the Liberal Party. Big business, which in the past had been staunchly liberal, became increasingly unhappy with traditional Liberal doctrines and began to gravitate towards the Conservatives. It was no coincidence that the man who led the revolt over Home Rule, Joseph Chamberlain, was himself an immensely rich Birmingham industrialist who questioned the sacred Liberal doctrine of free trade. He advocated a protective tariff, preached the "civilizing" as well as the economic benefits of imperialism, and viewed the Empire as a closed market for British industrial goods, all positions far closer to the Conservative than to the Liberal Party.

Gladstone going on and on

Pax Britannia and the World's First Superpower

Joseph Chamberlain (1836–1914) was born into a world when it was good to be alive, especially if you were British and wealthy. The 19th century is often called the British century, the Pax Britannia, and the generation between 1850 and 1875 is known as Britain's golden age, when industrial technology and the capitalist work ethic, heavily reinforced by a demanding Calvinistic Deity, united to fulfill Thomas Carlyle's call to "Produce! Produce! Were it but the pitifulest, infinitesimal fraction of a product, produce it in God's name!" The age-old problem of production was solved, and suddenly not only did the tight little island become the workshop of the world, but the world also came, purse in hand, knocking at its door. The market value of British exports between 1840 and 1870 rose by a staggering 282 percent, representing 33 percent of the world's manufacturing capacity. Britain controlled 25 percent of the world's trade while 60 percent of all steamships flew the Union Jack. The earth was shrinking, very much to Britain's economic and imperial advantage. By 1870, direct telegraph contact had been established between London and Calcutta, and the change from sail to steam and the construction of the 104-mile Suez Canal (1875) reduced the voyage to India from months to weeks.

During her golden age, Britain produced 50 percent of the world's cotton goods, 60 percent of its coal and 70 percent of its steel. As exports soared by a multiple of seven, so did imports, and one awe-struck economic commentator boasted that "the several quarters of the globe" had become "our willing tributaries." With little competition, it was a seller's market, and the profits came flooding in, to be reinvested abroad to make yet more money. By 1870, £800 million had been sent overseas to industrialize the world, a shortsighted policy, but immensely profitable. British capital financed the U.S. railroad system, and in 1857 her holdings in American railroad stock amounted to £80 million. By the turn of the century, her foreign investments totaled £20 billion, with France and Germany poor seconds at 8.7 and six billion respectively.

At home, wages rose far faster than prices creating not only a growing domestic market, but also social quiet and optimism:

> *Blessings on science and her handmaid steam!*
> *They make utopia only half a dream.*

The world's first international fair, the Great Exhibition of 1851, was organized by Queen Victoria's technologically and scientifically minded husband, Prince Albert. Its centerpiece was the Crystal Palace, a 1,848-foot-long, 408-foot-wide, and 108-foot-high iron and glass structure looking more like a giant greenhouse than an exhibition hall. The structure was designed by Joseph Paxton, the Duke of Devonshire's head gardener, and it resolved an environmental controversy that very nearly killed the exhibition. All previous plans for the building had required cutting down trees in Hyde Park; Paxton's glass house simply enclosed them. The exhibition's purpose, as one historian has written, was not merely to exhibit British industrial superiority, "but to proclaim to all foreign visitors the gospel of free trade and universal peace and the glories of the British constitution."

The "universal peace" so proudly proclaimed in 1851 was, alas, more wishful dreaming than reality. The 19th century had more than its fair share of "small" wars with dire consequences. The Opium War (1839–42), a preemptive and undeclared strike conducted mostly by British gunboats, humiliated the 4,000-year-old Chinese empire and opened the country up to Western (largely English) economic penetration, giving Britain a 150-year lease on Hong Kong, and guaranteeing the immensely profitable, if still illegal, flow of drugs to 350 million Chinese. (By 1866 nine out of ten adult Chinese in Canton smoked the "foreign mud" called opium.) The Austro-Prussian and Franco-Prussian wars (1864 and 1870) unified Germany under Prussian domination and deprived France of the province of Alsace-Lorraine, thereby poisoning German-French relations for the next 75 years. And the American Civil War (1861–65), which Britain almost entered on the side of the South because of her dependence on Southern cotton, changed the course of U.S. history. (Amends were later made by placing a replica of August St Gauden's Chicago statue of Lincoln in Parliament Square.) A series of mini-wars during the first half of the century more than doubled the size of British holdings in India. At the same time the crushing of the Sepoy Mutiny (1857–58) within the Indian army (240,000 native troops to 40,000 British commissioned and non-commissioned officers) changed the character of British rule from semi independent merchant princes and nabobs like Clive of India, into rigid, if well meaning, civil servants bent on bringing Western civilization to the subcontinent. E. M. Forster's famous 20th-century novel of interracial tension, *A Pas-*

sage to India (1924) catches the flavor of this new and "improved" Raj when he has his major protagonist say, "We're not here for the purpose of being pleasant. . . . We're here to do justice and keep the peace. . . ." When these sentiments are criticized as "those of a god," he answers, "India likes gods."

The great exception to the importance of 19th-century wars was the Crimean conflict (1854–56); a more improbable and inconsequential struggle is hard to imagine. Britain, with France and Turkey as difficult allies, went to war with Russia over issues which were never clear to contemporaries or later historians—something to do with Greek Orthodox monks and preventing Turkey, the "sick man of Europe," from being gobbled up by Russia. The conflict was rather as if an elephant and a whale had decided to war on each other. There was much costly splashing about on the Crimean peninsula in the Black Sea, and sensational headlines in the British yellow press, but few results. Both sides had a terrible time supplying their forces, and Britain had to rely heavily on French soldiers commanded by a prickly French commander who, with considerable justification, dismissed the British war effort in general and the heroic but idiotic charge of the Light Brigade into the teeth of Russian guns, in particular, as a splendid spectacle, but scarcely serious war. (*"C'est magnifique, mais ce n'est pas la guerre."*)

The only Brits to emerge with a scrap of honor were Florence Nightingale (her statue with an inappropriate oil lamp in her hand stands at the bottom of Lower Regent St. on Waterloo Place) and her nurses who sought to relieve as best they could the suffering of the neglected British enlisted men. At the main British hospital conditions were appalling: cholera, typhus, dysentery, maggots, rats and 20 chamber-pots for 2,000 men. The war's only lasting contributions to history must be measured in terms of three articles of clothing: the Balaclava helmet (a knitted cap reaching to the shoulders) worn by British troopers; the raglan overcoat designed by Lord Raglan, the British commander-in-chief; and the cardigan sweater invented by Lord Cardigan, the leader of the Light Brigade, who had purchased his lieutenant colonelcy for £35,000 in 1836, had spent another £10,000 dressing his men in cherry-colored pants to make them the best-dressed regiment in the British army, and during the Crimean campaign had lived on his private yacht. Cardigan rode at the front of his men and miraculously escaped death in a slaughter from which only 195 men out of 673 riders returned. (After the war Cardigan had his horse's hoof turned into a silver embossed inkwell and its head mounted on the wall of Deene Park in Northamptonshire, the family ancestral home. They are still there for the visitor to inspect.)

PATIENT HEROES
"Well, Jack! Here's good news from home. We're to have a medal."
"That's very kind. Maybe one of these days we'll have a coat to stick it on!"

Dangerous and insecure as the century was, Great Britain, as the world's only global power, was in a position to ignore continental unpleasantness, and wrap itself in the satisfying mantle of splendid and snobbish isolation. Armed with a three-ocean navy that was unchallenged throughout the world, Britain could, in the words of Lord Palmerston, speaking as Foreign Secretary in 1850, confidently maintain that "a British subject, in whatever land he may be, shall feel confident that the watchful and strong arm of England will protect him against injustice and wrong." (The USA, the closest approximation to a superpower which exists today, could never make such a statement with any expectation of fulfilling its promise.)

Optimism, Classical Liberalism, and Victorian Morality

There was much to be both proud and optimistic about. In medicine, human suffering was dramatically curtailed by the use of anesthetics, while, thanks to Joseph Lister, the realization that wounds had to be kept clean in order to prevent infection, transformed surgery from a deadly into a life-saving procedure. Two of the worst killers, smallpox and cholera, were under control by 1870, and the death rate dropped from 24.1 to 18.8 per thousand during the century. Progress was in the air, and everything from the iron law of wages to the Newtonian law of gravity was viewed as the work of a benevolent, albeit mechanically minded, Deity. Even the universe was said to be so orderly and simple that "in its motions there is no uncertainty, no mystery."

In politics, the world seemed to be on the verge of a new era. Classical Liberalism with its four panaceas for mankind's troubles was the unquestioned gospel of the day: free trade between nations (a matter of considerable self-interest to Britain), free movement of ideas and individuals, free education, and the principle that the government which governs least, governs best. John Stuart Mill epitomized the doctrine when he wrote: "Over himself, over his body and mind, the individual is sovereign. . . . The only freedom which deserves the name, is that of pursuing our own good in our own way . . ." Mill, however, added an awkward proviso that was the cause of endless debate: "so long as we do not attempt to deprive others of theirs, or impede their efforts to obtain it."

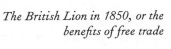
The British Lion in 1850, or the benefits of free trade

In the name of liberating the individual and encouraging him to help himself (and incidentally save the state money) a new concept of society emerged, one seeking to introduce utilitarian principles into government and maximize efficiency. The age of statistics and "rational" planning was dawning. Poor relief was reorganized in 1834, and the subsidization of wages and price controls were done away with, as unwarranted and meddlesome interferences in the free and natural operation of the economy. Government-run workhouses were established, partly as a last resort for the desperately poor, partly as a social lesson that it was pleasanter to hold down a job than to go on public relief. The purchase system in the military gave way during the 1870s to promotion based on merit; flogging was abolished within the ranks; and splendidly colorful, but militarily more efficient, regimental uniforms were introduced to reflect the new social status of the army. No wonder Gilbert and Sullivan's heavy dragoon in the operetta *Patience* (1881) sang:

> *When I first put this uniform on,*
> *I said, as I looked in the glass,*
> *"It's one to a million*
> *That any civilian*
> *My figure and form will surpass . . ."*

The secret ballot was adopted as a means of curbing private influence in public elections, and by 1880 elementary school education had become free and compulsory to assure all children a chance to compete in the new industrial society. Competitive examinations were introduced into the civil service during the 1860s, and as a consequence the quest for government office was transformed from a stampede for private profit into a service inspired (at least most of the time) by honesty, professionalism and efficiency, and presumably dedicated to the public good. All classes grew more respectful of the law, London after 1850 becoming one of the safest cities in the world. The laboring man suddenly became respectable, organizing unions of highly skilled workers who preached not social revolution but better wages and working conditions under the capitalist sun.

Most of these changes were accomplished in the spirit of liberal reform, but equally important was the presence of Victorian morality, a virulent mixture of evangelical religion, Benthamite utilitarianism, sexual prudery, romanticism, and a stern sense of self-improvement. Religious publications exploded (one in four books published during the first half of the century dealt with divinity), and Henry Fielding's rollicking narrative of Tom Jones's sexual escapades was replaced by the Victorian novel, which sought "to instruct while it amuses." Thomas Bowdler gave his name to a new word—"bowdlerize"—when in 1818 he published his "family" edition of Shakespeare in which all words and expressions "which cannot with propriety be read aloud in a family" were omitted, a goodly percentage of the Bard's vocabulary! Medievalism captured the Victorian imagination, Sir Walter Scott's romances—especially *Ivanhoe* and *Rob Roy*—becoming instant best sellers. The buildings of Parliament (officially the Palace of Westminster) after their destruction by fire in 1834 as a consequence of burning old tax records, were rebuilt in the new romanticized fairy-tale Gothic style. Railroad terminals (London boasted 15 of them, almost twice the number of any continental metropolis) were built like medieval cathedrals, combining Victorian aesthetics and technological achievement and symbolizing God's blessings and human progress. (The best example is St. Pancras, which stands in gingerbread contrast to its next-door neighbor, the very modern British Library.) That "radical, infidel college," London University, was founded in 1825 in defiance of Oxford's and Cambridge's monopoly of English education (Scotland had four universities) and their Anglican bias which excluded Catholic, Dissenter and Jew, and ignored physics, chemistry and medicine. The new university's curriculum was non-sectarian, no clergymen sat on its governing board, and it was heavily supported by middle-class Classical Liberals, including J.S. Mill and the utilitarian philosopher Jeremy Bentham, who bequeathed to the new institution his skeleton and stuffed effigy dressed in his second best suit. (Both are still there on display.)

Sports were tamed from public street brawls into gentlemanly games, cricket discarding its rowdy audiences and heavy gambling to become the quintessential English pastime. Even boxing became a civilized sport, changing from a dangerous, no holds barred, punch and wrestling match into an encounter with padded gloves, confined to a 24-foot square and regulated by the Marquis of Queensberry's rules. Bear baiting, cock fighting and public hangings gave way in popularity to organized athletics, music halls and weekends at the seaside. Britain's prestigious public schools (in U.S. parlance, private boarding schools) ceased to be "nurseries of vice" and became cultivators of "first, religious and moral principle; secondly, gentlemanly conduct; thirdly, intellectual ability," in that order of importance.

Sports were tamed from public street brawls into gentlemanly games

Not even the laissez faire state, so beloved by Classical Liberals, could withstand the moral, religious and humanitarian onslaught. The plight of children of six and seven working in cotton mills and coal mines caught the public imagination and produced a howl of journalistic and parliamentary outrage, largely orchestrated by the seventh Earl of Shaftesbury, on the grounds that "what is morally wrong can never be politically right." (Shaftesbury Avenue was named for him and the statue of the Angel of Christian Charity, better known as Eros, in Piccadilly Circus, was erected in his honor.) In 1833 the employment of children under nine in textile factories was outlawed, and their working hours reduced to eight a day with an additional three hours for daily schooling. Nine years later, children under 13 and all women (what was so shocking was their semi-nudity) were prohibited from working in the mines. And finally, in 1847 the ten-hour day was mandated, a bill adamantly opposed by John Bright, a Quaker cotton manufacturer and avid Classical Liberal reformer, on the grounds that it was "a delusion practiced on the working classes"; that all these laws deprived men and women of the right to choose their own working hours, and worse, they fostered idleness and crime by leaving children without jobs to get into trouble.

What upset Bright more than the social legislation itself was the presence of government inspectors, armed with irrefutable facts and figures, who arrived in droves to enforce the new laws. The specter of state interference was waiting in the wings, and the *London Times* noted in 1850 that "the government of the physical and moral well-being of every class of the labouring population . . . is one of the most humane and distinguishing characteristics of the present time." The state that regulates its citizens in the name of social welfare was slowly taking shape. The national budget in 1830 was £50 million: 29 million to service the debt (the cost of winning the Napoleonic War), 15 million for the armed services, and 6 million for everything else—the cost of tax collection, law enforcement, the Crown, the diplomatic corps, and the civil service. Thirty years later the budget for everything else had more than doubled, jumping to 15 million, the civil service being responsible for most of the increase.

Nineteenth-century Britain, however, held firm to its priorities: animals, especially dumb animals, came before humans. Parliament first enacted legislation against "the improper treatment of cattle" in 1822, and two years later the Society for the Prevention of Cruelty to Animals was founded. (Royal was not affixed to its name until Victoria gave it her blessings in 1840.) Children, on the other hand, were not offered the same protection until 1884. There are still today Brits who clearly prefer dogs to children, and not long ago Lord Somers complained in the House of Lords about the banning of canines from public parks. "I wonder," he said, "why it is that local authorities always seem to attack the unfortunate dogs. I notice that they do not say anything about uncontrolled small children, of which there are many, who go into food shops sucking their fingers and then go around handling the food. I consider that to be far less hygienic than a dog sniffing."

Human suffering, especially if it was on a relatively small scale or the product of human evil that could not be ignored, touched Victorian hearts, but suffering, when it had natural causes, was on a gigantic scale, and far from respectable middle-class homes, was greeted with indifference and misunderstanding. Such was the fate of the 1.5 million Irish who died in the Great Famine of 1845–46. Overpopulation (8.2 million), a one-crop economy (the potato), a medieval infrastructure, and a potato blight that destroyed crops for two consecutive years, produced catastrophic starvation and disease. Nearly 20 percent of the population perished (more than all the British killed in World Wars I and II) and another 1.7 million migrated, mostly to the United States, taking with them their conviction that the famine was a deliberate English plot to solve the Irish question by exterminating the population. It wasn't a conspiracy but, as Victoria confessed in her diary, merely a matter "too terrible to think of." Nevertheless, the memory lingers on to this day, and in part explains the extensive unofficial American support given to the Irish Republican Army in the recent conflict over the future of Northern Ireland.

Respectable Victorian households could close their minds to starvation across the Irish sea and complacently conclude that famine was the price that Ireland had to pay for having economically remained back in the 13th century. But Charles Darwin (1808–82) was far more difficult to ignore. He was solidly English, the embodiment of upper-middle-class respectability, yet his ideas struck at the spiritual roots of Victorian England: its deeply held conviction that man was "the heaven descended heir of all the ages," and that life, despite the material comforts wrought by industrial technology, was still a spiritual odyssey directed by a benign Deity whose purpose was revealed in Scripture. Darwin's two volumes—*On the Origin of Species by Means of Natural Selection* (1859) and *The Descent of Man* (1871)—upset the religious apple cart. "My theology," Darwin confessed, "is a muddle; I cannot look at the universe as the result of blind chance, yet I can see no evidence of beneficent design." Darwin was the last of the great 18th-century enlightened thinkers. As Newton had removed the Deity from the operation of a mechanical and soulless universe, so Darwin removed Him from the biological world, postulating the existence of the uniform and universal law of evolutionary change: all species, including mankind, were interrelated and evolved over time as a consequence of the need to survive. Eighteenth-century England had been willing to honor Sir Isaac Newton with a knighthood, but 19th-century Britain drew the line at conferring the same dignity upon Charles Darwin, although it was willing to bury him in Westminster Abbey along with Newton, and knight three out of four of his sons for distinction far less weighty than their father's. (A hint of what mid-19th century Britain was like can be gleaned by visiting the cathedral city of Rochester in Kent during its early June Dickens festival when the city dresses up in the clothing of the novelist's most famous characters.)

The genealogist who went too far. Darwin's ideas struck at the
spiritual roots of Victorian England

The Economic Facts of Life
(1875–1914)

Classical Liberalism with its insistence on free trade, free competition, and no government interference, suited nicely Britain's industrial head start. But after 1875 the absolute upset of the economic balance of power began to shift back to a more normal state of affairs. During the final decades of the century, Britain not only paid the price for having been the first industrial nation on earth, but also reaped the dragon seeds of having financed the industrialization of the rest of the world. Suddenly she had to face three new industrial giants—Germany, Japan and the United States—against whom Britain had to compete with antiquated machinery and old-fashioned techniques. The U.S. and most of Europe turned to high tariffs to protect their nascent industries, but Britain clung doggedly to the doctrine of free trade, forcing her industries to compete both at home and abroad with foreign commodities. Although the United Kingdom's gross national product grew impressively, its relative economic position plummeted. In 1880, Britain manufactured one million tons of steel or one-third of the globe's output; by 1902, her steel production had risen five-fold, but represented only one-seventh of the world's production.

The same percentages applied to the economy as a whole: by 1900 her percentage of the world's manufacturing output had dropped four points to 18.5 percent, while that of the U.S. had jumped nine points to 23.6 percent and Germany five points to 13.2 percent. The same was true of her carrying trade which fell from 30 to 21 percent. The world's industrial and commercial pie was growing, but Britain's slice of it was getting smaller and smaller, and at the same time her dependence on the rest of the world for raw material and food was increasing. The old axiom that the world could not get along without British exports was being replaced by a new equation: Britain could not survive without the rest of the world.

Why Britain was unable to capitalize on her industrial head start and did so poorly in the industrial race, is difficult to explain. It clearly had something to do with old-fashioned equipment and vested interests. While the U.S. leapt from the oil lamp to electricity, Britain remained in the gaslight age, largely because of the power of the gas companies. Her coal mines were becoming less and less productive as the mines went deeper and deeper, and the mine owners failed to introduce new coal-cutting machinery. As a consequence, profits dried up, wages stagnated, and the industry became the seedbed for 20th-century labor unrest. Equally important, British manufacturers failed to recognize that the industrial revolution had moved from its production to its marketing stage; they refused to develop aggressive sales practices, not realizing that a ready supply of spare parts was just as important as the quality of the original machine in keeping customers happy.

*One possible reason why Britain failed to capitalize
on her industrial head start*

Britain also fell behind in the educational race. She failed to educate her work force or maintain the necessary connection between the scientist and engineer, let alone expose her ruling elite to science and technology. A classical curriculum for talented amateurs reigned supreme, and Eton, that spawning ground for "effortless superiority," boasted, as late as 1884, 28 classic masters, but only six mathematics teachers and no modern language or science instructors. Little wonder then that at the turn of the century one observer was complaining that the "best brains of the upper classes will go anywhere but into industry—into a bank or a merchant's office perhaps, but not into horny-handed manufacture." The British social ideal was never the engineer, scientist or industrialist, but remained the landed country gentleman, who did not have to work very hard, was educated in the humanities, and gave his time to public service. With such an ideal as its model and a social system that encouraged the upper echelons of management to get to work at 10 am, regard business as something of a game, and always conduct itself in a gentlemanly fashion, British industry was ill-prepared to survive in a brutally competitive environment.

The new economic facts of life and industrial atmosphere stand behind most of the major events and policies of the late 19th and early 20th centuries. They inspired the new imperialism and scramble for world markets that divided up Africa among the great nations of Europe. They were closely related to Britain's decision to end splendid isolation and search for European and world allies. And the growth of giant cartels in restraint of trade and the Liberal Party's jettisoning of its opposition to government interference in the economic and social life of the country, were both closely tied to the Kingdom's changing economic position.

The New Imperialism

Late 19th-century British imperialism was different in form and spirit from any colonial expansion in the past. The American colonies, Canada, and later Australia (except for the criminals sent there as punishment) and New Zealand had been settled by private enterprise with colonists determined to establish replicas of the mother country, new Englands overseas. The result had been the extermination of the native population by war, disease, or enforced migration—"the only good Indian is a dead Indian." In India, a trading company had been transformed into an Empire almost by default. British traders had come to the subcontinent only to be confronted with a political vacuum which, if they wanted to preserve their profits, they had to fill. In contrast, the new Imperialism was public and political from the start. Britain sent out to Africa and other parts of the globe administrators and soldiers to govern and "civilize," and the motive was blatantly imperial and geopolitical. Between

1870 and 1900, 165 million people and four million square miles were added to an Empire that became the largest in world history, covering 12 million square miles and encompassing some 400 million inhabitants. But far from reflecting the industrial vigor of the mother country, these new acquisitions were signs of Britain's economic decline and growing insecurity in a world filled with new international predators.

British administrators, soldiers and missionaries
being sent to govern and "civilize" the Empire

For the first two-thirds of the century, Britain followed a policy of imperial devolution, and even Disraeli in 1852 complained that "these wretched colonies will all be independent in a few years and are millstones round our necks." In this spirit, Canada received self-governing dominion status by the British North American Act of 1867 which caused no debate in a Parliament anxious to get back to the really important issue of whether or not to impose a tax on dogs. By 1870, however, Disraeli had changed his mind, and a decade later, public opinion followed suit. Suddenly British policy makers became obsessed with statistics, judging national power in terms of global trade, manufacturing percentages, and population figures. (In 1900, the German population stood at 56.7 million, Russia's at 103 million, and both were growing rapidly, while Britain was cresting at 41 million.) The teeming millions of India and the other peoples of the Queen's Empire had to be called in to redress the population imbalance in Europe. Cecil Rhodes, who dreamed of English colonies stretching from Egypt to South Africa with a rail connection between Cairo and Cape Town, and a global alliance of all English-speaking peoples (thus his funding of Rhodes scholarships for

Americans to study at Oxford) stated the new policy best. "This is what England must do or perish: she must found colonies as fast and as far as she is able . . . seizing every piece of fruitful waste ground she can set her foot on," and then teach her colonists that "their first aim is to advance the power of England by land and sea."

THE RHODES COLOSSUS
Striding from Cape Town to Cairo

Britain feared that she was slipping in the industrial race. She worried that Russia was expanding southeast toward Afghanistan and Persia (today's Iran), and that Germany had predatory eyes directed at Africa. More and more the demand was heard to secure safe markets for British exports—"There are forty million people beyond the gateway of the Congo, and the cotton spinners of Manchester are waiting to clothe them." All these pressures contributed to the new Imperialism, but so also did jingoism and romance. Britain suddenly became inordinately proud of her Empire. Victoria and her subjects basked in the Royal Title Bill of 1875 that conferred upon her the title "Empress of India." The Queen-Empress could now stand tall in the community of European monarchs: the Kaiser of Germany, the Emperor of Austria-Hungary, the Tsar of Russia and the Sultan of Turkey.

Spurred on by a sense of innate superiority, British youth responded with enthusiasm to Rudyard Kipling's appeal:

> *Take up the white man's burden*
> *Send forth the best ye breed*
> *Go bind your sons to exile*
> *To serve your captive's need.*

G. A. Henty and Henry Rider Haggard deluged young readers with tales of peril, heroism and adventure in outposts of Empire while extolling those stalwart Victorian qualities: duty, restraint, obedience and discipline. And Kipling's *Kim* (1901) captured for all age groups the romantic thrill of growing up in Imperial India. Missionaries went forth to Christianize the heathen (of course, teaching them to wear British cotton), and the tabloid press sold millions of newspapers whenever these preachers were eaten by cannibals. Zanzibar was taken over as a protectorate in 1895 because public and religious opinion was outraged by the existence of slavery in that African country. When the medically trained missionary-explorer David Livingstone disappeared, much to the delight of the press, into "darkest Africa," the English-speaking world held its breath until Henry M. Stanley, sponsored by the *N. Y. Herald*, found him and phrased the world's most memorable greeting on encountering that eminent divine—"Dr. Livingstone, I presume." (Livingstone's body rests in Westminster Abbey, and his statue stands across from the Albert Memorial at the top of Exhibition Road.)

The new imperialism, however, was not without its dark underbelly: arrogance, hysteria, cruelty and death. Largely because of the Suez Canal's importance as the vital lifeline to India, the crown jewel of the Empire, Egypt had been turned into a British dependency. When in 1884 Egyptian troops got into trouble in the Sudan battling religious fanatics, the British government felt obliged to send General Charles Gordon, a Bible-packing eccentric who cheerfully confessed that "if I was chief, I would never employ myself, for I am incorrigible," to evacuate Egyptian personnel. Unfortunately, Gordon disobeyed orders, tried to defend the city of Khartoum from Sudanese fundamentalist forces led by a religious leader called the Madhi (the guide), and was killed along with all his men for his folly. Rather belatedly (13 years later) the British got around to dispatching an army of 25,000 to avenge his death. At the battle of Omdurman (1898), General Kitchner lost 50 men and slaughtered nearly 30,000 Sudanese. The Mahdi's head (he had died before the British arrived) was taken from its coffin and mailed to General Gordon's nephew (he later gave it to the London College of Surgeons) while his finger- and toenails were kept by British troops as souvenirs. Gordon, true to British love for quirky heroes, and Kitchner both earned statues near the heart of Empire in London. (Gordon, replete with Bible, swagger stick, and army binoculars, stands on the Victoria Embankment; Kitchner, in riding boots and field marshal's uniform, is behind 10 Downing Street in the Horse Guards Parade.)

Suddenly an Egyptian-British affair erupted into an international incident that brought Britain and France to the brink of war. As Kitchner was mopping up at Khartoum, 120 French Senegalese riflemen under the command of the audacious Captain Jean-Baptiste Marchand appeared at Fashoda (today's Kodok) on the upper reaches of the Nile River and claimed the Sudan for France. As Kitchner's and 20,000 of his men confronted Marchand's 120 riflemen, the two nations, goaded on by hysterical newspapers in both countries, postured over a wasteland 3000 miles from either London or Paris. *The Scotsman* stated that "no impudent French pretensions must be tolerated," and the French press announced that the arrival of Marchand at Fashoda was a "glorious achievement for France" while *Figaro* fanned the fire by sanctimoniously writing that France "can afford to be calm, while the English, knowing that they are wrong according to their own maxims, find it necessary to bluster." War was averted because France backed down; as the French Premier confessed, "We have nothing but arguments, they have the troops."

British expansion northward from South Africa was just as brutal as the move southward from Egypt and a great deal more costly. British South Africa was originally limited to the Cape Colony. Blocking the path northward were two Boer (descendants of the original Dutch settlers) republics, the Orange Free State and Transvaal. At stake was not simply Anglo-Saxon manifest destiny, but also the presence of diamonds and gold in both Boer states which were being flooded with English-speaking settlers in search of riches. Orchestrated by Cecil Rhodes, one of the world's first self-made multimillionaires and founder of the De Beers Diamond Company, and secretly abetted by Joseph Chamberlain in his capacity as Foreign Secretary in a Conservative government, Britain manufactured a war (1899–1902) with the Boers that she eventually won at the price of appearing to be the world's bully. The British army, used to 80 years of colonial wars against ill-armed and worse-organized enemies, did not distinguish itself—"People here do not seem to look upon war sufficiently seriously. It is considered too much like a game of polo with intervals for afternoon tea." The conflict cost Britain 22,000 dead and that same number wounded. Like Vietnam for the United States, it badly mauled her world image, and introduced into the English language two unpleasant terms—"commando" (the Boer word for their guerrilla troops) and "concentration camp" (the concentration of Boer civilians by the British into crowded, tightly guarded quarters). It also led in 1910 to the self-governing Union of South Africa within the British Commonwealth under circumstances highly favorable to the Boers: nothing was said about the rights of the black population, and the first two presidents of the union were ex-Boer generals.

A German satirical depiction of British colonialism in Africa

The End of Splendid Isolation
(1900–1914)

Of all the major powers, Britannia was the most successful in spreading its version of Western civilization throughout the earth and painting the globe imperial crimson, but success came with a heavy price tag. By 1900, she had scarcely a friend in the world, and was thoroughly disliked and envied by almost everybody.

British aptitude for building empires

It was extremely ominous that Admiral Von Tirpitz, Commander of the German navy and adviser to the Kaiser, recounted the anecdote of the British Admiral who, encountering a bay he had never visited before, dipped his finger into the water and, tasting it, arrogantly announced, "Salt water: English territory." It was not, however, imperial rivalry that led to the end of splendid isolation and caused the diplomatic revolution of the first decade of the 20th century, but two other inter-related matters of much greater concern to the tight little island. First was her inability in a world of rapidly changing technology—where the United States, Germany and Japan had the industrial potential to challenge her naval supremacy—to maintain sea power equal in strength to any combination of her rivals. Second was the presence of a belligerent, parvenu and highly insecure Germany that was using its new industrial strength to create the most efficient war machine in Europe. It was building an army of 4.5 million and was determined to match, ship-for-ship, Britain's new super battleship, the *Dreadnought* with 12-inch guns and oil-fired turbines, and by 1914 the balance was Germany 13, U.K. 18. Britain had to concentrate its entire fleet in the North Sea to keep even that superiority. As Admiral Sir John Fisher confessed, "Ten years ago we not only had command of the sea, but we had command of every sea. We have the command of no sea in the world except the North Sea at this moment."

By 1900, Britannia had begun to retrench throughout the world and to look for allies. She patched up her territorial disputes with the United States, allowed the Caribbean to become an American lake, and established a "special relationship" which has lasted to the present day. In 1902, she entered into a defensive alliance with Japan and withdrew her navy from the Pacific, and two years later she turned her back on 700 years of warring with France and began to negotiate an *"entente cordiale"* with her old rival. She even came to an understanding with Russia whereby the Russian bear ceased to growl at India, and the two countries divided Persia into equal zones of influence. By 1912, relations with France had grown so cordial that the two nations had reached a naval understanding—France took over the protection of British sea lanes to India in the Mediterranean, while Britain guarded the French Channel coastline. In guaranteeing the defense of the French coast, Britain, almost without realizing it, entered a continental alliance system in which Germany, linked defensively with Austria-Hungary (with Italy as a flabby ally), confronted France, which was allied to Russia. Relations among the great powers was becoming increasingly militaristic and inflexible; their binding alliances made certain that any small war was likely to explode into a full-scale conflict; and militarily the two sides were so evenly balanced that both France and Germany felt obliged to back up their junior partners no matter how irresponsible and inflammatory their actions, especially in the Balkans.

Confidence Shaken
(1900–1914)

Europe was sitting on a powder keg, and periodic shudders of anticipation ran through the Continent, but no one seriously thought that any nation would be silly enough to light the fuse. The historian Charles M. Andrews, in his inaugural address in 1899 to the American Historical Association, confidently told his audience that if college students would only study "European history of the last thirty years," they would dismiss "war, the frequently occurring universal war" when they encountered it in the newspaper headlines. After all, Victoria was "the grandmother of Europe": George, King-Emperor of Britain, and Willy, the Kaiser of Germany, were her grandsons; Nicky, the Tsar of Russia, was married to one of her granddaughters; and the crowned heads of Spain, Denmark, Sweden, Norway, Romania, and Greece were related to her by blood or marriage. More important than family solidarity was economic self-interest. Britain and Germany were each other's best customers, and Russia was Germany's most important source of food and raw materials.

No one could imagine a prolonged, devastating international war, but under the upper-class polish and prosperity of Edwardian England (Edward VII mounted the throne in 1901), so delightfully depicted in the upstairs half of the television program *Upstairs, Downstairs*, there lurked a nagging sense that all was not well, especially at home. As the 19th century gave way to the 20th, Victorian respectability and restraint, morality and godliness seemed to be under assault from every direction. And when, on a Sunday night in April of 1912, the luxury liner *Titanic*, that miracle of British engineering and mirror of material progress, struck an iceberg and sank on her maiden voyage to New York, to become the world's most ominous symbol of fallen pride, even God seemed to be renouncing His Englishness and forsaking His chosen people.

Politically the Kingdom began to polarize; the spacious middle ground, upon which both 19th-century Liberals and Conservatives could agree, and which was the comfortable hallmark of Victorian politics, was disappearing. The Liberal Party, forsaken by big business and Whig aristocrats, became the party of the little people and the "honest broker" of the working man, jettisoning many of its Classical Liberal doctrines and advocating social reform. In 1905, it won a smashing electoral victory and inaugurated the first great bout of welfare and equalizing legislation—unemployment and old age insurance, free meals for schoolchildren, a graduated income tax, and death duties—all the bills the House of Lords committed political suicide to prevent in 1911.

The Boiling Point

But even with a government in charge that preached compassion and reform, the country was convulsed by labor unrest and violence triggered by a steady drop in real wages and an upsurge of class hatred unimaginable in Victoria's reign. The economy was paralyzed by labor violence, and in 1912, 41 million workdays were lost in strikes. Worse was being planned for the autumn of 1914: a general strike of all miners, dockers, and railroad workers to bring capitalism to its knees.

Even the women were misbehaving in their incessant demand for the vote, and 20th-century Britain awoke to the unpleasant truth that the female of the species could be just as destructive as the male. Militant suffragists determined to win electoral equality with men, and, led by the redoubtable Emmilene Pankhurst and her two daughters, chained themselves to the iron fence outside Parliament, poured acid into mailboxes, broke priceless china in the British Museum, smashed the windows of No. 10 Downing Street, and went to jail by the hundreds. Mrs. Pankhurst was convinced that "broken glass" was "the most powerful argument in modern politics," and she might have prevailed had not the far greater violence of World War engulfed the nation. As it was, the ladies rallied behind King and country, and a grateful nation in February of 1918 offered them the vote, but with the cautious proviso that they be a sensible 30 years of age.

Militant suffragist (after long and futile efforts to light a fire for her tea-kettle).
"And to think that only yesterday I burnt two pavilions and a church!"

Of all the domestic troubles besetting Britain, Ireland proved (as always) to be the most difficult and lasting. The Liberal Party under Gladstone had failed in 1886 and 1893 to achieve Home Rule for Ireland (a separate Irish Parliament and executive with authority over everything except foreign policy, defense and coinage); and when it returned to power in 1905, it once again advocated Irish political reform but could do nothing until the House of Lords had been chastened. In 1912, Commons passed an Irish Home Rule bill, but an unrepentant Lords exercised its delaying veto and postponed enactment until September of 1914. During those two years Ireland exploded. Now that self-government was about to become a reality, Ulster (Northern Ireland) with its Protestant majority refused to become part of Catholic Ireland and insisted on remaining in the UK, while Catholic Ireland announced that any Home Rule which failed to include the entire island was unacceptable. Both sides began to arm, and the Liberal Government was confronted with the prospect of military action to force Home Rule on Northern Ireland. The army balked at such a possibility; there was talk of mutiny; and the leader of the Conservative Party actually hinted at condoning civil war. "There are things stronger than parliamentary majorities," he warned. "I can imagine no length of resistance to which Ulster can go in which I should not be prepared to support them." The Liberal Government seemed paralyzed, unable to decide between three unacceptable alternatives: force Home Rule on the Protestants, force partition on the Catholics, stand aside and let the two sides fight it out.

Then, suddenly and unexpectedly, everything changed. The cabinet had been struggling with the Irish crisis when Sir Edward Grey, the Foreign Secretary, began reading a note handed him from the Foreign Office; it was Austria-Hungary's July 23rd ultimatum to Serbia in response to the assassination of Archduke Ferdinand while visiting Sarajevo (in today's Bosnia) a month before. In the gripping words of Winston Churchill, First Lord of the Admiralty, "the parishes of Tyrone . . . faded back into the mists and squalls of Ireland, and a strange light began immediately . . . to fall and glow upon the map of Europe." That glow was war which would convulse the globe in two bloody and traumatic seizures—1914–18 and 1939–45—for the next 30 years, banishing forever Europe's well-bred semi-aristocratic leadership, killing at least 35 million Europeans, and rewriting the map of the Continent twice over. Only one major European nation escaped without military occupation, revolution or humiliation—Great Britain—and the price she paid was the end of Empire and an exhausted retreat from world power status into shaky second-class standing. Sir Edward Grey was devastatingly correct when, on August 4, 1914, he spoke the epitaph of not just Victorian England, but of 19th-century Europe, when he sadly forecast that "the lamps are going out all over Europe. We shall not see them lit again in our lifetime." When the lights came on again after 1945, they shone on a very different world, one in which Imperial Britain had no place.

Total War, The First Go Around
(1914–1918)

The nations of Europe were swept into the vortex of total war by an intermix of motives regarded by each as being perfectly sensible. A collapsing Austria-Hungarian monarchy, torn by nationalistic forces and in need of the prestige of a military victory in order to survive, was determined to crush Serbia on the grounds that "if the monarchy must perish, it should at least perish with decency." An equally unstable Russia felt obliged to come to the rescue of her fellow Slavs in the Balkans. Germany, confronted with the prospect of a war on two fronts, expected to polish off France in a six-week invasion if it moved swiftly before Russia could fully mobilize, but to do so her war plans required a sweep through Belgium. France itched to get back her lost province of Alsace-Lorraine, and Britain, worried lest all of Europe fall under the domination of her greatest trade and naval rival, felt bound by "obligations of honor" to back up her 1839 guarantee of Belgium neutrality when that country was overrun by German troops en route to Paris. Turkey, fearful of a British-Russian entente, entered the fray in October on the side of Germany, and the following May, an opportunistic Italy reneged on its treaty with Germany and joined Britain and France. In retrospect and given the horrendous consequences, none of these motives make much sense, but at the time only the Kaiser's personal motive would have been dismissed as ridiculous. He was shocked that his cousins had turned on him. "To think that George [of Britain] and Nicky [of Russia] should have played me false! If my grandmother had been alive, she would never have allowed it." (She might well have balked when George V changed his family name from Hanover to Windsor in order to dissociate himself from his German cousins.)

Alas, the old lady had been dead for 13 years, and the rules of diplomacy and conduct of war were changing rapidly. Far from the seizure of Paris in six weeks, the conflict bogged down into an agonizing war of human and industrial attrition on the western front, in which the nations of Europe bled to death while squandering the profits of the Industrial Revolution to achieve their bloody purpose. No matter the carnage, nothing either side could do seemed to break the stalemate. The British offensive of the Somme in 1916 cost 20,000 dead and 40,000 wounded on the first day of battle, and more shells (two million) were exploded in a single week than during the entire three years of the Boer War. A year later at Passchendaele, 240,000 British soldiers died, while at Verdun, the bloodiest encounter of the war, France and Germany each left behind 300,000 mangled corpses. Little wonder French troops mutinied at such tactics. Even the British attempt to turn the German flank and penetrate the so-called "soft underbelly of Europe" was stymied by Turkish defenses on the Dardanelles. The generals had no answer to the killing except to call for more human gun fodder. One survivor of the war years wrote that he had the "sensation of taking a profitless part in a game played by monkeys and organized by lunatics."

In order to survive in a war in which both human and material efforts had to be reckoned in the millions, a wartime Coalition Government under Lloyd George (of 1911 Peoples' Budget fame) transformed Britain into a nation in arms. The railroads and munitions plants were placed under government control, food rationing was introduced, and compulsory military service imposed (but only after two years of war). Even the cherished English principle of free speech was sacrificed—a man was actually arrested for calling King George "a bloody German" which, of course, was absolutely true. (He was three-quarters German.) The grayness of peace was replaced by the black and white of war. Any discussion of the conflict that did not blame the Germans became a criminal offense. Stories of German atrocities were widely circulated, and the image of the friendly beer-drinking German was replaced by the Prussian tyrant, a veritable Attila the Hun. British sacrifices and economic mobilization, however, were to no avail. Until the late spring of 1918, Germany seemed to be winning the war. German victories on the eastern front in April of 1917 triggered the Bolshevik Revolution and removed Russia from the war. German submarines brought Britain to the edge of starvation; she lost 38 percent (7 million tons and 60,000 seamen) of her merchant marine.

HOW A PRUSSIAN ST. GEORGE WOULD HAVE DONE IT.
"The friendly beer-drinking German was replaced by the Prussian tyrant,
a veritable Attilla the Hun."

The only silver lining to these grim statistics was that German unrestricted submarine warfare—especially the torpedoing of the British passenger liner *Lusitania* and the death of nearly 1200 passengers of whom 100 were children—swung American public opinion heavily to the British-French side. Public opinion was further inflamed when British intelligence intercepted, decoded and sent on to Washington a message from the German Foreign Minister to his Ambassador in Mexico proposing that the two countries "make war together" on the understanding that Mexico regain her "lost territory in Texas, New Mexico and Arizona." On April 6, 1917, the United States declared war. Two million fresh American lives to squander overwhelmingly tipped the balance, and Germany formally surrendered at the eleventh hour of the eleventh day of the eleventh month of 1918. Significantly, November 11, not June 28, 1919, the day the Versailles peace treaty was signed, is the day of remembrance (called Veterans' Day in the U.S.) because the Great War, as it was called, brought not peace, but only fruitless sacrifice. No victory monuments in the tradition of Waterloo were raised; only long lists of the names of the 750,000 British war dead. The Empire, despite German predictions to the contrary, gave the mother country impressive support, and Australia, Canada, New Zealand, and India added another 250,000 names to be remembered.

A Weary Giant; The Inter-War Years
(1918–1939)

National exhaustion is difficult to measure. Economically, the evidence is mixed and appears worse on paper than in reality. Britain spent $35 million a day not to lose the war; the debt soared from $3.2 to $37 billion and took three-fourths of the prewar budget to service; and although Europe (mostly France and Russia) owed her $10.5 billion in war loans, which were never repaid, Britain was in debt to the United States to the amount of $4.2 billion, of which she eventually paid half. But relative to other countries (except the U.S.) Britain emerged from the war with her economic potential still high; the death rate during the war was far less than the emigration rate to her colonies during the 1870s, '80s, and '90s; and her Empire was more spectacular than ever. What are today Palestine-Israel, Jordan and Iraq became protectorates carved out of the Turkish Empire, and the control of Germany's colonies in Africa finally linked Cairo and Cape Town in one splendid band of Imperial crimson.

Economic exhaustion proved to be less debilitating than spiritual malaise. In France, the will to fight died in the carnage of Verdun, paving the way for her humiliation and conquest by Nazi Germany 21 years later. In Britain, victory was overshadowed by two decades of apathy, disillusionment, economic retrenchment, pacifism and appeasement. There was little sense of triumph, especially among the troops, and when the Armistice finally arrived, "out came the inevitable cigarette but there was no cheering." In one sector of the front, a little American doctor from Vermont, who had been in the trenches only a fortnight, tried to cure the apathy. As one British observer put it: "He broke his invincible teetotalism, drank half a bottle of whisky, and danced a cachucha. We looked at his antics with dull eyes and at last put him to bed." The future belonged to the United States, not the United Kingdom.

What hurt the most was the speed with which the world forgot the goals for which millions had been asked to die: a war to end war, a war to make the world safe for democracy, and a war to make a home fit for returning heroes. Not one came close to being realized, and the sense of failure and waste was highest in those ranks expected to lead the next generation. One in five Cambridge-Oxford graduates perished in the war; in one public school, 720 "old boys" died, leaving behind them only 80 sons; and the will to take chances, the will to change, and the imagination to see that prewar standards and solutions no longer applied, all died with them.

In Ireland, Britain was confronted with a dilemma: "Go all out or get out." She had the will to do neither, mixing mismanagement, ill timing and overreaction in proportions that eventually guaranteed full Irish independence. During the war, most of Ireland had been surprisingly loyal to its island neighbor and patiently waited for Home Rule until the fighting was over. A tiny minority, however, consorted with the enemy, and on Easter Sunday, 1916, stormed the Dublin post office building and declared that the "Irish Republic" had arrived and avowed "the right of the people of Ireland . . . to the unfettered control of Irish destiny," including Ulster's. The rebellion lasted only a week and found almost no support, but with the help of the British, who stupidly executed, military style, 15 of the leaders—one and two at a time for ten days—the Easter Rebellion achieved its purpose. Fifteen martyrs rose from their graves, the sacred soil of Ireland was "warmed with the red wine of the battlefield," and public opinion swung heavily against any kind of Home Rule and in favor of unconditional independence.

The party of Sinn Fein (Ourselves Alone) swept the Irish election of 1918 and its delegates refused to sit in Westminster. Instead, they set up their own parliament (the Dail), and with the help of the party's military counterpart, the Irish Revolutionary Army (IRA), established an alternative structure of government. The British refused to legitimize the rebel government by acknowledging the existence of internicine war and sending the army in to crush it. They treated the "unpleasantness" as a police action and hired demobilized veterans as mercenaries (called Black and Tans because of the color of their uniforms) to reinforce the local Irish constabulary. Brutal civil war ensued until both sides were exhausted.

Eventually Britain offered full independence on two conditions: Ireland to acknowledge itself as part of the Empire and give allegiance to the Crown; and Northern Ireland to be separated from the south and be given its own parliament and Home Rule. It took two more years of even more atrocity-ridden fighting among the Irish themselves to achieve an agreement, but in 1922 the Irish Free State was established with the quiet understanding, at least on the part of the Irish, that it would eventually transform itself into today's Republic of Ireland (excluding for the time being its six northern counties). Irish nationalist purists still regret, however, that their island remains divided, that it is economically tied to Britain, and that English, despite legislation to the contrary, is still the dominant language.

Old ties were all but severed in Ireland, but 10,000 miles away in India, historic habits died more slowly. British India was a political accident held together by force of arms, force of custom and respect for the sovereign. The Raj was a ramshackle political structure, possessing no ideological purpose except to keep the peace. Slowly, however, but never purposefully, the Raj transformed a geographic expression into a political body endowed with a sense of its own national identity. After 1918, Indian nationalism was fanned by Britain's sweet wartime promise of Home Rule to justify a million Indian soldiers fighting to save the world for democracy. Thereafter the call for independence was orchestrated by a "seditious fakir" (Winston Churchill's unflattering description) named Mohandas K. Gandhi, whose education in England allowed him to recite (not quite accurately) Lord Byron's lines "'Freedom's battle once begun' is 'bequeathed from bleeding sire to son,'" and to develop the doctrine of non-violent disobedience. During the inter-war years the jewel of the Empire, Britain's proof of world-power stature, was slipping from her grasp. The moral creditability of the Raj and the self-confidence of its rulers began to dwindle, awaiting the shock of a second World War for the Imperial structure to collapse and the British to decide that they had no business—economically or morally—in India.

At home, the same forces of change and rebellion were at work on every level of society. Working men sought to better their condition or save what they had won during the war years. In one of the worst examples of British class and labor bloody-mindedness, coal miners and owners came to blows when the industry, already with 300,000 men out of work, was faced with further cutbacks. The Government tried to negotiate, but concluded, "It would be impossible to say, without exaggeration, that the miners' leaders were the stupidest men in England if we had not had frequent occasion to meet the owners." The miners went on strike on May 1, 1926, and the Trade Union Congress, the national confederation of British labor unions, called a general strike three days later. For nine days the trains, newspapers, dockyards, steel mills, power plants and gasworks closed down, but in an oddly British fashion: there was little violence. Shopkeepers, businessmen and college students rushed to man the trains, fulfilling their childhood dreams of becoming locomotive engineers, and strikers, confronted with unexpected spare time, elected to play soccer with a police team. (The strikers won 2 to 1.)

The general strike collapsed not so much because the Government, with enthusiastic middle-class support and the use of military personnel, kept the nation's vital services operating (moored submarines supplied electrical energy to the refrigerators of the London docks and prevented millions of pounds of meat from spoiling) as because its organizers were appalled by the thought that "if a force arises in the state which is stronger than the state itself, then it must be ready to take on the functions of the state." Even in the midst of the Great Depression and three million unemployed workers, British labor was never willing to stage a revolution, and remained loyal to the parliamentary process.

The upper classes were also riddled with rebellion, either in the form of pacifism or scorn for decorum and past authority. The flapper age of shock and impropriety had arrived, and the newly enfranchised (1928) female voters of 21 (finally equal to men) recited with gusto:

> *If the skirts get any shorter, said the flapper with a sob,*
> *There'll be two more cheeks to powder and a lot more*
> *hair to bob.*

A new generation was emerging which was determined that it would never again allow the kingdom to be led down the garden path of 19th-century false promises into war. At Oxford in 1933, the university debating society overwhelmingly passed the resolution "that this house refuses to fight for king and country." Similar resolutions were proposed and passed in universities throughout Britain and the empire.

Pacifism and a sense of apathy and retrenchment stand behind British inter-war foreign policy as the nation's leaders tried to negotiate with a revitalized Germany, now transformed into the Third Reich by Adolph Hitler and bent upon a policy of international gangsterism and blackmail. In response, Britain seemed to be "a frightened, flabby old woman." The Versailles Peace Treaty of 1919 had left the major powers of the world frustrated and angry. Britain and France were determined at almost any cost to maintain the status quo; Italy and Japan were opportunistic and restless; Germany and the Soviet Union were openly revengeful and set upon changing the terms of the treaty; the United States was isolationist; and the League of Nations without teeth or U.S. support, was helpless in keeping the peace or curbing aggression. In 1938, Prime Minister Neville Chamberlain, deeply suspicious of the Soviet Union's ultimate intentions and receptive to Germany's argument that it had been unfairly treated at Versailles and that the principle of self-determination justified its demand that all Germans be allowed to join the Fatherland, decided to assure the peace of Europe by negotiating directly with Hitler. Chamberlain made the terrible mistake of judging the German Führer by himself: Hitler was a gentleman and a rational human being whose word could be depended upon.

British tendency to keep out of foreign politics

Hitler had already violated the terms of the Versailles Treaty by re-arming and reoccupying the Rhineland, had absorbed Austria, and was now threatening war if the three million Germans living in Czecho-slovakia were not immediately incorporated into a greater Germany. At Munich in late September, Chamberlain acceded to the Führer's demands on the firm promise that this was Hitler's last territorial demand in Europe. Happily believing that war had been averted and lasting peace achieved, he returned to London with what he proudly described as "peace with honor." The Czech Ambassador was far less sanguine and told the British Prime Minister and Foreign Secretary that "if you have sacrificed my nation to preserve the peace of the world, I will be the first to applaud. But, if not, gentlemen, God help your souls."

There was cause to worry, and, as a precaution, Chamberlain has-tened the construction of the Cabinet War Rooms, an underground bunker to house the Prime Minister and top military staff in case of war. (The rooms are located underneath the Office of Works on King Charles Street and are today open to the public. They survive as a vivid reminder of how desperate the war years were.) Hitler, to Chamberlain's dismay, broke his solemn oath almost before the ink was dry. Within the year, he gobbled up what was left of Czechoslovakia, entered into an agreement with the Soviet Union to divide up Poland, and on September 1, 1939, invaded that country. Two days later Britain and France, com-ing to the bitter realization that Hitler could be stopped only by force of arms, declared war. The 21-year truce was over, and Chamberlain's dreams were in shambles; everything he had worked for, everything he had believed in, had "crashed to the ground."

Winston Churchill called the Munich settlement "a disaster of the first magnitude," and many people agreed with him, but Chamberlain's apologists argue that Munich postponed war for a year, thereby grant-ing Britain 12 months in which to rearm. On the face of it, this is no justification for selling out a small central European country and bol-stering the German war machine by turning over the Czechoslovakian armament industry (its Skoda factories in 1938 had an output equal to that of Great Britain), especially since Germany made far better use of the time, spending 25 percent of her national budget on armaments to Britain's 7 percent. But in one area it is possible to argue that the ex-tra 12 months may have been crucial because, as in the 16th century and the defeat of the Spanish Armada, the Battle of Britain during the summer of 1940 was won by superior technology. Although Germany out-produced Britain plane for plane, by September of 1939 Britain had increased the number of her Hurricane and Spitfire fighters from 6 to 26 squadrons and had extended her chain of radar stations to protect all of southern and eastern England. Superior aircraft and an advanced radar warning system saved Britain's hide and secured her from invasion when German blitzkrieg tactics ("lightning war" in which tanks in unison with dive bombers were used to smash French defenses) brought France to her knees and to the surrender-table at the exact place where Germany had surrendered 22 years before.

One War Too Many: World War, The Final Phase (1939–45)

Eventually the combatants in the second eruption of World War were the same as in the first: Germany against Britain, France, Russia and the United States, but with the important difference that Italy and Japan sided with Germany. However, until 1941 the conflict was limited to Britain, France and Germany, and for the first nine months, the so-called "phony war," nothing happened, except that Hitler's appetite for Poland was satiated. Then on April 9, 1940, all hell broke loose. Germany overran Denmark and Norway, and a month later attacked France, pouring across the Belgian and Dutch borders to get at the unprotected French flank. On May 10, the day the invasion of France began, Neville Chamberlain's Government resigned with the words shouted by Oliver Cromwell 297 years before ringing in its ears: "You have sat here too long. . . . Depart, I say, and let us have done with you. In the name of God, go!" It was replaced by a Coalition Government headed by Winston Churchill (1874–1965), aged 65, with false teeth and a slight speech impediment.

   The man who guided Britain through its "darkest hour" was half-American and is one of the most controversial figures in Anglo-Saxon history, a man who could say with some justification, "We are all worms but I do believe that I am a glow-worm." Heavy drinking, cigar smoking, acid-tongued, Churchill was disliked and distrusted by his fellow politicians as a man who was twice a turncoat, having first joined the Conservative Party, deserted it for the Liberals, becoming First Lord of the Admiralty during the 1914–18 war, and then returned to the Conservative ranks. During the inter-war years, he had been the unpopular voice of Cassandra warning the Kingdom of the Nazi menace and demanding that it rearm. Churchill's model and hero was his ancestor John Churchill, Duke of Marlborough, the 18th-century war leader who had brought Louis XIV of France to heel, and his aim was to do the same to Hitler. He bluntly told the House of Commons that he had nothing to offer "but blood, toil, tears and sweat," but boldly added: "What is our aim? I can answer in one word: Victory—victory at all costs, victory in spite of all terror; victory, however long and hard the road may be." (Something of the man's pugnacious personality can be sensed in his famous statue on the doorsteps of the Houses of Parliament.)

In the midst of catastrophic defeat, Churchill's Government pulled off two coups—one, a miracle, the evacuation between May 27 and June 4—by over 650 coastal steamers, pleasure boats and naval transports—of some 350,000 British and French troops trapped in the French port of Dunkirk; and the other, the bitter but necessary decision in July to sink the French navy gathered at Oran, North Africa, after France surrendered to Germany. Both were crucial events because, along with Churchill's dogged determination to carry on the fight alone against overwhelming odds, they gave a massive electrical charge to British morale and, equally important, convinced Franklin Roosevelt that there was still fight left in the British bulldog. The American President's main concern until then had been that the British navy not fall into German hands, but after July he began to listen with greater and greater receptivity to Churchill's passionate request that he exchange 50 old U.S. destroyers for British islands in the Caribbean.

When Britain refused to listen to German peace overtures, Hitler decided, like Napoleon before him, to invade England—Operation Sea Lion—but, since Britain still ruled the waves, he had first to win air supremacy over the English Channel. And so on August 13th, the world's most momentous air battle began. Out-numbered more than three to one British Spitfires and Hurricanes, forewarned by radar, held off the massive German air attack aimed at Royal Air Force ground installations. In late August as an act of bravado, the British bombed Berlin, and in retaliation Hitler ordered the saturation bombing of London. It was a fatal mistake, because it redirected German planes away from RAF airfields, allowing the British time to rebuild their nearly destroyed ground facilities and to refurbish their shattered fighter squadrons, and it clustered German aircraft over a single target, which proved so costly that Hitler gave up day-time bombing for the relative safety of night-time attacks. For 200 days the air battle raged, with heavy German losses and profound consequences. Not only was it apparent that the British were winning and that there would be no invasion of the island, but equally crucial, American public opinion also swung away from isolationism to a pro-British position, allowing Roosevelt to risk asking Congress to sanction the destroyer-exchange deal even though a presidential election was only weeks away. Five months later, the newly reelected American President turned the United States into the arsenal of democracy, and in the Lend-Lease Act of March 1941, promised "unqualified, immediate, all-out aid." By the war's end, $27 billion worth of war materials had been shipped to the beleaguered island. (An appreciative nation erected a monument to Roosevelt in Grosvenor Square across from the U.S. Embassy.)

The British people were experiencing war as never before; it had entered their front parlors; the home front had become the war front. Sixty thousand civilians would die in air raids; two homes out of every seven, along with two schools out of every ten, would be destroyed; the Kingdom would be transformed into a "war machine" with unprecedented powers; and for five years all class, economic and occupational differences would be swept away. Never, before or since, has the tight little island been so united. In May of 1940 Clement Atlee, the Labor Deputy Prime Minister told the House of Commons that the Government "demands complete control over persons and property; not just some people and some particular sections of the community but of all persons, rich and poor, employer and worker, men and women, and all property." The wartime socialist state—the warfare state—was created, in which private interests gave way to public need, consumption and production were regulated by careful state planning, and all Brits were subject to conscription, either in the military and its support services or in industry and agriculture. Price control and Government subsidization of imported foods kept prices within reach of the poor. All foods except bread and potatoes were rationed to equalize the effect of acute food shortage. Peers of the realm and London dock workers could purchase nothing except utility clothing and furniture, and inflation was checked by siphoning off excess funds into the war effort. The basic income tax was set at 50 percent and rose to 97.5 with a surtax on the remaining 2.5 percent. In the name of wartime survival, a social revolution transpired in which the standard of living became the same for everybody, as rich and poor huddled together in London subway stations to escape some 74,000 tons of German bombs or 3.5 pounds for every man, woman and child.

"I think somebody must have dropped this."

Despite total mobilization and U.S. aid, 1941 looked bleak for the British. They had not lost the war but it was clear that they could not win it alone. Germany had overrun the Balkans, the vital Suez Canal was in danger, and the summer months foretold nothing but an even more ferocious German air attack. Then, in June, everything changed. Hitler, seeking oil and grain resources and expansion room for the so-called Aryan race, sent his armies into the Soviet Union. Churchill detested Communism but he was willing to make a pact with the devil if that would insure victory. Six months later, on December 7, Japan attacked Pearl Harbor; the United States with her immense industrial strength now openly entered the conflict; and the British Prime Minister ecstatically wrote, "After seventeen months of lonely fighting . . . we have won the war. England would live; Britain would live . . . the empire would live. . . . Our history would not come to an end." Alas, Churchill was not quite correct: the grand alliance of Britain, the Soviet Union and the United States won the war and Britain survived, but not her Empire or her history, at least not as a world superpower.

It took a titanic effort. Russian sacrifices stalled and then defeated the German army. Britain and the United States, even after huge Imperial and American losses in South East Asia and the Pacific, checked and finally threw back Japanese conquests. Britain became an island fortress—the home of 1.5 million American soldiers—and on June 6, 1944 (D-day), British, Imperial and United States troops crossed the Channel and stormed the Normandy beaches. Eleven months later, Hitler was dead and the European war was over. In September 1945, the dropping of the atomic bomb brought the war with Japan to an unexpectedly swift conclusion, and the world was once again ready for another try at permanent peace, a peace in which Britain and her Prime Minister would play almost no part. Real power—military and economic—had long since shifted from London to Washington and Moscow, and Churchill, having been thrown out of office by the British electorate even before the war had ended, spent the next six years writing what is still the best account of the war years, his six-volume *History of the Second World War*.

Utopia Limited
(1945–1951)

Americans have always regarded Winston Churchill as the personification of the British spirit under duress—defiant, resilient, pragmatic—but the British who lived through the 1939–1945 war had trouble deciding whether their war-time leader was the savior of the kingdom or just another damn politician. Certainly the election of May 1945 made it dramatically clear that most Brits would not stomach a return to peacetime normality as defined by the standards of 1939. They demanded a new social system worthy of the sacrifices made during five years of total war, a home fit for returning heroes, a clean sweep of the old way of life, and the preservation of many of the wartime equalities. The only way to guarantee such a sweeping change was to vote Churchill's Conservative Party out of office and replace it with a Labor Government. As Churchill grimly described what many thought to be an "astonishing act of ingratitude": "I acquired the chief power in the state, which henceforth I wielded in ever growing measure for five years and three months of world war, at the end of which time, all our enemies having surrendered unconditionally or being about to do so, I was immediately dismissed by the British electorate from all further conduct of their affairs." What happened was totally unexpected; the Conservatives lost 173 seats in the House of Commons, the Liberal Party was almost annihilated—reduced to 12—and an upstart Labor Party, that had begun 52 years before as a one-man party, swept the election with just under 400 seats.

The Labor Party, drawing its votes and financial support from the trade unions and receiving its intellectual vigor from a small group of middle-class intellectuals called the Fabian Society, was organized in 1900 by James Kier Hardie. Hardie, a Scottish coal miner and leader of a nascent labor party, had entered Parliament in 1893 clad in his working man's cloth cap and tweed jacket and accompanied by a small brass band in defiance of the accepted dress code and proper decorum of the House of Commons: top hat, frock coat and gentlemanly restraint. By 1906, trade union money, organization, and votes, along with home-grown Fabian Socialist policies, transformed a party of one into a small but highly vocal cluster of 24.

The appearance of even 24 Labor MPs spelled the demise of the Liberal Party. By 1929 it had shrunk to 59, and middling class Britain found itself forced to vote either Labor or Conservative if it wanted a voice in national policy. In 1945 this middle group swung heavily to the left and voted Labor, partly because Labor in the Churchill Coalition Government had proved itself respectable and competent, and partly because Labor had a picture of the future that appealed to almost everybody, even conservative country gentlemen. Clement Atlee, the leader of the Labor Party and Deputy Prime Minister during the war years, was the product of a good public school and Oxford University, and so unobtrusively respectable that Churchill described him as "a sheep in sheep's clothing." The new Prime Minister outlined his party's dream: "Our task is to work out a system of a new and challenging kind which combines individual freedom with a planned economy: democracy with social justice." Few could disagree with such a goal.

Labor's approach to the problems that beset society was heavily bureaucratic in size and attitude. By 1951, 26 percent of the British labor force was toiling diligently in government offices to build the welfare state, in contrast to 17 percent in the United States. As early as 1929 *Punch* magazine delighted in satirizing the Labor Party's rigidity of mind by retelling the story of Beatrix Potter's *Peter Rabbit* as it might have been written by Beatrice Potter, the ardent and drearily "scientific" Fabian Socialist who along with her husband, Sidney Webb, were the intellectual godparents of the Labor Party:

JUVENILE OFFENDERS: Case B2957. Rabbit (Peter)
Age.—Uncertain. . . .
Parents.—Father (habitual criminal) deceased: G.S.W. See
    Registrar-General's returns of Deaths due to Accidents
    with Fire-arms; also Minority Report of the Royal Com-
    mission on the Composition of Rabbit-Pies, p. 341, H.M.
    Stationery Office. . . . Mother left to bring up four small
    children single-handed. Hereditary tendency to crime
    probably aggravated by lack of paternal control.
Environment.—The entire family occupy a basement room in a
    sand-bank. See Recommendations of the Housing Com-
    mittee, no. 5: Overcrowding.
Occupation—None. Female members of family (Flopsy, Mop-
    sy, and Cottontail) occasionally employed in blackberry-
    picking. See Proceedings of Committee of Investigation
    into Conditions of Casual Infant Labour, p. 483.
Offense.
    (a) Being on enclosed premises for unlawful purposes.
    (b) Theft of vegetable produce, the property of
         Mr. MacGregor. See Fabian Society Pamphlet No. 67
         "On the Private Ownership of Land;" also Report of
         the Ministry of Agriculture on Small Holdings.
Sentence.—Discharged with imprecation.
Deterrent Measures.
    (a) Nature of.—Camomile tea.
    (b) Efficacy of.—Nil. See case B2958: Bunny (Benjamin).

British bureaucrats at work

Labor's political style may have been bureaucratic and heavy-handed, but Britain was fortunate in the extreme that a Labor Government led it through the difficult postwar years of austerity, retrenchment, dissolution of empire, and cold war. Though its Socialist utopian dream was badly mauled by postwar reality, no other government would have been as successful in demanding the national sacrifices necessary to survival after a war that left the Kingdom exhausted and deeply in debt. Churchill's wife is said to have consoled her husband on the loss of the election of 1945 by suggesting that the defeat was a blessing in disguise. Winston grumbled that "the disguise was perfect," but his wife was right: the next five years were not easy for the British people.

For the first time, an avowedly Socialist party was in power and a working-class oriented government in control. Within the year the warfare state was transformed into the welfare state. With the National Insurance and Health Service Acts, the Government assumed full responsibility for protecting all citizens against unemployment, sickness, accident, and old age. (Health care was so generous that you could get a free wig if you could persuade your doctor to prescribe one, and free dentistry and glasses were offered to any resident of the isles. As a consequence, droves of Europeans took their vacations in Britain to improve their health.) A million-and-a-half state-subsidized homes were built, and public education, especially at the university level, was democratized and expanded, 25 new institutions of higher education being constructed. Nationalization of the means of production and communication, that fervently held Socialist panacea for all the ills of society, was introduced with doubtful results since 1) many of the nationalized industries, particularly coal and the railroads, were already in deep economic trouble; 2) state control meant neither worker control nor greater managerial efficiency or workingman loyalty; and 3) since only 20 percent of the economy (aviation, the Bank of England, coal, electricity, gas, railroads, and trucking) were affected, the concept of nationalization got tangled up in the debate over the over-all performance of British industry, which did considerably better after 1945 than it had before 1939, but markedly less well than post-war Germany, Japan, the USA or even Italy.

One of the most ironic lessons of the war, as far as Britain was concerned, was that to the victor belongs the obligations, to the losers belong the future. The industries of Germany and Japan were totally destroyed, and their peoples faced starvation, but in absolute defeat resided future hope. Bankruptcy liquidated past debts; their industries were reconstructed with new and more efficient technology; and starting fresh proved to be spiritually and economically advantageous in the postwar world. In contrast Britain's industry was old, exhausted and badly mauled by war, and her imperial and military responsibilities weighed heavily on the economy. Britain's military budget—troops to occupy Germany, defend the Empire, and later to support NATO—was the third highest in the world, exceeded only by Russia and the U.S. Maintaining great power status proved to be expensive far beyond Britain's means: after 1945 U.S. atomic research was closed to her, and she had to develop both the atomic and hydrogen bombs on her own. Worse, two bouts of World War and the rise of world food and raw material prices at the moment when American Lend-Lease ended, so completely liquidated Britain's ability to pay for imports to feed her peoples and supply her industries, that the island faced starvation and industrial collapse unless even greater sacrifices than during the war, were made. In a word, the utopia of the welfare society had to give way to the dictates of survival. As the austere and vegetarian Labor Chancellor of the Exchequer confessed: you can't divide up the economic pie equitably if there is no pie to cut up.

Wartime austerity not only did not end, it grew worse. Food became scarcer than ever before. Bread and potatoes were for the first time rationed. Sweets almost disappeared, and every Brit was limited to 13 ½ ounces of meat, eight ounces of sugar, two pints of milk, and one egg a week, and worst of all the beer supply was cut by half! The clothing shortage was so acute that the King, George VI, complained that his family's wardrobe was threadbare, and, when his daughter Princess Elizabeth married Lieutenant Philip Mountbatten, a Greek great grandson of Victoria, the Government allowed the bride only 100 extra clothing coupons for her wedding and honeymoon. Gasoline was prohibited for civilian use, tobacco and American films were heavily taxed to discourage their import, the King's subjects were urged to limit their bath water to a few inches and to share the hot water, and coal miners were asked to work an extra half hour a day. Not even the weather cooperated. The winter of 1947 was the worst in living memory. The Thames river froze over, and when spring finally arrived, two million sheep and the equivalent of a month's bread supply were lost when pasture land and wheat fields were flooded. In the nick of time, the United States awoke to the

The winter of 1947 was the worst in living memory

crisis and, through the Marshall Plan, pumped $5.6 billion in 1948 into Britain's and Europe's collapsing economies, Britain receiving the single largest parcel—$3.2 billion. (In all the U.S. distributed $17 billion.) The following year the pound was devalued from $4.03 to the pound to $2.80 to cheapen British goods on the U.S. market, and by 1950 exports had risen 77 percent and the trade deficit was finally closed.

The worst was over, but so was the Labor Government. It tore itself apart in a noisy debate over whether to allocate funds to maintain Britain's world status and military obligations and to support the United States in the cold war against Russia, or to unilaterally disarm the Kingdom, spend more money on the domestic benefits of the welfare state and refuse to allow U.S. atomic missiles on British soil. Britain could afford one policy or the other, but not both. As a consequence, in the election of 1951, Churchill won at the mature age of 77, and then three more Conservative Prime Ministers were returned to power for the next 13 years. They headed, however, a party which had bought into the welfare state and, like Labor, faced up to the reality that the Kingdom could no longer compete with the United States and Russia as a superpower and was better off as just another medium-sized European country.

Just before the Labor Party went belly up, it put on a national party—the Festival of Britain—to celebrate the end of postwar austerity (actually, rationing was not totally ended until 1954), give the country a much-needed pat on the back, and commemorate the 100th anniversary of the Great Exhibition of 1851 but, alas, without its spirit of extravagant confidence about the future. Architecturally, however, the festival produced the Royal Festival Hall, the only example of postwar British architecture worth looking at.

Finis Britanniae
(1947–1964)

Hugh Dalton, the first Labor Chancellor of the Exchequer, set the mentality for imperial dissolution when he said, "If you are in a place where you are not wanted, and where you have not got the force, or perhaps the will, to squash those who don't want you, the only thing to do is to come out." Both imperial will and force had been weakening ever since the 1914–1918 war, and in 1926 Britain recognized her self-governing dominions—Australia, Canada, New Zealand and South Africa—as equal "autonomous communities" within the Empire, and members along with Britain in "the British Commonwealth of Nations," a gathering of sovereign states whose Prime Ministers met regularly to discuss, but not necessarily to agree upon, issues of mutual concern.

After 1947, this concept was expanded to become the face-saving device for dismantling the Empire; as the various segments gained independence, they mostly signed on with the Commonwealth. The major exceptions were Burma, which was too prickly; Egypt, which had always been free at least in theory and was fed up with all things British; Pakistan which left the Commonwealth in a fit of pique when the Commonwealth recognized its breakaway province of Bangladesh; Palestine, which nobody wanted; South Africa, which was asked to leave in 1961 because of its policy of racial discrimination; and Ireland, whose independence was officially recognized by act of Parliament in 1949. (Oddly enough the Irish, though independent, are not foreigners and when resident in Britain have the right to vote.)

India, which represented well over half the population of the Empire, was the first to win independence. Though the last Viceroy, Admiral Lord Louis Mountbatten, worked desperately to preserve the unity of the Indian subcontinent, Hindu-Moslem religious hatred proved insurmountable, and on 15 August, 1947, India and Pakistan gained independence as separate states, the British Raj dividing itself between the two nations down to the last Imperial rifle and government pencil, but, unfortunately, not to the last Moslem or Hindu, and no division satisfactory to both was possible in Kashmir. Palestine proved to be even more difficult; so much so that Britain, confronted with a three-way war between 100,000 of her troops and Jewish and Arab terrorists, turned the Jewish-Arab conflict over to the United Nations and in 1948 simply pulled out, having created one of the world's worst headaches.

Imperial dissolution became a stampede in the late 1950s, when Harold Macmillan's Conservative Government decided to pull out of the business of Empire as swiftly and gracefully as possible, before world opinion and local nationalist military pressure forced it to do so. Between 1956 and 1964, Britain divested herself of all her African, West Indian, South East Asian and Mediterranean holdings except Gibraltar—still a blot on Spain's honor. The last Imperial plum, Hong Kong, was turned over to China when its lease ran out in 1999. The majestic halls of Empire—Canada House, South Africa House, the colonial and

India offices, the War Office—clustered around Trafalgar Square and Whitehall, still stand proud but faintly embarrassed in their new domesticated roles. Though the retreat from Empire was accomplished with Anglo-Saxon stiff-upper-lip graciousness, it was not without its moments of humiliation. When Egypt nationalized the Suez Canal in violation of its treaty obligations, Anthony Eden, Churchill's successor as Prime Minister, hysterically ordered out the troops and indulged in the extraordinary semantic sophistry of announcing that "we are not at war with Egypt; we are in armed conflict." Either way Britain backed down in the face of U.S. grumbles and Russian growls, and belatedly realized that with India independent, the canal was scarcely worth fighting over. (It took eight years to clear the canal of the debris of battle and added £20 million a month to the cost of British imports.)

W.C. Sellar and R.J. Yeatman conclude their satirically humorous treatment of British history, *1066 And All That*, with the provocative statement that at the end of the 1914–1918 war "America was top nation, and history came to a ." Or at least memorable history did. A far better date for the end of history as Western Europe has known it for the past thousand years, would be the end of the 1939–1945 war, when the United States and Russia emerged, at least for the time, as "top" nations and Great Britain slipped back into relative historical obscurity, ceasing to be a world superpower or have any memorable history. So that is where this brief historical overview will leave the tight little island, content to recount the passage of the past half-century in an even briefer addendum, neither tear-stained nor nostalgic, only mercifully short.

Chapter V

LESS AND LESS MEMORABLE HISTORY

Hard Times

D espite the brave new world forecast by the Festival of Britain
and the following year (1952) by the succession of an attractive, if unglamorous, young Queen and the advent of a second
Elizabethan Age, the decades following World War II were some of
the worst in the island's history. Deprived of its 19th-century industrial
head start and struggling to adjust to a diminished world status, but still
beset by out-of-date memories of Empire and economic hegemony, the
Kingdom lurched from one humiliation and crisis to the next.

Pound sterling, which had once been the monetary benchmark of
the globe, fell after 1948 in relation to the Yankee dollar from $4.05
to almost par. Britain's naval might, which only a decade before had
ruled the waves, was so diminished that when NATO was established
in 1949, the Kingdom had to accept the ignominy of an American Admiral in command of its warships. The anthem "Rule Britannia" had
become a joke. Victory, so heroically won, became a mockery as both
her enemies—Germany and Japan—rose from the ashes of defeat to
win the peace that broke out after 1945. In 1955 the British pound had
purchased eleven German marks; 40 years later, the German economy
was so robust and the British so flabby that the pound bought less than
three marks. Even that most stately and aristocratic of British trees, the
elm, was wiped out during the 1970s when 6.5 million fell prey to the
Dutch elm disease.

Culturally it seemed that the country that had spawned Shakespeare
and Newton was being reduced to an American overseas appendage.
Bill Haley's Comets, rocking noisily round the clock, bombarded the
land, and, while British teenagers, all appropriately dressed in American
Levis, were gyrating to the "devil's music" of Elvis Presley, their parents

were being mesmerized by the New World gospel of Billy Graham. Even the "drunkometer" to measure the alcoholic intake of fun-loving Brits hurtling down the highways was a cruel American import. In 1968, London Bridge was bought up and carted off to, of all places, Lake Havasu City, Arizona. Eight years later, McDonald's invaded the Kingdom to replace fish and chips with an even worse fast food diet of hamburgers and fries. By 1979 the skate board made its appearance, turning every sidewalk in Britain into a dangerous adolescent playground; and within the decade LSD found its way across the pond, accompanied by ear-shattering Acid House music. A totally fed-up former British Minister of Education lamented in 1997 that "America even influences the way we grieve." He was complaining that Elton John at the funeral of Princess Diana sang a song that he had originally composed for Marilyn Monroe and that "our singers sing in bastard Americanese."

Even the dubious distinction of being the home of the missing link between man and ape was taken away when in 1953 the Piltdown Man, discovered in a gravel pit in southern England in 1912, was declared to be a scientific hoax. But the worst humiliation of all came ten years later, when Britain belatedly decided to join the European Common Market, and was told by General Charles de Gaulle, the President of France, to go and peddle her wares elsewhere. Britain in 1957 had turned her back on European economic integration and refused to join West Germany, France and Italy in an economic union, preferring her insular isolation and fading images of 16th-century Elizabethan seadogs and world empire. By 1963, economic reality dictated a change of heart. Unfortunately, de Gaulle was intensely suspicious of Britain's "special relationship" with the United States and fearful lest France's ancient rival interfere with French dreams of once again dominating Western Europe as in the days of Louis XIV. The General was still bitter that England had burned his favorite heroine, Joan of Arc, at the stake and was confirmed in his Anglophobia by his treatment by Churchill (and Eisenhower) during World War II. He revenged himself and French honor by vetoing British entry. Britannia sulked and composed scurrilous poems telling the French where they could put their Eiffel Tower, boasting:

> *We're glad of what we did to you*
> *At Agincourt and Waterloo.*

Anglo-Saxons applauded when Mary Quant, a 20-year-old London art student, led an attack on French haute-couture and turned the British capital for the next ten years into the fashion center of the world with her miniskirts, violent colors, and page-boy haircuts—the swinging 60s were born in London. But, alas, neither a Carnaby Street "mod" clad generation, which proclaimed the liberating blessings of a "permissive society" and rapped to the Mersey beat of the Beatles, nor the ego-satisfying image of the unflappable James Bond, Ian Fleming's immaculately dressed super-hero who always triumphed over the bad guys (and dolls), could conceal the economic and structural malaise that beset the country.

Economic Suicide

Once de Gaulle was safely dead, and the French awoke to the realization that they needed Anglo-Saxon help to counterbalance German economic resurgence, Britain was allowed in 1971 to join the European Economic Community (today much enlarged and aspiring to political integration as the European Union). The decision, however, to become European and actually fulfill Napoleon's dream of a tunnel under the Channel linking England and France, failed to stop Britain's apparent determination to undo the Industrial Revolution and transform herself from a developed into an underdeveloped country. The well-behaved trade unions of the first post-war Labor Government fell prey to one of the worst legacies of the late Victorian-Edwardian years—bloody mindedness. Their managerial counterparts were not far behind in obtuseness and pigheadedness, and the entire realm was smitten with the belief that everything small was beautiful. For well over 20 years, the motto "I'm all right Jack" came close to paralyzing the economy. British business was hidebound, unimaginative, and scornful of the new science of econometrics and American business-school methods. Labor was fearful of any changes that smattered of efficiency lest they endanger jobs, and adamantly ignored the warning that one man's pay raise equaled another man's price raise. Business, labor and two decades of Labor and Conservative Governments failed to heed the basic economic lesson that if your industrial machine is becoming increasingly inefficient in relation to world competition, you should not be paying your work force more and more to produce less and less.

The result was near-disaster. Uncontrollable wildcat strikes, usually over wages, but often over the firing of a single laborer, drove up wages 240 percent, while the ensuing inflation made British goods that much more difficult to sell on the world market. In a showdown with coal miners, railroad engineers and electric power workers, Edward Heath's Conservative Government in 1974 declared a state of emergency. Electricity could not be used to heat homes, lighted advertising signs were shut down, the speed limit was cut to 50 miles per hour, and worst of all, television was shut off at 10:30 PM. The nation was put on a three-day week to save energy which, of course, further injured the economy by making it impossible for industry to compete or even fill back orders. Stalemate ensued, and Heath was obliged to call a general election, asking "who governs Britain." He lost. A Labor Government was no more successful at controlling the trade unions or revitalizing the economy. Strikes made London almost uninhabitable: uncollected garbage in the streets, hospitals forced to close for want of heat, and the dead unburied in graveyards.

As the economic crisis deepened, extremists in both parties flourished. Labor clamored for the end of the special relationship with the United States; unilateral disarmament; withdrawal from the European Economic Community; high protective tariffs; total nationalization of banking and industry, and the abolition of all private schools, private medicine and the House of Lords. The Conservatives were equally doctrinaire, demanding a fundamental reversal of the path Britain had been following ever since the semi-Socialist welfare state had been inaugurated in 1945. They called for a completely free market economy; steep reductions in government spending on social programs; the privatization of all aspects of banking and industry; the re-energizing of the economy by dramatic lowering of the income tax from the existing high of 83 to 40 percent, and the modernization of industry, even if that meant high unemployment.

In the end, good luck and economic forces, not ideology, saved the British bacon. It turned out that God was after all an Englishman (more accurately a Scotsman) for He found vast quantities of gas and oil in the North Sea, which helped stem the inflation (25 percent in 1975) and balance an annual trade deficit that at its height had reached $12.2 billion, the worst in British history. Equally important, time was running out for the coal miners who had spearheaded much of the labor militancy in an attempt to keep their mines from closing. As the country turned more and more to gas, oil and atomic energy for fuel and power, the number of miners shrank from a high of 1.2 million in 1920 (with a thousand fatal mining accidents a year) to fewer than 15,000 in 1994 with only 18 mines still operating.

Thatcherism

One of the vagaries of the British political system is that political parties can generate large parliamentary majorities and introduce sweeping, even revolutionary, changes without receiving a majority of the popular vote. In fact, no party since World War II has ever received greater than 48 percent of the popular vote. In May of 1979, just such a political revolution took place: 43.9 percent of the electorate, fed up with the arrogance of the trade unions and a decade of "stagflation" (economic stagnation accompanied by inflation), voted Conservative, and Margaret Thatcher, quoting Abraham Lincoln's words that "you don't make the poor richer by making the rich poorer," commenced her 11 ½ year reign with a handsome majority of 339 seats in the House of Commons, to Labor's 268. (Four years later, with only 42.4 percent of the popular vote, she increased that majority to 396 seats.)

Mrs. Thatcher, a purse-swinging chemistry major from Oxford and the daughter of a grocer from Grantham (Lincolnshire), was a triple whammy. She was Britain's first female Prime Minister; she held office longer than any political leader since 1820; and she was the first to lead a party to three consecutive elections. She was also the first in 150 years to be kicked out by her own party while still in office. She tamed the trade unions, reducing the number of days lost by strikes to the lowest since the 1950s; transformed the coal industry; returned nationalized services to the private sector; lifted controls on foreign exchange, and fought a cheap, short, successful war (the best kind) with Argentina. (The bone of contention was the Falkland Islands, an outcropping of heather-covered rocks 400 miles from the Argentine coast, but close to 7,000 miles from Britain, inhabited by some 1,800 sheep farmers who were determined not to become Argentinean and to remain British subjects.) The war displayed that there was still fight in the British lion and gave a huge boost to British morale—it could act (in a small way) as a great power. Industrial production soared by 30 percent; for the first time, Britain led the EEC in economic growth; and by 1985 she had become the largest investor in the United States, supplying 24 percent of all foreign capital, compared to Japan's 10 percent. The Russians called Thatcher "The Iron Lady" and the sobriquet stuck.

A rejuvinated Britannia and British lion take on Argentina in the Falkland war

Thatcherism was successful, but it came at such a high price that many thought that her cures were worse than the economic disease. Unemployment jumped to three million, the largest since the Great Depression of the 1930s. Thatcher's efforts to "modernize" higher education and cut away fat and complacency earned her the undying hatred of the academic establishment which sought revenge by destroying her standing in the history books. (Thatcher was the only retiring Prime Minister to be denied an honorary degree by Oxford, her own alma mater.) Her "reform" of local government taxation—she wanted to replace property taxes with a head or poll tax—led to a popular rebellion almost as violent as in 1381. She nearly destroyed her own party by her furious opposition to any further merging of Britain into the European Union, which she predicted would eventually destroy British historic identity just as effectively as any Napoleon or Hitler. The lady, as she proudly announced, "was not for turning," and in 1990 "she who must be obeyed" was forced to resign; not even her own cabinet could take any more of her authoritarian moralizing. Thatcherism, however, lived on without Thatcher under her successor John Major, the son of a circus performer, for another seven years until his Conservative Government was brought down by its reputation for sleaziness and hopeless inefficiency. There are, however, many people today who say that Tony Blair, the current Labor Prime Minister, is nothing more than the Iron Lady dressed up in beguiling Labor clothing.

The Irish Question Again,
or
Who Cares About the UK?

As if Thatcherism was not difficult enough to live with, Britain has had to endure for the umpteenth time the Irish question. Ireland has remained an unanswered problem ever since an ill-natured and worse-informed Deity placed the two islands adjacent to each other and arranged for the Pope back in 1172 to grant the Emerald Isle to Henry II of England as part of his divine right. Ever since, a myriad of English soldiers, politicians and churchmen have been trying unsuccessfully to resolve the question, and in 1921 when the British finally pulled out and left southern Ireland to its own devices, keeping only the northern counties as part of the UK, most people thought the Irish question had finally been settled. Northern Ireland was given its own Prime Minister and Parliament; it sent its own M.P.s to Westminster; and the Protestants enjoyed a substantial majority and a stranglehold over the economy.

By 1969, however, the situation had altered. Catholics were reproducing far faster than Protestants, and the Protestant majority became increasingly insecure and hysterical. The Catholics, tired of forever being economic underdogs, launched a civil rights campaign; and the radical, semi-Marxist wing of what remained of the IRA (the Irish Republican Army which had fought the British in 1918–21 but had later been outlawed by the Irish Republic) recognized a heaven-sent chance to realize its ultimate goal of a totally united Ireland. Protestant militants were determined that hell would freeze over before they would allow Northern Ireland to unite with its southern and Catholic neighbor.

They clashed with a Catholic extremist minority supported by the IRA, that in turn was heavily financed from America and trained and armed by Libya's General Gaddafi as an exercise in terrorism. As always happens, the moderate majority was caught in the middle. Violence ensued. The British sent in troops to restore order; Home Rule was suspended in 1972; and the northern counties were governed directly from London. The IRA, appealing to Irish manifest destiny and seeking to persuade the British to accept the inevitability of a unified Ireland, retaliated with bombs and terror directed not only at British soldiers but also at civilians in England.

Earl Mountbatten, World War II hero, last Viceroy of India, uncle to the Queen's husband, and great grandson of Victoria, was blown to bits while on a fishing trip to Ireland. (He was accorded a state funeral that equaled Nelson's and Churchill's.) Cars were exploded in front of Harrod's in London; mortars were lobbed into 10 Downing Street, breaking china and damaging the kitchen; a Northern Ireland MP to the British Parliament was assassinated; and in October of 1984 the Grand Hotel in Brighton was hit with a 100-pound bomb while Margaret Thatcher's cabinet was attending a Conservative Party convention. The Iron Lady herself escaped unscathed, but four people were killed and 30 others injured. That "shameless hussy," as both Catholic and Protestant extremists liked to call the British Prime Minister, was in no mood for mercy; she sternly allowed ten IRA prisoners, who were on a hunger strike, to starve to death. In all, over 3,600 people have died as a consequence of the violence over the future of Northern Ireland, 59 percent at the hands of the IRA, 29 percent by the Protestant diehards, and the rest by Ulster police and British troops. As Mrs. Thatcher confessed, it was difficult to imagine "a political initiative which would be acceptable to one side which would not be repugnant to the other. But we will have to keep on trying." Britain is still trying, with a glimmer of hope of success today.

While Protestant Unionists in Northern Ireland were clamoring (and killing) to stay in the UK, Scottish and Welsh nationalists were yapping to get out. For 800 years it had seemed as if the warring parts of the British Isles were destined to join together in an ever more centralized union. Then, in the 1950s, a reverse trend suddenly set in. The Scots stole back their Stone of Scone and started once again celebrating Robert Bruce's victory over Edward II at the battle of Bannockburn in

1314, the only major engagement the Scots ever won. Robert Burns was acclaimed to be a cultural hero and his Gaelic verses endlessly recited while everything worthwhile in British culture and society was said to be Scottish, including North Sea gas and oil. After all, James Barrie's Peter Pan, Conan Doyle's Sherlock Holmes, David Hume's philosophy, Joseph Lister's medical discoveries, Robert Stevenson's Long John Silver, and James Watt's steam engine, all had Scottish roots. With stern Highland logic, nationalists pointed out that Scotland already had its own laws, church, money and television, so why didn't it also have its own political identity? The Welsh were less jingoistic in their devotion to leeks and a language that nobody except themselves could spell or pronounce, but they resented seven centuries of exploitation by their Anglo-Saxon neighbors. They were particularly miffed that their coal mines had been pillaged (and then abandoned) to fuel an industrial revolution from which they benefited little, and that all the real estate with the best views was being bought up by the English for summer homes. Throughout the Celtic fringe, the cry went up that the time had come to rethink the constitutional links that joined original Celtic settlers to the Anglo-Saxon newcomers.

In 1999, a triumphant Labor Government, which had been swept into office with the help of Welsh and Scottish votes, responded to Celtic nationalism by introducing the principle of federalization, and granting Scotland and Wales their own representative organs—Scotland a parliament, Wales an assembly.

Whether watered-down federalism will suffice to stem the tide of nationalism remains to be seen. But for the moment at least, Scotland, as so often has been the case, has its cake and can eat it too; it is virtually independent in local affairs, but still sends MPs to a British Parliament in Westminster where they often have a deciding vote on their southern neighbor's private concerns. Understandably, the English are not pleased.

More Slings and Arrows

Just at the moment when the British had learned to live with Irish terrorism, believed that the worst of the economic crisis was over, and hoped that they had been sufficiently punished by outrageous fortune for whatever sins had earned the wrath of the gods—probably their having won

World War II—a new set of afflictions descended from on high. Bad judgment and worse luck brought Lloyd's of London, the most famous insurance company in the world, to the brink of bankruptcy, when between 1988 and 1991 it lost over £11 billion, largely from betting on the weather, which is never a smart thing to do. The bovine population during the late '80s came down with mad cow disease; 176,000 cattle died, eventually four million had to be slaughtered, and the market for British beef disappeared for the next decade. The year 1992 was for Queen Elizabeth II her Annus Horribilis—some of the most historic parts of Windsor Castle, including St. George's chapel, went up in flames; there was an unsavory squabble over who owned the castle and should foot the £11 million bill; and, worst of all, the royal offspring began to embarrass their parents by making spectacles of themselves in the yellow press.

Three out of four of the Queen's children have been divorced, a rate well above the national average, which is the highest in the European Union. Charles, the Prince of Wales and heir to the throne, made the mistake in 1981 of marrying the marvelously photogenic, teenaged Diana, who promptly won every heart (except Charles's), stole the limelight from the royal family (which it resented), and developed into the darling of the international media—poised, beautiful and dangerous to both a monarchy that was without glamour or sensitivity and a husband who at 44 was suffering from mid-life identity crisis. In taking on a young, vivacious bride, he was recapturing his youth, satisfying his parents and securing the succession, but also leaving behind his mistress, Camilla Parker-Bowles, the wife of a one-time close friend. The marriage started with a fairy-tale wedding in vivid Technicolor, watched by hundreds of millions throughout the globe. It rapidly deteriorated into a soap opera that shattered the carefully orchestrated aura of royal respectability and mystique of monarchy so important to the House of Windsor. The couple separated in 1992 amidst accusations of adultery on both sides, and the marriage ended four years later in an acrimonious divorce, leaving Charles to tend his organic garden and Camilla Parker-Bowles, and Diana to whirl to her destruction in September 1997 in a fatal car crash in Paris. The divorces of Charles's siblings, the equestrian excelling Anne and the helicopter pilot Andrew, were pale in comparison, but Elizabeth II, who inherited her throne because her uncle had not been allowed to marry a twice-divorced American, had cause to call 1992, and the years that followed, her Annus Horribilis.

Even as the tight, if beleaguered, little island crept into the 21st century, it was far from certain whether the gods had been fully appeased. The fireworks designed to welcome the new millennium embarrassingly failed to go off, British agriculture and tourist trade sustained an estimated $3.2 billion loss from the worst outbreak of foot-and-mouth disease in the Kingdom's history; so bad the entire countryside had to be closed to tourists. The Millennium Dome, heralded as an innovative architectural leap into the new century, was plagued with delays and mishaps; its appearance, which reminded many of some Darwinian aberration—a giant white poached-egg-shaped slug with gold spikes as antennas—was the subject of furious debate; and it is anybody's guess whether, as its supporters maintain, it is "a triumph of confidence over cynicism." And in 2001, Lloyd's suffered its largest single-event loss ever: $2.87 billion for the September 11 attack on the New York World Trade Center.

"We Happy Few"

The gods are notoriously capricious and have proved many times over that it is dangerous to write the British off too soon. The Millennium Dome may yet inaugurate a new age for Great Britain. Measured in terms of creature comforts and standard of living, the Kingdom is twice as prosperous as it was when the half-century of adversity set in. The Queen's subjects are today better housed, fed, educated and cared for than at any time in their history, and a peer of the realm can no longer expect to live a decade and a half longer and stand five inches taller than a commoner, as he did when Victoria sat on the throne. London is said to be once again the richest city in Europe (and the priciest), and though the tabloid press might make one think otherwise, the Kingdom enjoys the lowest violent crime (but not theft) rate of any Western industrial nation.

Politically, Britain moved in 1997 into an era of unusual good will in the wake of Tony Blair's unprecedented Labor majority of 419 seats (but only 43.2 percent of the popular vote) in the House of Commons. The Labor Party has turned its back, for the time being, on doctrinaire solutions, renouncing its commitment to the nationalization of banking and industry. Today the "New Labor" Government prefers to send chills up and down Tory spines, not with threats of Socialist takeover but with

animal rights legislation to abolish that favorite aristocratic pastime—
fox hunting. More important, Labor has divorced itself from the trade
unions, reducing their influence in the party's policies and announcing
that it has other constituencies and power bases to satisfy. Henceforth
the party owed the unions "fairness, not favors." The trade unions have
not been pleased with this new formula, but since their membership has
dropped precipitously, falling from a high of 53 percent of all workers
in the late 1970s to 28 percent in 2003, their political clout has shrunk
dramatically. If you can't get out the vote, you cannot expect politicians
to respond.

Labor has also given up its opposition to closer integration with the
Continent, accepting the opening of the Channel tunnel in 1994 as the
harbinger of the future. But not even an ebullient Mr. Blair has been able
to persuade the country to give up the image of the Queen as the symbol of British currency and adopt the Euro, the European Union's common money. Moreover, Britain's "special relationship" with the United
States still remains firm, as witnessed first by Mrs. Thatcher's friend-
ship with Ronald Reagan and her influence over George W. Bush when
Iraq invaded Kuwait (she claims to have told him: "Now, George, don't
go all wobbly on me"), and then by John Major's commitment of British forces in the Gulf War of 1991, and Tony Blair's more recent massive support of U.S. forces in Afghanistan and Iraq. Twenty thousand
British troops fought alongside American soldiers in the 2nd Gulf War.
The Prime Minister has paid a heavy political price for his backing of
President Bush's "preemptive" attack on Iraq in the name of destroying
weapons of mass destruction. In the May 2005 general election, anti-
war sentiment slashed Labor's overwhelming majority of 412 seats in a
House of Commons of 646 members, to 355, a loss of 57 seats. Labor
managed to win only 36.1 percent of the popular vote, one of the lowest
with which a party has ever won an election.

Reform of the House of Lords has disturbed the political atmosphere
almost not at all. Everyone agrees that an upper house stuffed with
hereditary lords of no distinction, most of whom having little interest in
the hard work of legislation, is a hopeless anachronism, but to date no
one has figured out whom to put in their place. Compromise legislation
has done away with the right of all but 92 of the 796 hereditary peers to
sit in the Lords, leaving some 550 life peers (ranging at one time from
Margaret Thatcher to the actor Laurence Olivier) and the 26 prelates

of the Church of England in control. So far the electoral principle, let alone submitting members to competitive examinations, has made little headway against the comfortable policy of stacking the Lords with the political castoffs and friends of the party in power.

That the future of the House of Lords and the death of the Queen Mother at the age of 101 are of any interest to the international media is surprising evidence of the cultural bonds that still tie the English-speaking world to an "Atlantic archipelago" off the northwestern coast of Europe. This may explain why London's Heathrow is the busiest airport in Europe, and British Airways is the largest global airline in the world. (Annually 14.2 million transatlantic visitors arrive in Britain, more than all the French and German tourists combined.) Britain may have lost her political empire and economic hegemony, but she still retains an unparalleled empire of words and history. English has become the lingua franca of the world. When Japan joined Germany and Italy in a tripartite defensive pact in October 1940, the language of negotiation was English, and today the Anglo-Saxon tongue is the international language of business, science, tourism, and the internet. It is the most commonly taught second language in the European Union, and is the common speech of the Commonwealth of Nations, a multiracial and multilingual collection of 54 nations (of which Elizabeth II is the head of state of 17) that shares a history of British parliamentary government and law. Little wonder Britain is second only to the United States as an exporter of TV programs; that Barbara Cartland's romantic novels (723 of them) have sold world-wide over half a billion copies; that hundreds of millions have delighted in Harry Potters' and Mary Poppins's spectacular proof of English magical ingenuity and happy insanity; and that English actors are busily turning Hollywood into a British colony. It is difficult to imagine a world without England: without the sandwich, the postage stamp, the Salvation Army, and the Christmas card, not to mention representative government, Common Law and the Boy Scouts. All of these give confidence that "there'll always be an England" and that the British will somehow continue to "muddle through," laughing both at themselves and their history. What one third-rate English playwright penned in the 18th century still holds true: "The people of England are never so happy as when you tell them they are ruined."

Chapter VI

THE ROYAL SOAP OPERA

B ritish economic, political and social history may have become
unmemorable to the point of oblivion, but the House of Windsor
has not. As a host of television documentaries, films and biog-
raphies on the royal family attest, the human factor still enthralls the
imagination and remains highly memorable. Nevertheless, all things
are relative: the marital scandals of Elizabeth II's difficult brood seem
deliciously marketable by today's tabloid standards, but placed within
the context of 31 generations of royal history, they pale into petty insig-
nificance. Elizabeth's bloodline, through the wives of both the Conqueror and his youngest son, goes back to the founding of the Wessex
dynasty, but, counting only from William I, she is the 42nd English-
British sovereign. During those 940 years, nine of her ancestors usurped
the throne or ignored the "rightful" succession; four, possibly five, were
murdered; one was publicly beheaded; two more were declared certifi-
ably insane; another was killed on the battlefield; and four "abdicated."
On the marital front, one executed two of his wives and divorced two
others, another kept his wife under lock and key for 20 years, and a third
renounced his throne to marry his twice-divorced American lover.
Royal mistresses were legion, and the number of bastards is beyond
reckoning: Henry I acknowledged twenty (nine sons and eleven daughters); Henry II had at two; John, Edward IV and Henry VIII at least
one each; Charles II a lusty fourteen (it is surprising how many people
today proudly claim descent from Charles's bastards); James II four;
George I two; George II one (but unrecognized); and William IV ten.
Thereafter, British sovereigns were both more faithful and more careful. As for doing their royal duty and begetting legitimate heirs to the
throne, William I had nine children, Henry II seven (his wife Eleanor
had two more daughters by Louis of France and a son who could have
been sired by either), Edward I fifteen (possibly seventeen), Edward III

191

twelve, Edward IV seven, Anne six (all died young), George III fifteen, and Victoria a modest nine. Finally, one wife engineered her husband's overthrow and murder, and another tried her damnedest but failed; she did, however, succeed in polishing off his mistress. No modern soap opera comes close to such a spectacular level of blood, intrigue, faithlessness, scandal and time in bed.

William I (1066–1087)

William I was called, generally behind his back, William the Bastard, and he could be extremely touchy about the subject. When rebellious townspeople in his native Normandy mocked him for his illegitimacy, he was "so stark a man" that he had them flayed alive and their skins hung from the town walls. He was the love child of Robert "the devil," Duke of Normandy and Herleve (also called Arlette), a tanner's daughter; not a propitious start for becoming a duke, but the sword, if not blood, prevailed. By the year of the Conquest, William was, as one historian has written, "a friendless man, suspicious, grasping and hard in his nature, unscrupulous and ruthless in his methods, formally devout in religion, yet withal indomitable in pursuit of his ends." That is why he conquered England and was able to hold both it and Normandy for 21 years. "Cold heart and bloody hand now rule the English land," wrote a Norse poet, but even the Anglo-Saxons had to admit the Conqueror made his new domain so secure "that any honest man could travel over his kingdom without injury with his bosom full of gold. . . . If any man raped a woman he was immediately castrated."

A contemporary described William as a man of tremendous presence. No one could "bend the bow on horseback at full gallop" as he did, and he never lost his dignity "whether sitting or standing, though the outward swell of his big belly deformed his royal person." What the writer did not say was that after his death, William was stripped of all his majesty and dignity.

William the Conqueror: "A friendless man."

His clothes were stolen and his body left naked on the floor, and by the time he was buried, his belly had swollen so large it was impossible to stuff him into his sepulcher. When force was applied, his body broke open, and priests and bishops fled the stench. Not even in the grave did the indignities of death cease. His tomb was broken into twice; once by Calvinist looters during the French religious wars of the 16th century, and again during the French Revolution. His bones have vanished, and all that remains is a stone slab in the Church of St. Stephen at Caen to indicate what might have been his original resting place.

William II (1087–1100)

William II had a far worse press than his father, because he didn't get along with priests and monks, which was a mistake for his future reputation; back then clerics did all the history writing, and they bellowed his inequities to the world. He was a King "hated by almost all his people and odious to God." The Conqueror had originally planned to give both England and Normandy to his eldest son Robert, but Robert was the prodigal son who never reformed. He was at war with his father when William died, and all he got was Normandy, England going to his younger brother William. William II possessed his father's astonishing strength, prowess at war, and bulging belly (but not receding hairline), and he spent most of his reign fighting Robert for control of Normandy. He even persuaded his brother to pawn Normandy to him for three years in return for 10,000 silver marks, so that Robert could go crusading. Normandy would have been gobbled up for good had William not died in New Forest while out hunting. He was shot "accidentally" by a henchman named Walter Tirel who wisely fled the scene and was never officially heard of again. The King was buried under the tower of Winchester Cathedral. It seemed to contemporary clerics justly symbolic that the tower collapsed the following year, but they had to admit "it had been badly built."

Henry I (1100–1135)

Henry I, the youngest of the Conqueror's three sons, was with his brother in New Forest when Tirel's arrow found its way into William's heart. Leaving the body where it fell, Henry galloped posthaste to

Winchester, seized possession of the royal treasury, and then took off for London and a hastily arranged coronation in Westminster Abbey. Finally, three days after the shooting (murder?), he gathered up his brother's body and had it properly buried. Poor Robert in the meantime was out in the cold a second time, having gotten only as far as Italy on his return from his crusade. The two brothers eventually fought it out, Robert coveting England and Henry desiring Normandy. Robert lost, and spent the last 28 years of his life—he lived to be 80—in Cardiff Castle in Wales. Henry, the first literate English King since Alfred, was a bookish man "not prone to personal combat." He possessed, however, a knack for ruling and maintaining the peace. He has come down in history as "the lion of justice," a beast not without its cruelty, as when he ordered that 80 of his minters, who had been caught debasing the royal coinage, should have their right hands and both testicles cut off. He sired three legitimate offspring and 20, possibly 21, bastards, and earned the title of "glorious father of his country."

When he died at 67 (legend says he exploded) of a surfeit of lamprey (eels) for which he had an uncontrollable passion, he left behind a succession crisis because his only legitimate heir was his headstrong and explosive daughter Matilda, and her unpopular husband Count Geoffrey of Anjou. Since Matilda had prompted her husband into a family quarrel with her father over feudal lands during the last year of Henry's life, the King at his deathbed was surrounded by supporters of two other candidates to the throne—his favorite bastard, Robert Earl of Gloucester, and his nephew Stephen. Matilda's timing was just as bad as her Uncle Robert's had been, and she too missed the throne of England.

Matilda and Stephen (1135–1154)

Most royal genealogies do not count Matilda as a proper British sovereign—this is why Elizabeth II is only the 42nd and not the 43rd monarch—because, although she fought her cousin Stephen for 12 years for the throne, she was never crowned, while he was. The best she could contrive was the title of "Lady of England and Normandy," not Queen. Matilda was not popular with the people who counted—mostly barons in England and Normandy. Although it was rumored she had "the nature of a man in the frame of a woman," Matilda was still a woman.

Stephen, on the other hand, was not only a man, but also the richest landowner in England, and he moved with lightning speed to secure the Crown, seizing the royal treasury in Winchester and arranging to be anointed King by the Archbishop of Canterbury. No one could now deny he was the legitimate monarch, but his anointing inaugurated almost a generation of anarchy and war in which nobody profited except possibly the barons. "Christ and his saints" indeed slept. Stephen was aptly reported to be "a mild man and gentle and good, and did no justice." Everyone gave a sigh of relief in 1153 when he was forced to accept Matilda's son Henry Plantagenet as his legitimate heir. Nine months later, Stephen died and even the barons, seemed to have been glad to see him go.

A generation of anarchy during which "Christ and his saints" slept.

Henry II (1154–1189)

The mixture of political power with murderous family wrangling and the presence of two attractive but immensely strong-willed personalities have proven to be irresistible to Hollywood film writers and dramatists alike. Henry II and Eleanor of Aquitaine have been the favorite subjects of both. Henry and Eleanor married on 12 May, 1152, two years before Henry became King of England. He was 19; she was 30 or 31. It was the most portentous union of the century, because Henry was Duke of Normandy, Count of Anjou and acknowledged heir to the English throne, and Eleanor was Duchess of Aquitaine and Countess of Poitou; their marriage joined more than half of France with England under a single ruler. Impulsive and lecherous, charming and charismatic, scornful of ceremony and rich attire, and such a omnivorous reader that he made "every day a school day," Henry's energy and restlessness exhausted everyone about him. He never sat down except to eat or ride, which meant that his courtiers had to stand whenever the King was present, and he was forever on the move, perambulating about his realms checking that his will was enforced. One can hardly blame an overworked servant for complaining that his court was "a perfect portrait of hell." The King needed all his strength and intelligence to keep his family and wife under control and his warring feudal empire together. In the end he failed at both.

Eleanor was a divorcée, the mother of two daughters by Louis XI of France, whom she had divorced on grounds of consanguinity and incompatibility: he was more monk than husband. Sharp, witty, highly educated and at home in high society from Paris to Rome and on to Antioch and the Holy Land, Eleanor attracted tales of adultery and intrigue like flies to sweet candy. She gave her young husband eight children—five sons and three daughters—and enough trouble to satisfy any modern soap opera. She allegedly murdered one of her husband's mistresses, the fair Rosamond, a "masterpiece of nature," and, after that lady's death, imprisoned yet another of his concubines. She acted as an agent provocateur, fanning family quarrels and setting her sons against their father, so much so that Henry's last words to his heir, Richard, were "May God not let me die until I have avenged myself on you as you deserve."

Henry in his turn tried to get the Pope to allow him to repudiate Eleanor and, when His Holiness refused, he clapped his wife in prison for the remaining 16 years of his life. But even behind stone walls Eleanor remained a dangerous enemy, because she was a great feudal magnate in her own rights with a thousand vassals owing her service, and she was the mother of sons whom she continued to influence against her husband. After his death, she set up her own court in Aquitaine and became one of the central political players during the reigns of her sons, Richard and John. She died at 82. As one chronicler understated her career, she was "a very intelligent woman . . . but unsteady."

Eleanor offering Rosamond her choice: death by dagger or poison

Richard I (1189–1199)

Richard I has had a mixed press. For his own generation, he was a paragon of a monarch—the embodiment of the Christian knight who dedicated his life to God, war and fine poetry—but for many modern historians he remains something of a villain: "a bad son, a bad brother, a bad husband and a bad king." Undeniably Richard was a bad son; certainly Henry II thought so. Whether Richard was also a bad brother is more doubtful, if only because his siblings were even less faithful than he. As for his husbandly behavior, in all probability Richard was a homosexual, and married Berengaria of Navarre at 34 solely for political purposes. Finally, his performance as a king is judged by English historians, uninterested in his chivalry, crusades and French possessions, as a total failure. It is invariably pointed out that in a reign of ten years he spent a total of less than six months in his island Kingdom. As an English sovereign, his sole contribution to government seems to have been his successful testing of the efficiency of the financial and administrative structure created by his father; the Kingdom was able to raise the staggering sum of £100,000 to pay his ransom when he was imprisoned by the Duke of Austria while en route home from crusading in the Holy Land. Richard died from an arrow in his shoulder, defending his possessions in France. He broke off the shaft and ignored the wound till the fighting was over; the physician botched the extraction of the arrowhead and was appropriately executed for malpractice; the wound became infected and Richard died begging that he be buried as close to his father as possible so, it was reported, "he might ask him forgiveness in another world."

John (1199–1216)

John rivals Richard III as the all-time wicked King, but unlike Richard, only the psychological historians have sought to reestablish his reputation. He was a psychotic, and that presumably absolves all. John was a Richard Nixon figure—immensely able and immensely flawed. Indeed, had he not been such a strong-willed and administratively capable sovereign, who could milk his feudal financial rights to their limits and beyond, there would have been no Magna Charter. John was Henry's favorite son, but this did not prevent him from joining the bandwagon of enemies and conspiring against his father. News of John's treason killed Henry, and his last coherent words were "It is enough . . . . I care no more for myself nor for ought in this world."

King John in one of his usual rages

John had been married for financial reasons to his half-first cousin Isabella of Gloucester, the richest heiress in England, but shortly after the coronation in 1199 he fell madly in love with another Isabella, heiress to the French county of Angoulême, a young girl of 18 already engaged to a neighboring lord. John arranged for the Pope to grant him an annulment of his first marriage—note Henry VIII asked no more than John but couldn't manage it—and married the young lady. Her outraged ex-fiancé immediately teamed up with King Philip of France and Arthur Plantagenet, John's 16-year-old nephew and rival claimant to the English throne. Together they started a war that eventually ended in the loss of all of John's French inheritance, except for a part of southern Aquitaine. In the early stages of this conflict, John was successful, and, with the help of his 80-year-old mother, succeeded in capturing Arthur, who promptly disappeared into captivity never to be seen again. Murder by order of John has never been proved, but among the other negative titles John has acquired over the years is that of "wicked uncle" which rivals that of Richard III. Possibly the kindest words that can be said of John are those of the 17th-century historian Sir Richard Baker: "Having his royal posterity continued to this day, we can do no less than honor his memory."

Henry III (1216–1272)

Henry III mounted the throne in 1216 at the age of nine. Given his youth, his life expectancy might not have been great had it not been for the lack of potentially wicked uncles to usurp his throne. Even with no ambitious relatives to plague him, his succession was difficult enough. There was no crown—his father had lost it in the quicksand—and he had to be adorned hurriedly with a makeshift crown because the barons were still in revolt and the French had sent over an army to help them. Fortunately, once John was gone to his doubtful reward, the barons' complaints died with him and most of them turned on their French allies, allowing Henry to begin his 56-year reign. The young King turned out to be an exceedingly pious, generally amiable, albeit erratic, monarch who, if not plagued by wicked uncles, was engulfed by rapacious relatives. His mother, deprived 14 years before of her fiancé Hugh de Lusignan, promptly married Lusignan and begot a gaggle of children who, as soon as they grew up, turned to their royal half-brother for the good things of life. Then there was Henry's wife Eleanor of Provence and all her relatives who crossed the Channel for the wedding and stayed. Her uncle Boniface of Bellay was named Archbishop of Canterbury and another uncle, Thomas of Savoy, was created Earl of Richmond and given land on the Thames River, where he built Savoy Palace, the present site of the Savoy Hotel on the Strand. An incompetent, over-generous and easily influenced King, Henry was exceptional both in his good taste in architecture and his fidelity. He was devoted and faithful to his wife and rebuilt Westminster Abbey in its present French High Gothic style in honor of his royal ancestor and favorite saint, Edward the Confessor (canonized in 1161) for whom he named his eldest son Edward, the first of the Norman-Plantagenet kings to bear an English name.

Henry III, an incompetent, overgenerous and easily influenced King

Edward I (1272–1307)

Whatever Henry's failings may have been as a sovereign, he was a highly successful father; his sons were singularly un-Plantagenet in their devotion to him and remained loyal throughout his long reign. The eldest, Edward, stood in for Henry as he declined into his dotage, and, by the time he succeeded at 33 to the throne in 1272, was a seasoned warrior and ruler. To celebrate his coronation there was eating and drinking for two weeks. Three hundred and eighty head of cattle, 430 sheep, 450 pigs, 18 wild boars and 20,000 birds of various kinds were consumed; a "good feed" to which the King of Scotland brought 100 knights to do homage to the new King.

Edward was everything his father was not. Tall—6'2" (we know, because his tomb was opened in the 18th century by curious antiquarians)—dark-haired and handsome, his presence and violent personality were so great that, when he raged at the dean of St. Paul's Cathedral, the unfortunate cleric dropped dead, literally. Edward has come down in history as the Justinian of England, the law-giver, and during his reign "the very scheme, mould and model of the common law was set in order," and the concept of statutory or legislated law, as opposed to customary law, emerged. But law without ruthless execution remains parchment law, and Edward did not hesitate to enforce his will via the law in a savage manner. Under Edward, a new punishment for treason was introduced: the traitor was ignominiously dragged behind a horse to the place of execution, hanged, cut down while still conscious, castrated, disemboweled and the body decapitated and quartered. In the case of really important criminals, the head was impaled on a pole and exposed on London Bridge. This is what happened to David Llewellyn, one of the heroes of Wales, and to William Wallace, the hero of Scotland. There is also gruesome evidence—a bit of skin was found in living memory—that Edward revived the old Saxon custom of flaying alive anyone who had robbed a church and of nailing the skin to its door. In 1303 this seems to have been the fate inflicted on some monks who sought to rob the King's treasures stored for safe keeping at Westminster Abbey.

On a more gentle note, Edward married Eleanor of Castile. He was 15, she was nine. Her title of Infanta of Castile caused the English endless pronouncing difficulties until it was corrupted into Elephant and Castle, thereby naming a pub and the last stop on the Bakerloo subway line. The marriage was a long and happy one, producing 15 children (possibly even two more). When Eleanor, aged 44, died at Harby in Nottinghamshire, Edward constructed stone crosses—"Eleanor crosses"—at every place her funeral entourage stopped each night en route to London. Charing Cross just outside the old City of London was the final stop, and that is how it got its name.

Edward I, a seasoned warrior and ruler at 33

Edward II (1307–1327)

Edward II, alone among British kings, has never found even a revisionist historian willing to defend him. Magnificent to look at—"fair of body and great of strength"—inwardly he was a disaster both as a man and as a king. He was a dilettante and "a trifler" who liked bricklaying, roof thatching, rowing and swimming—not accomplishments admired by his barons. Worse, he had a tendency, as one scholar has tactfully expressed it, "to engage in emotionally charged relationships with ambitious young men and to fall hopelessly under their influence." Unfortunately these "ambitious young men" also did not endear themselves to the barons, and they were certainly not popular with Edward's wife, Isabella of France. She gave him two sons and two daughters, which shows that Edward was quite capable of doing his royal duty and fathering children when he put his mind to it. Unfortunately this was not often, since Edward was enamored first of a young Frenchman named Piers Gaveston and then of Hugh Despenser the Younger, a handsome and able young Englishman. In the end the neglected Isabella contrived her husband's downfall. She and Roger Mortimer, a powerful lord of the Welsh border who had become her bedmate in the King's absence, and young Prince Edward, the 14-year-old heir to the throne, in league with a menagerie of disgruntled barons and a hired continental mercenary army, overthrew Despenser, captured the King, arranged for Parliament to depose him, forced him to abdicate in favor of his son, and had him murdered.

The story that he died from a funnel being placed up his rectum into which a red-hot poker was shoved so that no external signs of death would be observable is a fairly well-documented legend that can be neither proven nor denied. In fact, most people closely associated with Edward II met sticky ends. Gaveston was hanged and his body left to be eaten by starving dogs. Despenser was barbarously hanged, drawn and quartered, "chopping off his genitals and burning them before his eyes." The King's first cousin, the powerful Thomas Earl of Lancaster, was beheaded, and Roger Mortimer in his turn was overthrown in 1330 by young Edward III, who decided at 17 that it was time to rule in his own right. Mortimer was hanged at Tyburn as a traitor. Only Isabella, known by her detractors as the "She-Wolf of France," escaped with her life, being placed in comfortable imprisonment by her son for the remaining 28 years of her life.

Edward II, resigning his Crown

Edward III (1327–1377)

As a boisterous and optimistic young king of 17, steeped in the chivalric haze of King Arthur and his Round Table of heroic knights, Edward won the glory and renown he craved during the first decades of the Hundred Year's War. But the only lasting mark he made on British history was his founding of the Order of the Garter and his begetting of a plethora of sons.

Legend has it that Edward plucked from the dance floor the fallen garter of a damsel in embarrassed distress. Another version says it was the Countess of Salisbury who dropped her garter to attract the King's lecherous eye. Whichever way, Edward picked up the feminine apparel; as he returned it, he coined the motto *honi soit qui mal y pense* (disgrace to him who thinks evil); and immediately established the Most Noble Order of the Garter, consisting of himself, his eldest son and 24 knightly companions. Each knight was assigned a cubicle in St. George's Chapel at Windsor Castle where the regalia of the order is still paraded—one of the most magnificent displays of feudal pomp and circumstance anywhere in the world.

Two versions of the origin of the Order of the Garter

Edward's fecundity was almost as magnificent: seven sons and five daughters. Of his sons, six grew into Plantagenet giants—Lionel was the tallest standing 6'7"—and five sired offspring to confuse and confound the succession for the next 108 years. When the old King died in 1377, he left behind as his heir his grandson, the ten-year-old Richard II. It was a sad and inglorious end to a reign that had started with so much vigor and success. Senility (Alzheimer's?) set in as Edward reached his sixties, and he died a helpless and manipulated old man of 65 in bed with his mistress who immediately absconded with the rings on his fingers.

Richard II (1377–1399)

Richard had many of the faults of both John and Edward II—a bad combination. He was a strong King in that he conceived of royal power in the grand and medieval manner of Henry II and Edward I, but he exercised it ineptly, without regard to the changed political reality of his day. Barons and Parliament were far stronger than in any time in the past. He was like Edward II in that he also was something of a dilettante, was captivated by the regalia and symbolism of royal authority but ignored its substance, invented the pocket handkerchief (his barons preferred their sleeves), liked bathing (a most unmanly trait), and dressed up, it was said, in apparel covered with jewels worth £1,000 (a living yearly wage was about £2.5). In a sad way, his coronation symbolized his reign. The little ten-year-old boy King whose head was too small for his crown was expected to endure the entire exhausting coronation ceremony. He fell asleep before it was over and had to be carried out of Westminster Abbey and put to bed.

It speaks well for Richard's uncles that they let him grow to manhood, but from an avuncular perspective, their restraint turned out to be something of a mistake. In 1397 Richard had his uncle Thomas Duke of Gloucester murdered, and the next year exiled Henry Bolingbroke, the son and heir of his uncle John of Gaunt, first for six years, then for life. Since Bolingbroke was in his own rights and through his wife one of the richest barons in the land, and, on the death of his father, became Duke of Lancaster, he was a magnate more powerful than the King himself. So maybe it was wise to ship him off to France.

Richard had been devoted to his wife Anne of Bohemia, and when she died in 1394, he built in Westminster Abbey a magnificent double tomb with effigies of the two of them eternally holding hands. After Anne's death, Richard changed dramatically, becoming increasingly moody, unpredictable and despotic, qualities that led to his overthrow, enforced abdication and death in 1399. Lancastrian sources maintain that Richard "perished heartbroken" of sheer melancholy (aka starving or being starved to death); other sources name Sir Piers Exton as the murderer. Whatever the truth, there was no place among the living for an ex-King, now simply known as Sir Richard of Bordeaux, in the plans of the new Lancastrian monarch, born Henry Bolingbroke, but now Henry IV of England.

Richard II, now simply known as Sir Richard of
Bordeaux, dying of sheer melancholy

Henry IV (1399–1413)

Once an over-mighty subject had usurped the throne, a dangerous precedent had been set, and Henry spent most of his reign fighting to survive, especially when some of his erstwhile baronial friends decided that the new King was not being sufficiently grateful for their help in winning him a throne. Fortunately, Henry in 1399 was a veteran warrior of 42, skilled in war and government, and as anyone who has read the Shakespearean account knows, he triumphed over Welsh and baronial rebels who were attempting to divide his Kingdom among them. Victory, however, came at a price. The physical and nervous strain was too great, and Henry became a neurotic hypochondriac plagued by severe eczema which contemporaries confused with leprosy visited by God in punishment for his seizing his cousin's crown. The concluding years of his life were troubled by the dilemma of all monarchs—the relationship between a ruling sovereign and his heir who is a potential king. The story that young Prince Henry of Monmouth tried on his father's crown while the King still lived is Shakespearean fiction, but it symbolizes the strain between a dying King and a highly capable and impatient successor. The end came on March 30th, 1413, and one of England's most memorable and glamorous monarchs mounted the throne.

Henry IV under great physical and nervous strain

Henry V (1413–1422)

Richard Coeur de Lion remained the kingly ideal, not Henry II and the builders of strong royal government. Richard I had combined chivalry with piety, military prowess with crusading zeal. Young Henry V could do no less. The age of crusading was over in 1413, but the military code and the language of chivalry still held the 15th-century mind in bondage, and given the priorities expressed in Prince Hal's educational expenses—"eight pence for harp strings, twelve pence for a scabbard, four pence for seven books of grammar in one volume"—it is not surprising that the young King remembered Edward III's glorious victory over the French and his family claim to the French throne, and renewed the ancient conflict between the two countries. As a legendary ideal—loyal, honorable and chivalric—Henry does not bear too close inspection. His feet may not have been of clay, but they were certainly of iron. When at 25 he succeeded his father, he was already a veteran campaigner, a professional soldier possessed of endless energy and the mystique of leadership. He was driven by the conviction that victory in war was a matter not of numbers but of "the power of God." The new King was not just conventionally orthodox in his faith. He was a fanatic in the intensity with which he held to his creed, a quality the religious heretics of his nine-year reign learned to their sorrow. What Henry's reputation would have been had he lived to see the first glow of foreign conquest extinguished by the bloody ordeal and expense of defending his newly acquired French territories, cannot even be guessed—Henry was an extraordinarily able administrator as well as warrior—but at 35 he could not have expired at a more opportune moment with his renown untarnished. Lord Byron was right: "Heaven gives its favorites—early death."

Henry VI (1422–1461, 1470–71)

Henry VI cannot be said to have "mounted" the throne when his father died in 1422; he was after all only nine months old. He suffered two uncles and a clutch of Plantagenet cousins determined to give him "good" advice and/or relieve him of his crown. As a singularly unkingly, peace-loving, and dangerously prodigal sovereign with an exceedingly ambitious and strong-willed French wife, his reign staggered along off and on for 40 years, interrupted by spells of insanity and enforced abdication. No wonder he ended up murdered in the Tower of London. The only thing that is surprising is that he wasn't dispatched sooner. Bringing up and educating a king is a ticklish business—the schoolboy may grow up to avenge himself on his educators—and Henry's "very dear and well beloved" councilors thoughtfully arranged, when the infant monarch had reached the age of two, to have him grant them permission to "reasonably chastise us from time to time." Then to be doubly sure, they insisted on the assurance that his teachers would "not be molested, hurt or injured for this cause in future time." Their fears were groundless; Henry grew up caring far more for "his soul's health" than for revenge upon his educators. He did, however achieve a certain memorability. He founded King's College of Our Lady of Eton Beside Windsor (today contracted to Eton) arguably Britain's most prestigious public (really private) boarding school and an institution that confers upon its 1100-plus students "a lifetime's innate consciousness of effortless superiority." Henry eventually sired (rumor had it that his wife had considerable help from other sources) a son, and he finally expired in the fiftieth year of his life of what contemporaries cautiously described as "pure displeasure and melancholy" (aka death by unknown means).

Henry VI mounting the throne

Edward IV (1461–70, 1471–83)

The man who twice replaced Henry VI on the throne was his 19-year-old distant cousin Edward Duke of York, distant biologically—Edward was the King's third cousin twice removed—but dangerously close dynastically, for should Henry's son die, Edward was the legal heir to the throne. Edward, of course, did not wait for this happy event to occur. After his triumph in 1461 over Lancastrian forces at the Battle of Towton, he locked Henry up in the Tower and proclaimed himself king. For nine years England had two anointed sovereigns. What kept Henry alive was the presence in France of his young son, the Prince of Wales—no use dispatching the father if there were a son to claim his crown. Not until 1470–71, when the wars of the conflicting roses gave a final convulsion (Edward was overthrown and fled to the Lowlands; Henry was restored, but Edward returned to remount the throne and kill the Lancastrain Prince of Wales in battle), did the first Yorkist King secure his title for good by having poor demented Henry VI quietly finished off in the Tower.

Edward was everything his predecessor was not. Six foot three and a half inches tall, he was the perfect image of a king, not in the least worried about his soul, careful about money, and extremely fertile—five daughters and two sons. The only flaw in an otherwise perfect ointment was that Edward ate, drank, and wenched himself into an early and unexpected grave at the age of 40, leaving behind his 31-year-old brother Richard as Lord Protector to his 12-year-old son Edward V.

Poor demented Henry VI in the Tower of London

Edward V (April 9–July 6, 1483)

Since young Edward reigned only 98 days, there isn't much to say about him except to ask the five-century-old unresolved question: who finished him and his brother off? Uncle Richard of Gloucester remains the prime suspect. Once he arranged for his nephews to be declared illegitimate and for the citizens of London to "offer" him the Crown, Richard had motive, opportunity, and historic precedent for removing two potential threats to his newly acquired throne. Legend, however, is a trifle vague as to the precise method of execution. "Some said they were murdered between two feather beds; some said they were drowned in Malmsey [wine]; and some said they were pierced with a venomous potion." Moreover, since much of the evidence against Uncle Richard is suspect, there are those who vigorously argue that either the boys died of natural causes—the bubonic plague, cholera, smallpox, to name just a few—or someone else managed the dirty deed. High on that list is Henry Earl of Richmond, the future Henry VII, who might have had pressing cause to do away with Edward IV's sons if they were still alive after his victory over Richard III at Bosworth Field, but so far no one has come up with convincing proof of this crucial point. Rather doubtful motives have been assigned to the Plantagenet Duke of Buckingham, who might have hoped to advance his own claim to the throne by framing Richard with the murders, and to the Duke of Norfolk, who as a claimant to the Mowbray estates, originally assigned by Edward IV to his second son, presumably would have profited from the boys' deaths. Finally, there is the theory that the children escaped, and that the bones discovered under the Tower stairs were imported to confuse King Richard and prevent a search for the young princes. This is a solution dear to the hearts of both modern novelists and contemporary Yorkists who used the myth as an excuse for a series of artful impersonations and conspiracies to divest Henry VII of his crown.

Edward V, too small for his crown

Richard III (1483–85)

Along with Henry VIII, Edward VIII and currently Prince Charles, Richard III continues to command stage center in the royal soap opera. His death alone is still remembered, and every year on August 22nd—the date of Bosworth Field—there appears in the *New York Times* and elsewhere, a memoriam to a King who generates more partisan debate than any other British monarch. It all started when the new Tudor sovereign vindictively blackened Richard's reputation. To murder a man was indeed "odious" (the 16th century assigned three such deaths to Richard: Henry VI in the Tower, his son on the field of battle, and the Duke of Clarence in a keg of Malmsey wine); to kill a woman was "unnatural" (the rumor that Richard had poisoned his wife was carefully cultivated); "but to slay and destroy innocent babes . . . the whole world abhorreth." (No one could forgive a usurper who had won his throne through double infanticide.) In the hands first of Sir Thomas

More and then of William Shakespeare, Richard became a monster, the devil incarnate who enjoyed deceit, dissimulation, and murder for the sheer pleasure of doing evil. Slander on such a scale spawns doubt, and eventually passionate defense. Richard in the 20th century has become "the Faultless King and Martyr," his reputation ruthlessly crucified by historians and playwrights in the pay of the Tudor Crown.

Today Richard's good name is preserved by the Richard III Society (also called the White Boar Society) which militantly maintains that the last of the Yorkist Kings was a fair-minded, constructive, and efficient monarch who, had he lived, would have successfully made history forget the manner by which he acquired his crown. But, alas, his dead body was dragged naked from Bosworth Field, unceremoniously interred at Grey Friars in the city of Leicester, and, when that monastery was destroyed by the second of the Tudor monarchs, his bones thrown into the river Soar. All that constructive potential, if it ever existed, was never realized.

Richard III commanding stage center

Henry VII (1485–1509)

Henry VII was Shakespeare's closet hero. The victor of Bosworth Field joined the warring roses of York and Lancaster when he married Elizabeth, the elder sister of the murdered princes in the Tower, and the Bard was quite certain that heaven had smiled upon "this fair conjunction" and as a consequence England had been blessed thereafter "with smoothe-fac'd peace, with smiling plenty, and fair prosperous days." Yet Shakespeare never wrote a play about Henry, because he lacked the fatal flaws of Richard II, the heroics of Henry V, the villainy of Richard III or the flamboyance of his son, Henry VIII. The best the seventh Henry could achieve was to pluck his crown off a hawthorn bush where it was found after the battle of Bosworth Field. The first of the Tudors was simply too average and too successful to make good copy for any dramatist and, after his wife died in 1503, he became depressingly avaricious and faintly ridiculous when he offered himself as an eligible bachelor in the diplomatic game of exchanging marriage vows for fat dowries. Nevertheless, Henry made few political blunders, was willing to forgive his Yorkist enemies when they proved their loyalty to him, and could, in the face of great provocation, be surprisingly compassionate.

The greatest bane of his reign was a surfeit of pretenders. The younger of the little murdered princes refused to remain quietly in his grave, and the legend arose that he had miraculously escaped both death and imprisonment and was claiming his rightful place on the throne as Richard IV. Equally unsettling was the story that Edward IV's nephew, the child Earl of Warwick whom Henry had secured away in the Tower, was in fact abroad, claiming to be Edward VI. These tales took on political and military reality when a young boy named Lambert Simnel, who proclaimed himself to be the liberated Earl of Warwick and rightful King of England, appeared at the head of a large Yorkist army. At the Battle of Stokes in June of 1487, his Yorkist forces were defeated and Simnel demoted from potential king to scullery boy in the royal kitchen where, by dint of hard work, he rose to the rank of king's falconer. Four years later the reincarnated Richard IV appeared in the person of Perkin Warbeck, a 17-year-old Flemish lad, blessed with Yorkist good looks and a regal presence. He persuaded much of Europe that he was the mysteriously missing prince in the Tower. (As one of George V's grandchildren remarked, Warbeck was "some one who pretended he was the son of a king, but he wasn't really; he was the son of respectable parents.") Warbeck fared no better than Simnel. He was captured in an abortive invasion of England but allowed to live, at least until the incurably optimistic mountebank, in company with the actual Earl of Warwick, tried to escape from the Tower. At that point Henry had them both executed.

Lambert Simnel demoted from a potential king to a scullery boy

Henry VII made only one serious mistake during his reign; he refused to listen to the pleas of Bartholomew Columbus, who came to England on behalf of his brother Christopher to raise money for his proposed trip to China via the Atlantic Ocean. Had he done so, the wealth of the Indies might have belonged to England, not Spain, and the history of the world unrecognizably changed. He did, however, leave behind, if not a world empire, his spectacular chapel with its exquisite high Gothic fan tracery supporting the ceiling. There, attached to Westminster Abbey, the visitor will find Torrigiano's (famous for having broken Michelangelo's nose), magnificent gilded bronze effigies of the King and his Queen resting on a black marble base.

Henry VIII (1509–47)

The moment Henry VIII was stuffed into a great leaden chest and on February 16, 1547, buried under the floor of St. George's chapel in Windsor Castle, he became possibly England's most memorable, certainly its most notorious, sovereign. The American Medical Association targeted him as a frightful example of the consequences of overindulgence. (His waistline was 54 inches. We know because his final suit of armor is on display in the Tower of London.) His matrimonial calamities thrust their way into the privacy of every home in the TV series *The Six Wives of Henry VIII*, starring Keith Michell; and his table manners have been etched upon our minds by the Hollywood production of *The Private Life of Henry VIII* in which Charles Laughton is forever slobbering at the mouth and throwing his chicken bones over his shoulder.

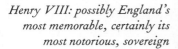
Henry VIII: possibly England's most memorable, certainly its most notorious, sovereign

In Henry, we are obviously dealing with a powerful and enduring personality, and over the centuries he has elicited the strongest kind of language, both pro and con. Charles Dickens accused the second Tudor of being "a disgrace to human nature and a blot of blood and grease upon the history of England." More recently, Jasper Ridley has turned the King into a modern dictator, modeled on Stalin, and warned that "Henry won the support of the majority of his people by appealing to their worst instincts—to their hatred of Scots and Frenchmen, of idealists, martyrs and 'do-gooders,' [and] to their willingness to denounce their neighbors to the authorities." (Not a pleasant portrait of the monarch or the English people!) At the other end of the language spectrum there is Professor A.F. Pollard's optimistic appraisal that Bluff King Hal "sought the greatness of England, and he spared no toil in the quest. . . . Surrounded by faint hearts and fearful minds he neither faltered nor failed."

Historians and moralists delight in passing judgment upon the past. Contemporaries, however, were considerably more cautious and restrained. William Thomas, writing shortly after the old King died, pronounced a verdict that is difficult to dispute: "He was undoubtedly the rarest man that lived in his time. . . . I say not this to make him a god, nor in all his doings I will not say he hath been a saint . . . [but] I wot not where in all the histories I have read to find one private king equal to him."

The battle, of course, still rages, and there are those who insist that syphilis changed Henry from an angelic-faced athlete blessed with boundless good heath into a tyrant, degenerate both in body and in soul. The syphilis theory is an invention of the late 19th century, and unfortunately there is not a hint of such an affliction in the French, Venetian or Imperial Ambassadorial reports. Foreign Ambassadors should have known; they were paid to report at length on the health of kings, and the Spanish Ambassador under Elizabeth I kept a spy in the royal laundry to check on the Queen's menstrual periods. Under the circumstance, it is probably best to leave the final word to the French Ambassador who knew Henry as well as anybody. The King, he said, was "a man to be marveled at and has wonderful people about him. . . . He is an old fox, proud as the devil and accustomed to ruling." (The place to imagine Henry is in his palace of Hampton Court which can be reached by car, bus or Thames riverboat from London.)

Henry VIII, a man "accustomed to ruling."

Edward VI, Lady Jane Grey and Mary I (1547–58)

The personalities and lives of Henry's descendants were irredeemably scarred and shaped by the constitutional and spiritual revolution he introduced. Edward grew from a frail and impish lad, who received the best humanistic education his father could supply, and who thanked his tutors for pointing out his faults, into a priggish teenager who paraded a puritanical conscience that allowed no one to "set light God's will" for the sake of political expediency.

Had he lived his allotted years, he might have turned into a savage Protestant Joshua—just and crusading but devoid of compassion. As it was, he died in the odor of Biblical sanctity four months short of his 16th birthday, crying out to God to save "this realm from papistry and maintain Thy true religion."

Had Edward VI lived his allotted years, he might
have turned into a savage Protestant Joshua

Given the boy King's religious ardor, Edward himself, not the Duke of Northumberland, may well have been the instigator of the King's famous "Device for the Succession." The traditional explanation is to portray Northumberland as "the evil duke" who, because he faced political ruin should Catholic Mary Tudor come to the throne, married his son, Guildford Dudley, to Lady Jane Grey, and then persuaded the dying Edward to exclude both Mary and Elizabeth from the succession and will his Crown to Northumberland's new daughter-in-law, Henry VIII's grand niece and a fervent Protestant. More recently, historians have begun to suspect that Edward himself composed this device exactly as he wanted it, leaving the Duke the thankless job of enforcing its provisions, which he did with such ineptitude that it almost guaranteed failure. Either way, a young girl of 16, who had to be beaten by her parents into marrying Guildford Dudley, suddenly and much against her will found herself Queen of England. She reigned for nine days before Edward's device collapsed; Mary was proclaimed Queen; and Jane and her husband carted off to the Tower. The new Queen was merciful. She did not immediately demand her cousin's head, but six months later, when faced with a rebellion that nearly toppled her throne, Mary changed her mind and the nine-day Queen and her husband were executed, a heavy price to pay for being accorded a place in the list of the Kings and Queens of England.

Mary persuaded herself to do away with her cousin, but despite endless advice to the contrary, she could never argue herself into executing a far greater danger to her crown, her half-sister, Elizabeth. The Spanish ambassador warned that "the Princess Elizabeth is greatly feared; she has a spirit full of incantation," and darkly suspected that her acceptance of Catholicism was faked. She was, he said, "too clever to get herself caught." But in the end, Mary's conscience and Tudor blood prevailed. Much to Elizabeth's delighted surprise, Mary drew the line at beheading Anne Boleyn's daughter, even though she regarded her as their father's bastard.

Elizabeth I (1558–1603)

"Fame," remarked Mark Twain, "is a rough business." On the face of it, Elizabeth I was a most improbable candidate for greatness. She was hopelessly anachronistic in her concept of government; her perspective was invariably parochial, never visionary; and, unlike her Protestant brother and Catholic sister, she was no crusader. God had given her the Crown of England and she intended to enjoy it.

The documents are laden with unpleasant evidence of her vanity, sarcasm, deceitfulness, ill temper, ingratitude, parsimony, and pride. She informed her early favorite, the Earl of Leicester, that the hand which had made him could "beat him to the dust," and she dismissed the entire House of Lords as "a collection of brains so light." She rewarded her ministers with temper tantrums and irrational tirades; delighted in showing off her wit and knowledge; and was forever fishing for compliments.

Elizabeth I: The documents are laden with unpleasant evidence of her vanity and pride

Though she never met Mary Stuart, she was intensely jealous of her cousin, asking the Scottish Ambassador who had the fairer hair, played better on the virginal, and was the better linguist. Wisely, the Ambassador avoided a direct answer, but when asked who was the taller, he admitted that Mary was. To which Elizabeth rejoined in a burst of Alice-in-Wonderland logic—then "she is too high, for I myself am neither too high nor too low."

Ministers bore their mistress's vanities, tantrums, and ill logic with patience, but what drove them to distraction was her procrastination. "For the love of God, madame," exploded Sir Francis Walsingham, "let not the cure of your diseased estate hang any longer in deliberation." Years later, the young Earl of Essex thought that the Bess of his generation was "no less crooked in mind than in body" and concluded that she "wrangles with our actions for no cause but because it is at hand."

How then did such an unlikely sovereign achieve fame both in her own lifetime and in the centuries to follow? As we have already seen, God performed a series of "unlooked-for-miracles" which assured that *Time* magazine would assign Elizabeth I as the most recognizable name of the 16th century. God, however, generally helps those who help themselves, and Elizabeth possessed three qualities that transformed the base metal of her personality into pure gold: she was a magnificent actress, her command of language rivaled Shakespeare's, and she was one of those rare princes who anguish over the relationship of means to ends—that is why she procrastinated so much. From the start, she understood her role as Queen. "We princes," she said, "are set as it were upon stages in the sight and view of the world." She demanded and held stage center and spoke her lines—always carefully rehearsed—with the grace of a consummate actress. "If ever any person," wrote Sir John Hayward of her coronation, "had either the gift or the style to win the hearts of people, it was their queen."

That gift was the product of talent and hard work, and Elizabeth warned that "to be a king and wear a crown is a thing more glorious to them that see it, than it is pleasant to them that bear it." The burden was not simply the drudgery of office—the scrutiny of detail that allowed her to know what Henry IV of France owed her down to the last half penny—but also the endless labor that went into producing the apparently effortless rhetoric that wrapped Her Majesty in a mantle of mystification so rich and colorful that no one knew exactly what she meant, but everybody agreed it was worth listening to—the sure mark of a brilliant politician.

Although Bess was a ruthless and calculating egotist, her conscience never fell victim to the theatrics of her office. She accepted her royal status as a marvelous dignity bestowed by God, but she assured her subjects "that the shining glory of princely authority hath not so dazzled the eyes of our understanding, but that we well know and remember that we also are to yield an account of our actions before the Great Judge." In her book of private devotions, she asked God to establish her Kingdom in peace, her Church in security, her reign in prosperity, her life in happiness, and for "myself at Thy good pleasure [to] be translated into immortality." The Deity may not have answered all of Gloriana's prayers to her full satisfaction, but given the enduring interest in "Elizabeth of good memory," she has certainly achieved a form of immortality.

Queen Elizabeth running through a "little thing" of her own composition to William Shakespeare

James I (1603–25)

Everyone in England was delighted to greet James VI of Scotland as the first English sovereign of that name. Government was a male prerogative, and the new King was eagerly anticipated as a happy change from the tiresome spinster ways of Elizabeth. Better yet, James had two sons to secure the succession and was known to be lavishly generous to his friends and supporters—a pleasant contrast to the parsimony of the late Queen. "The new broom," as James liked to call himself, although wise in the art of Scottish Kingship (which largely meant staying alive), was hopelessly lacking in the two qualities that spelled success south of the border: the gift of decorum and a sense of majesty. Revisionist historians have labored diligently to salvage James's reputation, but Thomas Macaulay's 19th-century words still remain embarrassingly close to the mark: he was a sorry excuse for a King, "stammering, slobbering, shedding unmanly tears, trembling at a drawn sword, and talking in the style alternately of a buffoon and a pedagogue."

James I, an unkingly King

Although James may have done nothing to cause the political and religious debacle of his son's reign, he bears a heavy responsibility for undermining respect for the Crown which was the rock upon which Elizabeth's government had rested. With the old Queen as the model, it is difficult to generate much respect for a King who refused to display himself to his subjects and crudely suggested that he might as well be asked to drop his britches and let them "see my arse"; who had a passion for costly clothing and jewelry, but always ended up looking ridiculous even by early 17th-century standards; who had a penchant for rewarding handsome young men of mean estate so long as they "frequently expressed their gratitude to their only begetter"; and who picked his nose in public and spoke out against smoking as "loathsome . . . and dangerous to the lungs" just at the moment that a lot of important people were acquiring the habit. The Scottish monarch was no fool, and he possessed considerable street smarts, but he was such an unkingly King and his reign so indecorous, crawling with "fools and bawds, mimics and catamites," that it was hard to maintain a proper reverence for monarchy. When James died, an observer commented that his funeral was "performed with great magnificence," but was hopelessly "confused and disorderly."

Charles I (1625–49)

Charles I was neither confused nor disorderly, and that was the source of most of his troubles. He possessed an exceedingly tidy and punctual mind, demonstrated exquisite good taste in everything save politics and human relations, and took with deadly seriousness his duties as the mystical father of his Kingdom and God's spokesman on earth. Unfortunately, he had the adaptability of a dinosaur, and so wrapped himself in the mantle of impenetrable divinity that he was incapable of the saving virtues that beset lesser mortals—affection, gratitude, forgiveness, and honesty. He was, noted one observer, "so constituted by nature that he never obliges anyone, either by word or deed." He was, confessed his staunchest supporter, Archbishop Laud, a "prince who knows not how to be or be made great." Charles's single obsession was his passion for decorum in politics, religion and the details of daily life. In an effort to make earthly reality conform to the cosmic theory of "degree, priority and place," he enforced for the first time in a hundred years the household regulations of Henry VIII: lesser officials could not dine in their own rooms at court but had to eat in the great hall, and the number of servants and horses they could keep was strictly regulated according to social rank and dignity of office. The most revealing decision the young King ever made was when he ordered the construction of a high wall around Richmond Park, his favorite residence, to keep the confusion and sordidness of the real world from encroaching upon the masques and murals of his fantasy world and upon his art collection, possibly the finest in the 17th century. (Most of it was sold by Oliver Cromwell and the military, but much was bought back after the Restoration and today constitutes the bulk of Elizabeth II's magnificent collection.)

In the recipe for governmental change, social, political and economic factors are clearly vital, but without the added ingredients of dullness, obtuseness, mental rigidity, and even well-meaningfulness on the part of kings and leaders, war and violent revolution would not occur.

Charles II (1660–85)

We have already seen that too much royal testosterone, resulting in a surfeit of claimants to the throne, as well as too few legitimate male off-spring can ball up the kingdom. Clearly the sperm count of a monarch and the fertility level of his spouse is an uncertain way to transfer political power from one generation to the next. In the case of Charles II, he achieved both extremes of danger: as a lover he was overly productive, as a royal stud he was a total failure. Charles possessed extraordinary sex appeal, but, of course, as King he had an unfair advantage over other men. Without counting the innumerable one-night stands, he possessed eleven recognized mistresses, and he sired 14 children, all illegitimate. Even his contemporaries were outspoken about their sovereign's sexual prowess and equipment, and John Wilmot, Earl of Rochester, always shocking, rhymed:

> *Nor are his high desires above his strength,*
> *His scepter and his p . . . are of a length,*
> *And she that plays with one may sway the other,*
> *And make him little wiser than his brother.*

. . .

> *Restless he rolls about from whore to whore,*
> *A merry monarch, scandalous and poor.*

Rochester was correct about the cost of Charles's mistresses, but not about their influence. There was little petticoat politics at court, and Charles was quick to announce that his interest in the opposite sex was confined to their bodies, not their souls. Nell Gwyn was a Prot-estant; Barbara Villiers, who was awarded the marvelous string of ti-tles—Duchess of Cleveland, Countess of Southampton and Baroness Nonsuch—was Catholic. Charles never allowed his sex life to interfere with his single political goal: never to go on his travels again. Despite exile and defeat, he escaped his mother's caustic Catholicism and his father's puritanical priggery. He emerged at 30 (a little like Elizabeth I) a ruler who was delighted to be alive to enjoy his throne, and he proved to be the most tolerant and civil monarch ever to wear the crown. His faith and his politics were both low-key. He worshiped a Deity who, he said, would "not damn a man for taking a little unregular pleasure by the way," and in the face of political and religious rudeness, he was invariably courteous. When the Quaker William Penn, out of egalitarian principle, kept his hat on while in the presence of the King, Charles removed his own bonnet. Penn rather unwisely asked, "Friend Charles, why dost thou not keep on thy hat?" Charles politely replied, "Tis the custom of this place that only one person should be covered at a time."

Wit and tact conjoined with deep cynicism about men's true motives, plus a great deal of salutary laziness, kept the political and religious beasts at bay, allowing Charles to concentrate on what he regarded as the really important things in life: first women, then tennis (at which he excelled), swimming, and gardening. He doted on clocks (he had seven in his bedroom); was fascinated with all aspects of science; founded the Royal Observatory at Greenwich, thereby creating zero meridian and Greenwich mean time; was the friend of Newton; and dabbled in alchemy. In fact, he may have died of mercury poisoning from one of his alchemical experiments.

The King's personality suited perfectly the political, intellectual and moral climate of his age, and he spoke the absolute truth when he laughingly assured his brother, who was criticizing him for his lack of security precautions: "Don't worry, Jamie. They'll never kill me to make you king."

Charles II possessed extraordinary sex appeal but as a King he had an unfair advantage

James II (1685–88)

Not even the first Charles, whose political insensitivity cost him his head, came close to his second son's level of religious obtuseness and political incompetence. James II was so inept he could not even arrange his own flight from the Kingdom without the help of the man who replaced him on the throne. The King's first try ended in failure and capture, and only when the future William III ordered everyone to look the other way was the second attempt successful.

James started off reasonably well as Duke of York and Lord Admiral of the Fleet. He was by far the handsomest of his Stuart clan, and diarist Samuel Pepys of the Admiralty was devoted to him, but then Mr. Pepys had some strange tastes. Actually, the Duke was not a bad administrator, but from the start he made a better bureaucrat than politician. He vastly admired the divinely inspired monarchy of his first cousin, Louis XIV of France, and James's conversion to Catholicism made his methodical authoritarian instincts all the more determined. All issues were either black or white, and his notion of debate was to state a proposition; if it was questioned, to reassert it exactly as before on the grounds that the truth needed no defense. "I will make no concessions," he often avowed; "my father made concessions and he was beheaded." Throughout the last half of his brother's reign, he was kept in virtual exile lest he say or do the politically incorrect thing.

Fortunately for England, and totally unlike his father, there resided behind James's graceless rigidity of mind and faith an exceedingly timid man who needed priest and minister to hold his hand. When both failed him, he panicked and fled in his hour of need to the safety of the Sun King across the Channel.

The Last of the Stuarts
William III/Mary II (1689–94); William (1694–1702); and Anne (1702–14)

It is surprising that the film industry has not latched on to the Stuart family; it has all the ingredients of grand-scale drama—family calamity confounded by high politics unto the fourth generation. The first James came into his Scottish inheritance in the wake of his father's murder, instigated by his mother, who promptly ran off and married his assassin.

That marriage led to civil war, abdication, and a series of events which ended 19 years later with Mary Stuart's execution by her Tudor cousin. James's son Charles brought down upon himself the destruction of his royal family in civil war and violence and was executed (family members would say murdered) as a traitor to his subjects, the "good people of England." Charles's second son James II managed in only four years to make possible his own enforced abdication, while two out of three of his children, plus his nephew, successfully committed regicide tainted with patricide.

The history of the last Stuart monarchs is usually told in terms of constitutional struggle, politics, and international war, as England emerged between 1689 and 1714 the dominant power in Europe. But from a family perspective, those years are the emotionally charged story of the efforts of Mary and Anne, the Protestant daughters of James by his first wife Anne Hyde, in league with Mary's husband, their first cousin William of Orange, to deprive their father of his throne and prevent his Catholic son from inheriting the Crown (see the chart on p. 248). Anne detested her cousin William, and as a consequence the sisters ended up barely speaking to each other. Of course, it did not help their relations that Anne had 18 pregnancies in 18 years while Mary proved to be barren. After Mary's death in 1694, Anne thought the Crown should have gone to her, not kept by her brother-in-law. Add to this that Mary always did precisely what her husband told her to do; that Anne was not very bright and was easily influenced; and that William judged every political issue and human relation solely in terms of how they helped or hindered him in protecting his Dutch provinces from Louis XIV's aggression; and you have the plot for a spectacular Hollywood script. Especially so if you reckon that Louis was a first cousin once removed, thereby making even international war a family quarrel.

The Great Seal of William and Mary

Of the three grandchildren, William III was the most enigmatic and interesting. He was a moody, taciturn, tactless man who had been flung into the whirlwind of Dutch rivalries and European politics. His father, Prince William of Orange and Stadholder of Holland, died of smallpox eight days before William's birth in 1650. Young William struggled with ill health, was severely asthmatic, and survived on sheer will power that belied his frail body. He was a man driven by a mission. He accepted the friendless and unpleasant role of a Dutch alien in England and usurper of the English Crown because that was the only way he could diminish the dangerous light of the Sun King of France. He learned to trust no one; turncoats had brought him to power; and they could just as easily evict him. His reign crawled with plots to unseat him. He hated the English court with its endless bickering and intrigue and vastly preferred the solitude and order of camp life. Yet for all his paranoia, William possessed a quietly wry sense of humor that enabled him to rhyme:

> *As I walk'd by myself*
> *And talk'd to myself,*
> *Myself said unto me,*
> *Look to thy self,*
> *Take care of thy self,*
> *For nobody cares for Thee.*
>
> *I answer'd myself*
> *And said to myself*
> *In the self-same Repartee*
> *Look to thy self*
> *Or not look to thy self*
> *The self-same thing will be.*

Mary was William's silent partner, both as a wife and a Queen. She was every inch a Stuart in her pride of lineage as the daughter of a King and in the passion with which she maintained her convictions. She had shed a torrent of tears at her wedding to Prince William, whom she could not abide, but she soon reversed her position, learned to like Holland better then England, and eventually wrote that her love for her husband was so great it could only end "with her life." Mary provided emotional and dynastic strength to William and his cause. She backed unconditionally the invasion and bid for the English throne, and was his greatest, possibly only, true friend in England. Equally important, she supplied the gloss of legitimacy to regicide, accepting with stoic dignity that her father had disowned and cursed his daughters, and she used her considerable charm to soften her husband's tactlessness and win him popular support. When Mary died of smallpox at 32, she left William personally stricken, alone, and dynastically vulnerable.

There is little to be said about Anne Stuart, except that she was the last of her Stuart line, was severely overweight, suffered terribly in later life from gout, and was hopelessly slatternly in her dress and hygiene. What made her reign important was the presence of General John Churchill. William III, her brother-in-law, had viewed the General with deep suspicion—he had betrayed James II, and treated his new Dutch King with only marginal respect—but with William's death in 1702, the Churchills—husband and wife—came into their own. Sarah Churchill became the satin eminence behind the throne, directing the executive power to support her husband's military policies and talents. There were, however, two ugly flies in an otherwise perfect ointment. Anne's affection for and dependence on her female favorites were passionate but volatile. She endured 12 miscarriages in her Herculean efforts to secure an heir, and all six of her children died. When the last child died, Parliament established the succession in the Protestant line, and Elector George of Hanover became the heir apparent to the English Crown. Unfortunately, Anne did not care for George; he had come to England years before to propose to her, had taken one look, and quickly returned home. As the Queen's children died off, Anne began to sense God's wrath at her part in dethroning her father and barring his son. When her affection for Sarah Churchill (now the Duchess of Marlborough) turned to "indifference and aversion," Marlborough lost his influence at court, and this allowed the peace party to negotiate a settlement with France in 1713. Peace permitted Anne to approach her Catholic half-brother, known to his Stuart friends as James III, but to his Protestant enemies as the Pretender. If James would renounce his Catholicism, Anne would pressure Parliament into revoking the Protestant-Hanoverian succession. Fortunately for Hanoverian George, James did not consider England worth an Anglican communion, and the Stuart dynasty died with the Queen.

The Four Georges: I (1714–27), II (1727–60), III (1760–1820), IV (1820–30)

James III may not have figured a British Crown worth a Protestant conversion, but he was more than willing to fight for his regal rights, at least in a dithering and dilatory manner. By the time he got himself to Scotland in December of 1715 to lead the clans to victory, his Hanoverian opponent was firmly entrenched in England. James's bid for the throne lasted scarcely three months, and he wisely returned to France, always a Pretender, never a King. George I at the age of 54 had arrived in London the year before, replete with his two ugly mistresses, known as the Maypole and the Elephant because of their respective height and weight. Also in his entourage were a bevy of German chamberlains and secretaries and George's two black slaves, Mustapha and Mahomet. The new King, however, left behind him his wife Sophia Dorothea, whom he had divorced and imprisoned 20 years before for alleged adultery with a handsome young Swedish Count who mysteriously disappeared—fate unknown.

George I preparing himself to be King of England

History knows more about the first four Georges than about any previous dynasty, because the 18th century was the age of memoir and letter writing par excellence when gossip and scandal were recorded with the avidity of modern investigatory journalism. We know that George II had his chair pulled out from under him by his mistress as a practical joke; that when George III went swimming from his bathing machine he entered the water to the refrains of "God Save the King"; and that after George IV's death, 500 pocketbooks were found filled with £10,000 of forgotten money.

We also know that the first George did not want to leave Hanover, and the story is told that he had to be awakened when the news of his succession arrived; he grunted his acknowledgement and promptly went back to sleep. What upset George was that he could not take Hanover with him. There he was the absolute ruler of a thoroughly organized petty German principality, modeled not on the English system of government but on the court of Louis XIV of France. "Put," wrote the novelist William Thackery, "clumsy high Dutch statues in place of the marbles of Versailles," and fancy "French songs [sung] with the most awful German accent," "image a coarse Versailles, and we have a Hanover before us." In his German Electorate, George was supreme—witness what happened to his wife's lover. In Britain he was a limited monarch, limited by a dull Germanic mind, by almost no English (communication was done mostly in French), and by a loathing for everything British. As a consequence, George went back to Hanover every chance he got, which was generally every year, and left his Kingdom to be governed by his ministers—usually Robert Walpole. As Lord Chesterfield remarked, George was "an honest, dull, German gentleman" who was lazy, "diffident of his own parts," and preferred "the company of wags and buffoons." "If," he grudgingly concluded, "he does not adorn, at least he will not stain the annals of the country."

Like father, like son. George II emotionally and intellectually belonged in Hanover, except that he spoke better English (but with a heavy Teutonic accent), expressed fewer invidious comparisons between England and his Hanoverian paradise, and made more of a pretense of being a proper King. In fact, however, he left the government of the realm to Walpole and Pitt, and everyone understood that, if you wanted to manipulate the King, you spoke first to his wife, the redoubtable Caroline of Anspach, who endured her husband's boorish behavior in public to rule him in private. As Lord Chesterfield caustically put it, the King "was governed by the Queen while she lived [and] she was governed by Sir Robert Walpole; but he kept that secret inviolably, and flattered himself that nobody had discovered it."

George was known among the other sovereigns of Europe as "the dancing master." He was a dapper little man who strutted and posed but, under the mask of the disciplinarian, concealed a timorous personality and sluggish mind, inadequate to his regal responsibilities. His two passions in life were military strategy and genealogy, subjects on which he bored everyone as only a king can do. He loved routine, and Lord Hervey noted that the King on all occasions "seems to think his having done a thing today an unanswerable reason for doing it tomorrow." It is hard to find a kind word about the second George. He had few favorites, no friends except his wife, and made matters worse by living to age 77.

George III should have been a happy change, and up to a point he was. He was young—only 22—determined to please, and entirely English in education and pride of country. Yet George's reign crippled both the Crown and Empire, and he died deaf, nearly blind and insane. Like so many monarchs before him, George was filled with good intentions, but lacked the cerebral and psychological means to realize them. He had been brought up to be king and that is always a disadvantage. His father, Frederick Prince of Wales, died when George was 13 and for the next nine years his educators told him that he had to be great because he was soon to become sovereign of a great nation. Unfortunately, George knew that he could never live up to such high expectations, and as a consequence he clung to others like a vine to a pillar, and when things went wrong, as they always did, he invariably blamed those on whom he depended.

George was the first British sovereign to be obsessed with the duties as opposed to the rights of his office. The 22-year-old monarch was determined to be a "real King," and that, in his estimation, entailed not so much exercising his royal rights to enhance his own prestige, as fulfilling his obligation to protect the British constitution and authority of Parliament from corruption from within and encroachment from without. No one gainsaid his aims, but they were accompanied with such high-minded inflexibility that they were doomed to failure. As he confessed, "I never assent till I am convinced what is proposed is right, and then . . . I never allow that to be destroyed by after-thoughts which on all subjects tend to weaken, never strengthen the original proposal."

George III has had a rotten press. In the American colonies, he was (and often still is) pictured as a tyrant, and in London he was regarded as a meddlesome incompetent. But in the countryside, Farmer George, as he was known because of his affection for agriculture, was far more popular than his Hanoverian predecessors. He was a model husband, the embodiment of what would later be called middle-class Victorian virtues (he and his wife liked to call each other Mr. and Mrs. King), and as the poor man endured the ravages of hepatic porphyria (a liver imbalance that produces insanity), sympathy for the old demented King grew apace, so much so that he became the symbol of British perseverance in the face of French radicalism and Napoleonic aggression. Certainly few people, not even George, sane or insane, looked forward to the succession of the fourth George.

Farmer George and his wife

All the Georges detested their eldest sons; it seemed to run in the Hanoverian genes. George I was not on speaking terms with his heir, and had him evicted from St. James Palace. The second George and his wife could not abide Frederick, Prince of Wales (but, of course, few people could) and treated him abominably. And George III had all his sons whipped regularly (he thought it democratic) and much preferred his second son to the future George IV, whom he regarded as a spoiled, unfeeling delinquent. To make matters worse, the poor King had to stand by, often straight-jacketed, and watch the Prince of Wales govern in his place as Regent for the last nine years of his life.

William Thackeray did for the fourth George what William Macauley did for the first James: ruined his reputation forever, except that revisionists have had a harder time rehabilitating George than they have James. For Thackeray, the King was a hollow poltroon—nothing but padding, corsets, silk stockings, immensely high-collared, elaborately braided coat, a stock or scarf that reached to his chin, smirky smile, and false teeth. He was not simply a stuffed shirt but a stuffed man, and even the stuffing was nothing but a frothy mixture of alcoholic indolence, tearful sentimentality, sexual indulgence, and ridiculous vanity. Ever since, George has been the tasteless benchmark by which to compare the scandals surrounding Victoria's eldest son, the future Edward VII, and, more recently, the activities of Charles, the current Prince of Wales. But to be fair to the fourth George, compared to his eight brothers, Prinny, as he was called (he was Prince of Wales until he was 58), was something of a paragon. He could be charming when he chose, was by far the brightest of George III's offspring, and when he was sober was never a bore. The trouble with George IV's standing in history is that his marital and extramarital encounters make such marvelous copy that his reign, otherwise inconsequential, is unforgettable.

After George wearied of the Drury Lane actress Mary Robinson, his father had to come up with £5000 to prevent her from publishing her princely lover's lurid correspondence. Still as Prince of Wales, he secretly married the widowed Mrs. Mary Anne Fitzherbert, a staunch Catholic, in order to entice her into his bed. He knew the marriage was illegal, since it violated two acts of Parliament: one that prevented a member of the royal family from marrying without the King's consent; the other that barred the heir apparent from wedding a Catholic without forfeiting the Crown. In 1795, in order to get Parliament to pay his debts, which at his age of 24 had reached the impressive sum of £260,000, he accepted his father's advice to marry his first cousin, Caroline of Brunswick. The marriage was an immediate disaster. George was drunk when he first met the lady and walked out on her when he discovered that she was afflicted with appalling body odor. He was even drunker when he reluctantly married her. A year later they were separated, Caroline leaving for the Continent and the Prince returning to the bed of Mrs. Fitzherbert and spending most of his time devising ways of ridding himself of his legal wife. When George finally mounted the throne in 1820, Caroline returned to England to claim her royal title. George promptly ordered his government to introduce a bill into Parliament permitting him to divorce her and depriving her of her title as Queen. The bill got tangled in party politics and had to be withdrawn before it was voted down, but George consoled himself by barring the doors of Westminster Abbey to his wife during his coronation. The scandal was finally resolved when Caroline, much to everyone's relief, died the following year. George, however, did not return to Mrs. Fitzherbert; he had already dished that "wife" and found pleasure in a number of other ladies of the court.

George IV will always be remembered in history for the magnificence of Regency architecture and the splendid folly of his Brighton Pavilion (like Blenheim Palace, it must be seen to be believed), but for his contemporaries the best that the staid *London Times* could say on the day of his funeral in 1830 was, "There never was an individual less regretted by his fellow creatures than this deceased king." Popular sentiment was less restrained: "When George the fourth to hell descends, thank the Lord the Georges end."

"When George the fourth to hell descends, thank the Lord the Georges end"

William IV (1830–37)

In 1817, a Hanovarian family crisis occurred; on the death of Charlotte, the only child of George IV as a consequence of his one-night-stand with his wife Caroline, the dynasty was in danger of terminating. Of George III's 15 sons and daughters, not a one had produced a legitimate heir. Under great family pressure, George's three youngest sons, the Dukes of Cambridge, Kent, and Clarence reluctantly rose to the occasion. Cambridge wed a German princess but produced nothing. Kent was more fruitful: he gave up his mistress, married yet another German princess (he hoped Parliament would pay off his vast debts as a consequence), had a girl child—Victoria—and then promptly died. William Duke of Clarence, the eldest of the three brothers and heir presumptive, at the age of 53 took on yet a third German princess, half his age. Expectations ran high because the Duke had already had ten children—ten little FitzClarences, all of whom married into the British nobility—by his mistress, the comic actress Dorothy Jordan, but no heirs materialized (two daughters died within a month), all of which made Victoria's prospects both hopeful and insecure.

William IV's reign is immensely important, but the man himself is entirely forgettable. The great Reform Bill of 1832 took place, which changed Britain politically forever, but William remained a "Silly Billy."

Britain's Sailor King, starting as a midshipman and holding every other naval rank up to Lord High Admiral, had been hopelessly incompetent and royally meddlesome, but as a King aged 64 he wisely, if reluctantly, did exactly what his ministers told him to do. In the correspondence of the age, he seems to have been remembered largely for his endlessly boring after-dinner speeches (often in French), and the elegant Beau Brummell summed up contemporary opinion when he quipped William was "only fit to walk about on a quarter-deck and cry 'Luff'!"

Victoria (1837–1901)

Although she had the longest reign in British history, was the only monarch to keep an extensive and intimate journal, and was the first Queen to wear virginal white at her wedding, thereby establishing the modern tradition of white for all brides, there is little to say about Victoria. Her full name was Alexandrina Georgiana Augusta Victoria. She was to have been christened Elizabeth, but George IV so detested his brother that he refused, when he was Regent for his father, to permit his niece to assume the name of the great Queen. Until she ascended the throne at 18, Victoria had been engulfed in a suffocating cocoon of care and seclusion. She never slept alone, but always with her mother or governess. She was not allowed to walk down a flight of stairs unless someone held her hand. And no one was permitted to talk to her unless she was accompanied by her mother. Although she could not become Electress of Hanover (the title descended only in the male line), her first language was German, she married a first cousin of German stock, and throughout her life she was partial to all things German. Her education, rigidly supervised by her German mother, was deficient in the classics, politics, geography, and the sciences, but heavy on needlework, music. painting, and improving literature, and mountainous on Christian morality. Victoria at a tender age announced that she was resolved "to be good," and to make matters even better she married Albert Saxe-Coburg-Gotha, a serious young gentleman who had an even more developed sense of duty. Together they dutifully produced nine children. As a consequence, British royalty parted company with the carefree, disreputable ways of aristocracy to become the model of middle-class respectability and morality.

Victoria and Albert, models of middle-class respectability and morality

Victoria was young, popular and a pleasant change from her shabby royal uncles, and she displayed surprising strength of character—she evicted her mother and governess from her bedroom. Her instincts were always Hanoverian and heavy-handed, and for a minority of her subjects she remained an "ugly parsimonious German frau," but under Albert's quiet tutelage the Queen emerged as a reasonably gracious constitutional monarch in a Kingdom that was rapidly becoming a democracy. But when her darling Albert died in 1861, Victoria retired from public life, an "utterly brokenhearted and crushed widow of forty-one" (her words), and in his memory erected in Hyde Park a spectacular medieval shrine whose artistic value has been the subject of endless debate. For two decades she entombed herself in a castle in Scotland, was never seen by her subjects, and saved some £824,000 from the moneys Parliament voted her each year to sustain her government and perform her public duties. (This money in part explains why Elizabeth II is today such a wealthy woman. She is the direct beneficiary, without inheritance taxes, of her great-great grandmother's private estate, which at her death in 1901 was valued at £2 million.)

As the popularity of the monarchy—the Queen hardly seemed to be worth her cost—declined, republicanism grew. The size and cost of the royal household came under attack:

> *Grand children not a few*
> *With great grand children too,*
> *She blessed has been.*
> *We've been their sureties*
> *Paid their gratuities,*
> *Pensions, annuities.*
> *God save the queen.*

And in Parliament, members complained that it was ridiculous for the Kingdom to pay taxes to sustain an immensely rich old lady who did nothing, and refused all public responsibilities.

The Queen hardly seemed to be worth the cost of her
many children and grandchildren

Disraeli, not Victoria, eventually stemmed the tide of republicanism by luring his sovereign out of mourning and back into public life, and by associating love of monarchy with pride of Empire. By the time the old Queen died at 82 on January 22, 1901, she had become more an institution than a monarch, the symbol of domestic virtue, British motherhood, and Imperial greatness.

Edward VII (1901–1910)

Edward VII's reputation as Prince of Wales was such that a member of Parliament actually wrote that he hoped that "the present Prince of Wales should never dishonor this country by becoming king." But after waiting 60 years to be King, Edward turned out to be a highly effective, if not always reputable, sovereign. Unlike his mother, he doted on pomp and circumstance and sensed that the purpose of monarchy was not to meddle in government but to perform at official occasions. The task of a King was purely ceremonial and ritualistic, and Edward, marvelous conversationalist that he was, was excellent at the job. Also unlike his mother, he educated his son to be King. Victoria had clearly loved her eldest son, but she thought him such a ne'er-do-well that she refused to share with him a single iota of power or responsibility. As a consequence, he was bored and got into trouble—sex, gambling, debts. The Queen was particularly not amused when she discovered he was selling for extra pocket money her voluminous epistles about the virtues of frugality, written in response to his begging letters for more money to maintain his expensive college lifestyle.

Edward was rightly concerned about the future of the monarchy in a democratic, industrial society and once introduced his heir as the future "last king of England." He was wrong. George V, despite World War, unprecedented labor unrest, and global depression, was one of the most popular sovereigns Britain ever had.

George V (1910–36)

George V was the first sovereign to see, speak and hear no political evil. In contrast to his grandmother, who had been highly opinionated and tiresomely meddlesome, George set out to convince his Kingdom that a King who was totally outside and above politics, was nevertheless essential to the stability and operation of the political system. In brief, Britain deserved an excellent return on the high cost of monarchy in a world that was rapidly divesting itself of Kingship. The life expectancy of European monarchy was not good. In the years following the First World War, five emperors, eight kings and 18 minor dynasties vanished.

Ex-King of Greece, "Hullo, Ferdie! Seen anything of Kaiser William?"
Ex-King of Bulgaria, "He's somewhere behind. He'll join us a bit later."

Quite consciously, George and his equally conscientious wife Mary, Princess of Teck, became the parent image of the nation: sober, considerate, disciplined, and dull. The King proved to be extraordinarily adept at keeping the mystery and remoteness of royalty sacrosanct, while at the same time reaching out to what had become the real foundation of modern monarchy, the common person. He did this through his annual Christmas broadcast. He became the first radio monarch, oozing sincerity, sobriety and piety over the airways. George was every inch a King, but he was also a man to whom everybody could relate because he was such a solid citizen, such a family man, and such an avid stamp collector. What could be more endearing and enduring?

George not only recreated the British monarchy but also renamed it. His mother and father had detested the German side of the family, and when World War I broke out, George found the German Kaiser to be a highly embarrassing first cousin. Though the fifth George had no political power, he was still the absolute head of the English royal family, and on July 17, 1917, he issued a proclamation declaring that the "Name of Windsor" was henceforth to be borne both by "His Royal House" and by all "the descendants of Our Grandmother Queen Victoria," and that "the Use of All German Titles and Dignities" was to cease. At a stroke of the royal pen, 200 years of German ancestry—every British sovereign from George I to Victoria had married a German spouse, while George's own wife was more than half-German and his mother was Danish German—were abolished, along with such names as Saxe-Colburg-Gotha, Hesse, Battenberg (which became Mountbatten), Brunswick, and Teck. George was willing to accept that he was not very inspiring, but he was "damned," he said, "if I am an alien."

George died under circumstance that became public only 50 years after his death. His doctor, Lord Dawson, was determined that, when death was close upon the King, his sovereign should die with "dignity and serenity" becoming his regal status, and consequently hastened the King's demise with drugs (euthanasia) so that the news could be announced "in the morning papers rather than the less appropriate field of the evening journals." Even in death, timing, staging, and the media had become the Cerberus of the British monarchy.

Edward VIII (1936)

Despite the length of his name—Edward Albert Christian George Andrew Patrick David—Edward VIII reigned only 325 days. If Edward's many names reflected the Crown's efforts to endear itself to every ethnic group within the Kingdom (the influx of Commonwealth peoples had not yet begun), his decision to give up the Crown reflected the growing tension between the King's private and public life.

Edward was a bachelor of 41 when he came to the throne in 1936. For many, he was a refreshing change to the disciplined Victorian standards of his mother and father. (Neither his father nor mother ever spoke on a telephone, and she lived until 1953.) As Prince of Wales, he had traveled the length and breath of the Empire, was constantly in the news as an excellent athlete and horseman, and owned and flew his own airplane. He did his share of ceremonial duties, but confessed in his diary "what rot and a waste of time, money and energy all these state visits are."

Edward VIII regarded his ceremonial duties as
"rot and a waste of time, money and energy."

Whether he would have made an adequate sovereign is anyone's guess. As it was, he met Wallis Warfield Simpson, a twice-divorced American from Maryland, fell desperately in love, and clashed with his Prime Minister, Stanley Baldwin, who, in close alliance with the Archbishop of Canterbury and the Queen Mother, was adamantly opposed to the head of the Church of England marrying a divorced woman. (Baldwin may have had a hidden agenda—he thought Edward an unsuitable King who voiced social and economic concerns that the Conservative Government found politically embarrassing.) At issue were two interrelated rights, that of the monarch to have a private life and make decisions independent of his public office, and his right to go against the advice of his Government and act contrary to the will of the Prime Minister. Edward was no fighter. He chose to abdicate and avert what could have become a constitutional crisis. He and Mrs. Simpson simply faded out of public life and view, he as the Duke of Windsor with the title of "Royal Highness," she as his Duchess but without the right to royal rank, an insult that Edward never forgave Baldwin or the brother who succeeded him upon the throne.

George VI (1936–52)

Edward VIII's younger brother was called Albert, or Bertie for short, but he also had a long list of appellations, and when he became King, chose the name of George to associate himself with the comfortable stability and respectable domesticity of his father. His reign was a continuation of George V's style of monarchy, but with a difference. The sixth George was more folksy and informal; his title shrank from King-Emperor to King only of Great Britain and Northern Ireland; and most important of all, 13 of his 16 years as sovereign took place during wartime, and the equally unpleasant years of adjusting to post-war reality when even a King's family was subject to rationing, clothing coupons, and food shortages. George VI was a godsend to his Kingdom and the concept of monarchy. Even his defects were assets: his reticence, stutter, and shyness endeared him to a nation also being asked to face overwhelming disadvantages. His wife—Elizabeth Bowes-Lyon, Britain's first completely English Queen in citizenship and blood since James II married Anne Hyde back in 1660—was an even greater asset. The Germans had good cause to call her "the most dangerous woman in England." She was the perfect wartime Queen; her clothes, even before war broke out, looked as if they had been bought at Marks and Spencer with coupons, and her quiet, upbeat personality complemented her husband's dogged determinism to succeed in the job of Kingship. During the war both stayed in Buckingham Palace, and when their home was bombed, the Queen's reaction was simply to say the destruction made it easier for her "to look the East End [of London which was hit the hardest] in the face." One time, as the royal couple was viewing bomb damage, a voice called out "You're a good king." George countered: "You're a good people." He died at 57 of circulatory problems and lung cancer, brought on by exhaustion and chain smoking.

Announcing a new King and his greatest asset—his wife

Elizabeth II (1952–)

Elizabeth came to the throne in a "blaze of glorious Technicolor." If her grandfather George V had been the first radio King, she was the first television Queen presenting the historic grandeur of royal pageantry to a national and world audience. Westminster Abbey became the television stage for the royal family—the two most spectacular performances being the Queen's coronation in 1953, and the fairytale wedding of her son, Prince Charles, to the dazzling Diana in 1981. Almost as lavish was the marriage of her sister Margaret in 1960. Ex-Conservative Prime Minister Winston Churchill arrived in a Rolls Royce driven by a chauffeur; ex-Labor Prime Minister Clement Atlee arrived in a tiny Mini Minor driven by his wife; such were the conflicting political styles the Queen had to handle.

Until the 1980s, the media worked faithfully with monarchy to convert Elizabeth's crown into a halo: the BBC might criticize God all it wanted but not the royal family. Then things began to change with alarming speed. In converting the Royals into television celebrities, constantly under the theatrical spotlight, the Crown gained an avid world-following, but it also exposed itself to the lurid standard of Hollywood, where the private lives of screen personalities are subject to salacious public scrutiny. And it turned out that the Kingdom's perfect family—respectable, hardworking, and dutiful—had no intention of living up to Victoria's probably apocryphal advice to one of her daughters who objected to the thought of connubial bliss in bed with a lesser German prince: "My dear, close your eyes and think of England." A more tawdry, scandal-ridden, self-indulgent set of children, along with their spouses, has rarely been inflicted on any parents as upon the Queen and her husband, Philip Mountbatten (Battenberg), Prince of Greece, Earl of Merioneth and Duke of Edinburgh, but significantly not Prince Consort. The malapropism of an American undergraduate searching for the expression "limited monarchy" catches the standing of the British crown: it has become a "limited mockery."

To make matters worse, the press, so long such a dutiful guardian of a wholesome image of royalty that the British public was unaware of Edward VIII's relations with Mrs. Simpson until days before his abdication, has become increasing hostile, refusing to maintain the mystical distinction between the monarchy's public persona and its private reality. Even as late as 1989, the editor of the *Sunday People* was fired for publishing a photograph of Prince William, the seven-year-old heir presumptive, taking a leak in the park with the headline "The Royal Wee" and the caption "Willie's Sly Pee in Park." But that, of course, was before his parents' sex lives became international news.

British Royalty will probably survive scandal, paparazzi, and investigatory journalism so long as its scandals remain glamorous in the Hollywood tradition. But what is eating at the soul of Kingship is not moral outrage, but boredom. Bereft of political power, the job is unexciting, and except for the late Princess Di and (if you discount her hats), the Queen Mother, the Royal Family has been without a spark of charisma. Once the soap is taken out of the Royal Soap Opera the audience, so vital to modern monarchy, may simply get up and leave. What remains, however, is custom, history, and time-honored pageantry, and these may be enough to guarantee the future of the British Royals. King Farouk, the last sovereign of Egypt, may have spoken the truth when he predicted that at the rate things were going "there will soon be only five kings left—the king of clubs, diamonds, hearts and spades, and the King of England."

Elizabeth II, a thousand years of history but zero charisma

The Tudor Claim to the Throne

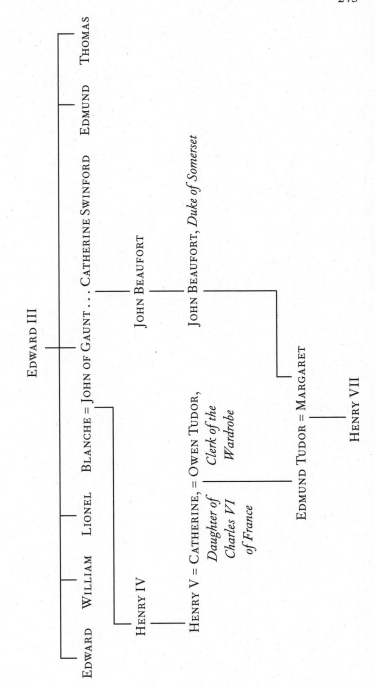

The Tudors: 1485–1603

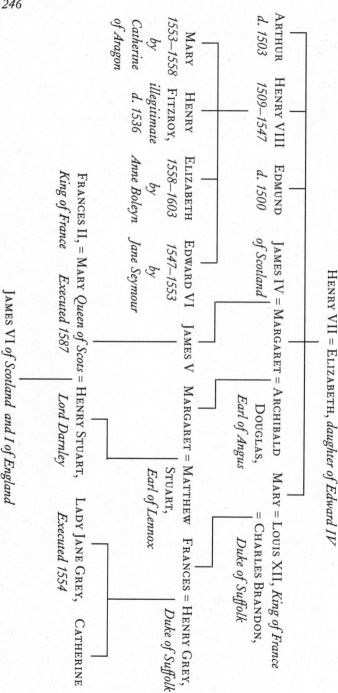

The Habsburg Dynasty

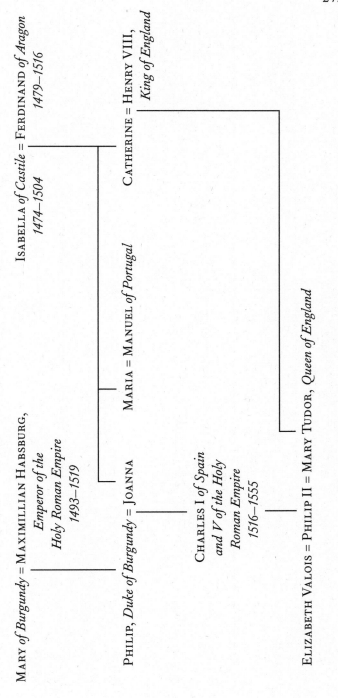

The House of Stuart

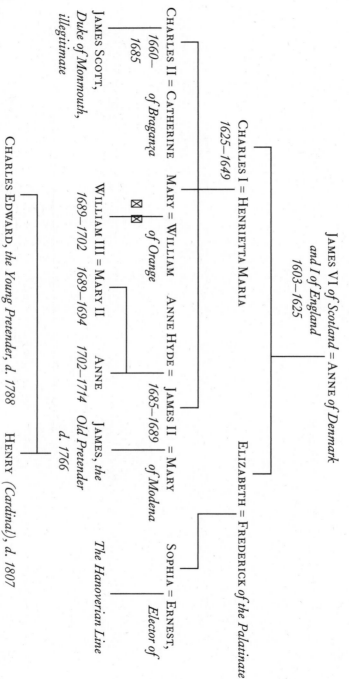

A BRIEF BIBLIOGRAPHY

The four volume series *A History of England*—C. W. Hollister and Robert and Robin Stacey, *The Making of England To 1399*; L. B. Smith, *This Realm of England 1399–1688*; W. B. Willcox and W. L. Arnstein, *The Age of Aristocracy 1688–1830*; W. L. Arnstein, *Britain Yesterday and Today 1830 to the Present*—is a lively and available survey, and each volume has an extensive bibliography.

GENERAL WORKS LISTED IN HISTORICAL ORDER

Green, Miranda J. *The World of the Druids* (1997)

Arnold, C. J. *Roman Britain to Saxon England* (1988)

Barlow, Frank. *William I and the Norman Conquest* (1965)

Holt, J. C. *Magna Carta* (2nd ed. 1992)

Keen, Maurice. *England in the Later Middle Ages* (1973)

Allmand, C. T. *The Hundred Years War: England and France at War, c. 1300–1450* (1988)

Guy, John. *Tudor England* (1990)

Smith, L. B. *The Elizabethan World* (2nd ed. 1991)

O'Day , R. *The Debate on the English Reformation* (1986)

Mattingly, G. *The Armada* (1962)

Tillyard, E. M. W. *The Elizabethan World Picture* (1934)

Clarkson, L. A. *The Pre-Industrial Economy of England 1500–1750* (1971)

Laslett, Peter. *The World We Have Lost* (1965)

Coward, B. *The Stuart Age* (1980)

Richardson, R. C. *The Debate on the English Civil War Revisited* (1989)

Plumb, John. *England in the Eighteenth Century* (1963)

Ashley, Maurice. *The Glorious Revolution* (1966)

Briggs, Asa. *The Power of Steam* (1982)

Brewer, John. *Sinews of Power: War, Money, and the English State, 1688–1783* (1989)

Black, Jeremy. *War for America: The Fight for Independence, 1775–1783* (1992)

Perkin, Harold. *The Origins of Modern English Society 1780–1880* (1969)

Mingay, G. E. *The Gentry: The Rise and Fall of a Ruling Class* (1976)

Briggs, Asa. *The Age of Improvement, 1783–1867* (2nd ed. 2000)

Young, G.M. *Victorian England: Portrait of an Age* (1936)

Woodham-Smith, Cecil. *The Reason Why* (1954)

Tuchman, Barbara. *The Guns of August* (1962)

Graves, Robert. *Goodbye to All That* (1929)

Clarke, Peter. *Hope and Glory: Britain 1900–1990* (1996)

Cannadine, David. *The Decline and Fall of the British Aristocracy* (1990)

Wiener, Martin J. *English Culture and the Decline of the Industrial Spirit, 1850–1980* (1981)

Porter, Roy. *London: A Social History* (1995)

Girouard, Mark. *Life in the English Country House: A Social and Architectural History* (1978)

Ferguson, Niall. *Empire: The Rise and Demise of the British World Order and the Lessons for Global Power* (2002)

Paxman, Jeremy. *The English: A Portrait of a People* (2000)

BIOGRAPHIES LISTED IN HISTORICAL ORDER

Smyth, Alfred P. *King Alfred the Great* (1998)

Owen, D.D.R. *Eleanor of Aquitaine: Queen and Legend* (1993)

Warren, W. L. *Henry II* (1973)

Hutchinson, H. F. *The Hollow Crown: A Life of Richard II* (1961)

Kendall, P. M. *Richard III* (1955)

Smith, Lacey B. *Henry VIII:The Mask of Royalty* (1971)

Johnson, P. *Elizabeth I: A Study of Power and Intellect* (1974)

Bowles, C. *Charles the First* (1975)

Ashley, Maurice. *Charles I and Oliver Cromwell: A Study in Contrasts and Comparisons* (1987)

Hibbert, Christopher. *George III, A Personal History* (1998)

Plumb, John. *The First Four Georges* (1956)

Arnstein, Walter L. *Queen Victoria* (2003)

Somervell, D. C. *Disraeli and Gladstone, A Duo-Biographical Sketch* (7th ed. 1932)

Gilbert, Martin. *Winston Churchill: A Life* (1991)

ILLUSTRATION CREDITS

Page 2: *Punch* (22 Mar 1911), p. 209.

Page 3: Ibid. (7 Feb 1912), p. 99.

Page 4: John Leech, *Pictures of Life and Character from the Collection of Mr. Punch, 1843–64*, vol. 1.

Page 11: *Punch* (18 Aug 1937), p. 181.

Page 12: *Billy Nye's Comic History of England* (Chicago, 1906), p. 24.

Page 14: *Punch* (1 Sep 1912).

Page 15: *Billy Nye's Comic History*, p. 35.

Page 16: Ibid., p. 49.

Page 18: Ibid., p. 78.

Page 19: Gilbert A'Beckett, *Comic History of England* (London, 1852), p. 53.

Page 21: W.H. Ainsworth, *Windsor Castle* (London, 1847), p. 32.

Page 23: *Billy Nye's Comic History*, p. 91.

Page 26: Ibid., p. 104.

Page 27: Ibid., p. 71.

Page 29: Ibid., p. 129.

Page 31: Ibid., p. 127.

Page 33: A'Beckett, *Comic History of England*, p. 133.

Page: 34: Walter C. Sellar and Robert J. Yeatman, *1066 and All That*, illustrated by John Reynolds (London: Methuen, 1930).

Page 35: *Billy Nye's Comic History of England* (Chicago, 1906), p. 138.

Page 37: Ibid., p. 144.

Page 38: A'Beckett, *Comic History of England*, p. 81.

Page 39: *Punch* (1851), p. 122.

Page 41: Ibid. (1896).

Page 42: A'Beckett, *Comic History of England*, p. 203.

Page 43: *Billy Nye's Comic History*, p. 148.

Page 45: Ibid., p. 163.

Page 46: A'Beckett, *Comic History of England*, p. 80.

Page 48: *Punch* (17 Nov 1937), p. 552.

Page 52: Ibid. (18 Dec 1912), p. 503.

Page 53: A'Beckett, *Comic History of England*, p. 62.

Page 55: *Billy Nye's Comic History.*

Page 56: Thomas Wright, *A History of Caricature and Grotesque in Literature and Art* (London, 1875), p. 256.

Page 57: A'Beckett, *Comic History of England*, p. 98.

Page 59: Ibid., p. 113.

Page 60: *Punch* (Jan 1851), p. 18.

Page 63: William Brannon.

Page 70: *Punch* (20 Jul 1938), p. 61.

Page 73: A'Beckett, *Comic History of England*, p. 157.

Page 74: Ibid., p. 168.

Page 77: Sellar and Yeatman, *1066 and All That*, p. 64.

Page 79: Arthur Moreland, *Humors of History* #148 (London, 1903).

Page 84: *Punch* (28 May 1930), p. 613.

Page 87: W. S. Gilbert, *'The Bab' Ballads* (London, 1868).

Page 88: *Punch* (7 Dec 1927), p. 635.

Page 91: Roduelph Ackermann, *Microcosm of London* (London, 1808–11).

Page 94: Adapted from an 18th-century engraving.

Page 96: Thomas Wright, *England Under the House of Hanover*, vol. 1 (London, 1848), p. 368.

Page 98: Burr Shafer, *The Wonderful World of J. Wesley Smith* (New York: Scholastic Book Services, 1960. Fourth printing, 1971). By permission of Vanguard Press, Random House.

Page 99: A'Beckett, *Comic History of England*, p. 279.

Page 102: Sellar and Yeatman, *1066 and All That*.

Page 107: Thomas Wright, *England Under the House of Hanover*, vol. 2, p. 22.

Page 108: Burr Shafer, *The Wonderful World of J. Wesley Smith*. By permission of Vanguard Press, Random House.

Page 113: *Punch* (1845), p. 49.

Page 118: A. M. Broadley, *Napoleon in Caricature 1795–1821*, vol. 2 (London, 1911), p. 12.

Page 120: *Punch* (May 1843).
Page 121: Ibid., vol. 9 (1845), p. 188.
Page 123: W. S. Gilbert, *More Bab Ballads* (London, 1872).
Page 126: *Punch* (28 Feb 1874), p. 89.
Page 128: Harry Furniss, *The Confessions of a Caricaturist*, vol. 1 (New York and London, 1901), p. 165.
Page 132: *Punch* (1855), p. 64.
Page 133: Ibid. (1846), p. 69.
Page 136: Ibid. (22 Apr 1936), p. 457.
Page 139: Ibid. (21 Jun 1933), p. 689.
Page 141: Ibid. (23 Nov 1938), p. 567.
Page 143: W. S. Gilbert, *'Bab' Ballads*.
Page 144: *Punch* (1896).
Page 147: *Simplicissimus Illustrierte Wockenschrift* #6 (Speczial Nummer: Kolonien, 1904), p. 55.
Page 148: *Punch* (17 Feb 1937), p. 177.
Page 151: Ibid. (2 Oct 1912).
Page 152: Ibid. (4 Jun 1913), p. 437.
Page 156: Ibid. (29 Jan 1941), p. 119.
Page 161: Ibid. (2 Mar 1938), p. 237.
Page 166: Ibid. (20 Sept 1939), p. 311.
Page 170: Ibid. (8 Nov 1939), p. 507.
Page 172: Ibid. (9 Dec 1936), p. 653.
Page 182: Adapted mostly from *Punch* with a few hand drawn additions by the author.
Page 192: *Billy Nye's Comic History*, p. 80.
Page 195: Sellar and Yeatman, *1066 and All That*.
Page 197: A'Beckett, *Comic History of England*, p. 90.
Page 198: Ibid., p. 110.
Page 200: Ibid., p. 244.
Page 201: Ibid., p. 129.
Page 203: Ibid., p. 153.
Page 204: Sellar and Yeatman, *1066 and All That*.
Page 205: *Billy Nye's Comic History*, p. 151.
Page 206: A'Beckett, *Comic History of England*.
Page 208: Ibid., p. 115.
Page 209: *Billy Nye's Comic History*, p. 166.

Page 210: A'Beckett, *Comic History of England*, p. 289.

Page 211: Ibid., p. 297.

Page 212: Sellar and Yeatman, *1066 and All That*.

Page 213: A'Beckett, *Comic History of England*, p. 18.

Page 215: Ibid., p. 25.

Page 216: *Billy Nye's Comic History*.

Page 217: Ibid.

Page 219: *Punch* (1896).

Page 220: A'Beckett, *Comic History of England*, p. 125.

Page 223: Ibid., n.p.

Page 225: Ibid., p. 253.

Page 228: Ibid., p. 281.

Page 231: Thomas Wright, *A History of Caricature and Grotesque*, p. 470.

Page 233: George Cruikshank, *The Political House That Jack Built* (London, 1819), p. 86.

Page 235: Sellar and Yeatman, *1066 and All That*.

Page 236: *Life* (5 Apr 1883).

Page 238: *Punch* (Oct 1918).

Page 240: *Punch* (29 Jan 1936), p. 139.

Page 242: *Punch* (30 Dec 1936), p. 740.

Page 244: CartoonStock, Ltd.

INDEX